AF669423

ENERGY CONSERVATION AND AUDIT

AUTHOR (S)

Dr. M. Rizwan
Professor
Department of Electrical Engineering,
Delhi Technological University,
Delhi, INDIA

Dr. Majid Jamil
Professor
Department of Electrical Engineering,
Jamia Millia Islamia,
New Delhi, INDIA

REVIEWER

Dr. Sekar Kandasamy
Professor,
Department of Electrical and Electronics Engineering,
Hindusthan College of Engineering and Technology,
Tamil Nadu, India.

KHANNA BOOK PUBLISHING CO. (P) Ltd.
4C/4344, Ansari Road, Darya Ganj,
New Delhi, India

All India Council for Technical Education
Nelson Mandela Marg, Vasant Kunj,
New Delhi, India

Dear Readers,

To prevent the piracy, this book is secured with HIGH SECURITY HOLOGRAM on the front title cover. In case you don't find the hologram on the front cover title, please write us to at contact@khannabooks.com or whatsapp us at +91-99109 09320 and avail special gift voucher for yourself.

Specimen of Hologram on front Cover title:

Moreover, there is a SPECIAL DISCOUNT COUPON for you with EVERY HOLOGRAM.

How to avail this SPECIAL DISCOUNT:

Step 1: Scratch the hologram

Step 2: Under the scratch area, your "coupon code" is available

Step 3: Logon to www.khannabooks.com

Step 4: Use your "coupon code" in the shopping cart and get your copy at a special discount

Step 5: Enjoy your reading!

ISBN: 978-93-5538-486-7

Book Code: DIP501EN

Energy Conservation And Audit

by Dr. M. Rizwan and Dr. Majid Jamil

First Edition: 2026

Originally Published by:

All India Council for Technical Education, Ministry of Education, GOI

Exclusively Published & Distributed by:

Khanna Book Publishing Co. (P) Ltd.
4C/4344, Ansari Road, Daryaganj,
New Delhi (INDIA)

Visit us at: **www.khannabooks.com**
Write us at: **contact@khannabooks.com**

To view complete list of books, Please scan the QR Code:

KPH

Printed in Bharat.

प्रो. टी. जी. सीताराम
अध्यक्ष
Prof. T. G. Sitharam
Chairman

सत्यमेव जयते

आज़ादी का अमृत महोत्सव

अखिल भारतीय तकनीकी शिक्षा परिषद्
(भारत सरकार का एक सांविधिक निकाय)
(शिक्षा मंत्रालय, भारत सरकार)
नेल्सन मंडेला मार्ग, वसंत कुंज, नई दिल्ली–110070
दूरभाष : 011–26131498
ई–मेल : chairman@aicte-india.org

ALL INDIA COUNCIL FOR TECHNICAL EDUCATION
(A STATUTORY BODY OF THE GOVT. OF INDIA)
(Ministry of Education, Govt. of India)
Nelson Mandela Marg, Vasant Kunj, New Delhi-110070
Phone : 011-26131498
E-mail : chairman@aicte-india.org

FOREWORD

Engineers are the backbone of any modern society. They are the ones responsible for the marvels as well as the improved quality of life across the world. Engineers have driven humanity towards greater heights in a more evolved and unprecedented manner.

The All India Council for Technical Education (AICTE), have spared no efforts towards the strengthening of the technical education in the country. AICTE is always committed towards promoting quality Technical Education to make India a modern developed nation emphasizing on the overall welfare of mankind.

An array of initiatives has been taken by AICTE in last decade which have been accelerated now by the National Education Policy (NEP) 2020. The implementation of NEP under the visionary leadership of Hon'ble Prime Minister of India envisages the provision for education in regional languages to all, thereby ensuring that every graduate becomes competent enough and is in a position to contribute towards the national growth and development through innovation & entrepreneurship.

One of the spheres where AICTE had been relentlessly working since past couple of years is providing high quality original technical contents at Under Graduate & Diploma level prepared and translated by eminent educators in various Indian languages to its aspirants. For students pursuing 2nd year of their Engineering education, AICTE has identified 87 books, which shall be translated into 12 Indian languages - Hindi, Tamil, Gujarati, Odia, Bengali, Kannada, Urdu, Punjabi, Telugu, Marathi, Assamese & Malayalam. In addition to the English medium, books in different Indian Languages are going to support the students to understand the concepts in their respective mother tongue.

On behalf of AICTE, I express sincere gratitude to all distinguished authors, reviewers and translators from the renowned institutions of high repute for their admirable contribution in a record span of time.

AICTE is confident that these outcomes based original contents shall help aspirants to master the subject with comprehension and greater ease.

(Prof. T. G. Sitharam)

प्रो. टी. जी. सीताराम
अध्यक्ष
Prof. T. G. Sitharam
Chairman

अखिल भारतीय तकनीकी शिक्षा परिषद
(भारत सरकार का एक सांविधिक निकाय)
शिक्षा मंत्रालय, भारत सरकार
नेल्सन मंडेला मार्ग, वसंत कुंज, नई दिल्ली-110070
दूरभाष : 011-26131498
ई-मेल : chairman@aicte-india.org

ALL INDIA COUNCIL FOR TECHNICAL EDUCATION
(A STATUTORY BODY OF THE GOVT. OF INDIA)
(Ministry of Education, Govt. of India)
Nelson Mandela Marg, Vasant Kunj, New Delhi-110070
Phone : 011-26131498
E-mail : chairman@aicte-india.org

FOREWORD

Engineers are the backbone of any modern society. They are the ones responsible for the marvels as well as the improved quality of life across the world. Engineers have driven humanity towards greater heights in a more evolved and unprecedented manner.

The All India Council for Technical Education (AICTE), have spared no efforts towards the strengthening of the technical education in the country. AICTE is always committed towards promoting quality Technical Education to make India a modern developed nation emphasizing on the overall welfare of mankind.

An array of initiatives has been taken by AICTE in last decade which have been accelerated now by the National Education Policy (NEP) 2020. The implementation of NEP under the visionary leadership of Hon'ble Prime Minister of India envisages the provision for education in regional languages to all, thereby ensuring that every graduate becomes competent enough and is in a position to contribute towards the national growth and development through innovation & entrepreneurship.

One of the spheres where AICTE had been relentlessly working since past couple of years is providing high-quality original technical contents at Under Graduate & Diploma level prepared and translated by eminent educators in various Indian languages to its aspirants. For students pursuing 2nd year of their Engineering education, AICTE has identified [illegible] books, which shall be translated into 12 Indian languages - Hindi, Tamil, Gujarati, Odia, Bengali, Kannada, Urdu, Punjabi, Telugu, Marathi, Assamese & Malayalam. In addition to the English medium, books in different Indian Languages are going to support the students to understand the concepts in their respective mother tongue.

On behalf of AICTE, I express sincere gratitude to all distinguished authors, reviewers and translators from the renowned institutions of high repute for their admirable contribution in a record span of time.

AICTE is confident that these outcomes based original contents shall help aspirants to master the subject with comprehension and greater ease.

(Prof. T. G. Sitharam)

ACKNOWLEDGMENT

The authors are grateful to the authorities of AICTE, particularly Prof. T.G. Sitharam, Chairman; Dr. Abhay Jere, Vice-Chairman; Prof. Rajive Kumar, Member-Secretary, Dr. Sunil Luthra, Director, and Reena Sharma, Hindi Officer Training and Learning Bureau for their planning to publish the books on **Energy Conservation and Audit**. We sincerely acknowledge the valuable contributions of the reviewer of the book Prof. Sekar K, Department of Electrical and Electronics Engineering, Hindusthan College of Engineering and Technology, Coimbatore for providing valuable inputs in all units of the book.

We would also like to extend our thanks to Prof. Prateek Sharma, Vice Chancellor, Delhi Technological University, Prof. Madhusudan Singh, Registrar, Prof. Rachana Garg, Head, Department of Electrical Engineering, Delhi Technological University, Delhi, Prof. Pragati Kumar, Vice Chancellor, Shri Mata Vaishno Devi University, J&K, Prof. Moinuddin (Former Professor, JMI), Prof. Sirajuddin Ahmad, Prof. M. Khan, Prof. A. S. Siddiqui, Prof. M. A. Khan, JMI, Jamia Administration, and Dr. Sheeraz Kirmani, AMU.

This book is an outcome of various suggestions of AICTE members, experts, and authors who shared their opinion and thought to further develop engineering education in our country. Acknowledgments are due to the contributors and different workers in this field whose published books, review articles, papers, photographs, footnotes, references, and other valuable information enriched us at the time of writing the book.

Dr. M. Rizwan

Dr. Majid Jamil

PREFACE

The book titled **Energy Conservation and Audit** is an outcome of the rich experience of two authors and a reviewer in the field of electrical engineering and energy conservation. Energy conservation is one of the most essential requirements globally in the present scenario as the demand of energy is increasing day by day. Conserving energy and reducing its consumption is crucial because excessive use of energy can be very expensive as well as harm to the environment. An energy audit is a comprehensive assessment, and evaluation of energy use in a structure, process, or system with the goal of conserving energy. The purpose is to identify ways to decrease the amount of energy required for operation without compromising the desired results.

Prime Minister, Shri Narendra Modi has pledged for wholehearted commitment towards energy conservation, on National Energy Conservation Day. "On this day, we pledge our wholehearted commitment towards energy conservation". The initiation of writing this book is *to bring awareness about the importance* of energy conservation among masses in our day-to-day life to achieve the objectives of energy conservation.

The main aim of this book is to enable diploma engineering students to understand the basics of energy conservation and energy audit and enable them to get an insight into the subject. Keeping in mind the purpose of wide coverage as well as to provide essential supplementary information, the topics recommended by AICTE have been included in a very systematic and orderly manner.

Efforts have been made to include the fundamental concepts along with necessary explanations of certain important topics in the simplest possible way. During the process of preparation, various standard text books, recent papers published in the field, case studies conducted apart from the latest information available on relevant websites have been considered and accordingly, incorporated in different units of this book.

While preparing the different sections, emphasis has also been laid on definitions and laws and also on comprehensive synopsis of formulae for a quick revision of the basic principles. The book covers fundamental as well as advanced knowledge in a very logical and systematic manner.

This book introduces the importance of energy conservation and energy audit. Efforts of the government in the promotion and implementation of energy conservation are included here. A lot of debates internationally are going on to find solutions for sustainable growth of energy and economy without affecting our environment. This book will provide an opportunity to explore means of energy conservation through well-defined procedures of energy auditing for large consumers of energy.

This book covers energy conservation methods and new technologies developed in the application of energy conservation in electrical appliances, in electrical installation systems, in lighting etc. Concepts of energy conservation in buildings, star labelling, opportunities and challenges in energy conservation are explained and presented. Energy auditing, and energy enterprises with some practical examples are presented in easy language to understand the fundamental concepts.

The Government of India has adopted the Energy Conservation Act in 2001 to provide a legislative framework and institutional mechanisms to improve energy efficiency. The implementation of this act resulted in the establishment of the Bureau of Energy Efficiency (BEE) as the central agency and State Designated Agencies (SDAs) at the state level to enforce the terms of the Act. Relevant laws and initiatives of government of India in practicing energy conservation by small and large energy consumers are presented in this book.

It is important to note that the QR code has been provided to collect the updated data and additional knowledge on the specific topic.

As far as the present book is concerned, **"Energy Conservation and Audit"** is meant to provide a thorough knowledge of the energy conservation and energy auditing. This book will prepare diploma engineering students to apply the knowledge to meet the challenges of protecting the environment and providing solutions for the development of sustainable, environment-friendly clean and green energy to tackle 21st century and onward engineering challenges and address the related aroused questions. The subject matters are presented in a constructive manner so that a diploma engineering student acquire sufficient knowledge of implementing energy conservation practices in different sectors to achieve sustainable human friendly development environment.

We sincerely hope that the book will inspire the students to learn and discuss the ideas of practicing energy conservation in day-to-day life and will surely contribute to the development of a solid foundation of the subject. We would be thankful to all beneficial comments and suggestions which will contribute to the improvement of future editions of the book. It gives us immense pleasure to place this book in the hands of the teachers and students. It was indeed a big pleasure to work on different aspects covered in the book.

Dr. M. Rizwan

Dr. Majid Jamil

OUTCOME BASED EDUCATION

New Education Policy, NEP-2020 based education comprises of outcome-based curriculum, outcome-based teaching-learning process and outcome-based assessment to achieve targeted learning outcomes. As per National Board of Accreditation, after completion of diploma program in engineering and technology the graduate will be able to:

PO1. Basic and Discipline specific knowledge: Apply knowledge of basic mathematics, science, and engineering.

fundamentals and engineering specialization to solve the engineering problems.

PO2. Problem analysis: Identify and analyse well-defined engineering problems using codified standard methods.

PO3. Design/ development of solutions: Design solutions for well-defined technical problems and assist with the design.

of systems components or processes to meet specified needs.

PO4. Engineering Tools, Experimentation and Testing: Apply modern engineering tools and appropriate technique to conduct standard tests and measurements.

PO5. Engineering practices for society, sustainability, and environment: Apply appropriate technology in context of

society, sustainability, environment, and ethical practices.

PO6. Project Management: Use engineering management principles individually, as a team member or a leader to manage.

projects and effectively communicate about well-defined engineering activities.

PO7. Life-long learning: Ability to analyse individual needs and engage in updating in the context of technological changes

COURSE OUTCOMES

Upon successful completion of the course, the students will be able to:

CO-1: Interpret energy conservation policies in India.

CO-2: Implement energy conservation techniques in electrical machines.

CO-3: Apply energy conservation techniques in electrical installations.

CO-4: Use Co-generation and relevant tariff for reducing losses in facilities.

CO-5: Undertake energy audit for electrical system.

Course Outcomes	**Expected Mapping with Programme Outcomes** *(1- Weak Correlation; 2- Medium correlation; 3- Strong Correlation)*						
	PO-1	**PO-2**	**PO-3**	**PO-4**	**PO-5**	**PO-6**	**PO-7**
CO-1	3	1	-	1	3	1	1
CO-2	1	2	2	3	3	1	2
CO-3	1	2	2	3	3	1	2
CO-4	1	2	2	3	3	1	2
CO-5	1	2	2	3	3	3	2

GUIDELINES FOR TEACHERS

To implement Outcome Based Education (OBE) the knowledge level and skill set of the students should be enhanced. Teachers should take a major responsibility for the proper implementation of OBE. Some of the responsibilities (not limited to) for the teachers in OBE system may be as follows:

- Within reasonable constraint, they should maneuver time to the best advantage of all students.
- They should assess the students only upon certain defined criterion without considering any other potential ineligibility to discriminate them.
- They should try to grow the learning abilities of the students to a certain level before they leave the institute.
- They should try to ensure that all the students are equipped with quality knowledge as well as competence after they finish their education.
- They should always encourage the students to develop their ultimate performance capabilities.
- They should facilitate and encourage group work and teamwork to consolidate newer approach.
- They should follow Blooms taxonomy in every part of the assessment.

Bloom's Taxonomy

Level	Teacher should Check	Student should be able to	Possible Mode of Assessment
Create	Students ability to create	Design or Create	Mini project
Evaluate	Students ability to justify	Argue or Defend	Assignment
Analyze	Students ability to distinguish	Differentiate or Distinguish	Project/Lab Methodology
Apply	Students ability to use information	Operate or Demonstrate	Technical Presentation/ Demonstration
Understand	Students ability to explain the ideas	Explain or Classify	Presentation/Seminar
Remember	Students ability to recall (or remember)	Define or Recall	Quiz

GUIDELINES FOR STUDENTS

Students should take equal responsibility for implementing the OBE. Some of the responsibilities (not limited to) for the students in OBE system are as follows:

i. **Students should be well aware of each UO before the start of a unit in each and every course.**

ii. **Students should be well aware of each CO before the start of the course.**

iii. **Students should be well aware of each PO before the start of the program.**

iv. **Students should think critically and reasonably with proper reflection and action.**

v. **Learning of the students should be connected and integrated with practical and real life consequences.**

vi. **Students should be well aware of their competency at every level of OBE.**

ABBREVIATIONS AND SYMBOLS

List of Abbreviations

General Terms

Abbreviations	Full form	Abbreviations	Full form
AAAC	All Aluminium Alloy Conductor	LFL	Linear Fluorescent Lamp
AC	Alternating Current	LT	Low Tension
ADLS	Automatic Delta-Load Switching	MCC	Motor Control Centre
AMI	Advanced Metering Infrastructure	MDC	Maximum Demand Controller
APFC	Automatic Power Factor Controller	MEDA	Maharashtra Energy Development Agency
ASCR	Aluminium Cored Steel Reinforced	MOSFET	Metal-Oxide-Semiconductor Field-Effect Transistor
ATC	Aggregated Technical and Commercial Losses	PCC	Power Control Centre
BEE	Bureau Of Energy Efficiency	PC-LED	Phosphor-Converted LED
BIS	Bureau Of Indian Standards	PF	Power Factor
BLDC	Brushless DC	PFC	Power Factor Controller
BMS	Building Management Systems	PT	Potential Transformer
CFLs	Compact Fluorescent Lamps	SDAs	State Designated Agencies
CHP	Combined Heat And Power	S&L	Standards And Labelling
CRI	Colour Rendering Index	T&D	Transmission & Distribution Losses
CRT	Cast Resin Dry Type Transformers	TDS	Total Dissolved Solids

CT	Current Transformer
DISCOM	Distribution Company
DC	Direct Current
EC Act	Energy Conservation Act
ECBC	Energy Conservation Building Codes
EEM	Energy Efficient Motor
EPI	Energy Performance Index
ESM	Excited Synchronous Motor
FACTS	Flexible A.C. Transmission Systems
HF	High-Frequency
HT	High Tension
HY-LED	Hybrid Mixes LED
IC	Internal Combustion
IEA	International Energy Agency
IGBTs	Insulated Gate Bipolar Transistors
IPFC	Intelligent Power Factor Controller
kVA	Kilovolt-Ampere
kVAR	Kilo Volt-Ampere Reactive
kWh	Kilowatt-Hour
kW	Kilowatt
LEDs	Light Emitting Diodes
UJALA	Unnat Jyoti By Affordable LEDs For All
UNFCCC	United States Framework Convention On Climate Change
UV	Ultraviolet
VA	Volt-Amperes
VFDs	Variable Frequency Drives
VPI	Vacuum Pressure Impregnated Transformer

LIST OF FIGURES

LIST OF TABLES

CONTENTS

1 Energy Conservation Basics

UNIT SPECIFICS

In this unit, the following topics have been discussed for a basic understanding related to energy conservation basics:

- Importance of energy, energy scenario in India.
- Concepts of energy conservation and energy audits.
- Indian Electricity Act 2001
- Role of BEE and MEDA, star labeling.

Here, in this unit, the main focus is to provide basic information on the importance of energy conservation. Energy is an issue that is intrinsically multidisciplinary in nature. The fundamental concepts of energy are found in almost all fields, if not all academic areas. This handbook is meant to be utilized by people from many fields. An integrated and system-based approach to energy conservation is described and recommended for practice in daily life.

Energy has played a critical role in human civilization, and the use of energy sources, notably fossil fuels, has drastically affected people's living conditions. The spectrum of human applications for various energy sources has grown to the point that contemporary living would be nearly impossible without them. To put it another way, human life has become increasingly reliant on energy consumption, yet the advancements it allows come at a high cost to the environment and vulnerable communities.

Therefore, it is essential to use energy optimally without compromising our needs and simultaneously without affecting our environment. Therefore, energy conservation is an important aspect of utilizing electrical energy for economic growth, prosperity, and technical, industrial, and sustainable development.

RATIONALE

This unit introduces the importance of energy conservation and energy audit. Efforts of the government in the promotion and implementation of energy conservation are also reflected in this unit.

PRE-REQUISITES:

Basic Knowledge of Physics of class Xth standard.

UNIT OUTCOMES

The outcomes of this unit are as follows.

U1-O1: To know the energy scenario and its resources in the country.

U1-O2: To understand the concepts of energy conservation and energy auditing.

U1-O3: Indian Electricity Act-2001 and relevant clauses of energy conservation.

U1-O4: To understand the roles of BEE and MEDA.

U1-O5: To understand the need and benefits of star labelling.

Unit outcomes	EXPECTED MAPPING WITH COURSE OUTCOMES (1- Weak Correlation; 2- Medium correlation; 3- Strong Correlation)				
	CO-1	CO-2	CO-3	CO-4	CO-5
U1-O1	3	-	-	-	-
U1-O2	3	1	-	-	1
U1-O3	3	1	3	-	1
U1-O4	2	1	2	-	1
U1-O5	3	1	2	-	1

1.1 Introduction

"Energy conservation refers to efforts taken to reduce energy consumption to preserve resources for future use and to reduce environmental pollution."

Electricity is the predominant and extensively used kind of energy worldwide. The topic of energy conservation is a significant issue for most energy consumers, especially those in the industrial sector. Energy conservation is particularly crucial for developing nations in the third world countries, as they face increasing energy prices. Therefore, such countries need to adopt efficient energy devices. Energy conservation is a major concern for both the industrial and utility sectors.

The areas where energy conservation may be used include power generating stations, transmission & distribution syst`ems, and consumers' premises. Measures should be implemented to improve the operational effectiveness of power plants.

Implementing energy conservation technology in the transmission & distribution system might potentially decrease energy losses, which account for around 35% of the overall losses in the power system. Adopting energy conservation technologies would improve the operational efficiency of electrical devices utilized by end-users. Implementing energy conservation technologies will result in energy savings, hence boosting the production of energy from existing sources.

1.2 Energy

Energy is "the ability to do work". The advancement of civilization is made feasible by humanity's ability to convert energy from one form to another and harness it for productive use.

Energy is used by individuals for a multitude of purposes, including walking and cycling, propelling automobiles on roads and boats across water, cooking meals on stoves, producing ice in freezers, illuminating our homes and workplaces, manufacturing goods, and launching astronauts into space.

Different types of Energy shown in Figure 1.1 and the significance of energy is presented in Figure 1.2.

There are several types of energy, including:

Figure:1.1 Forms of Energy

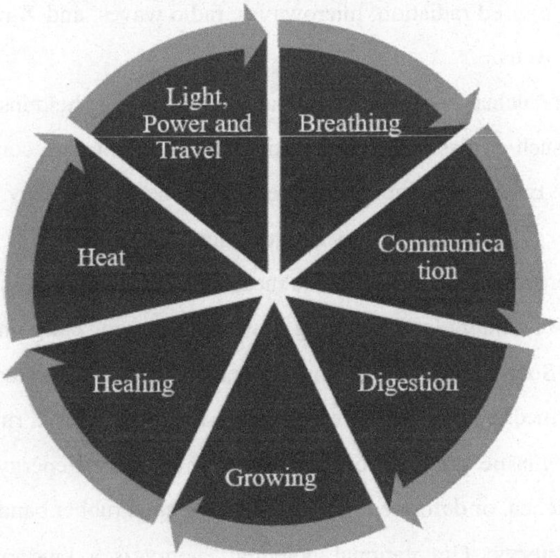

- Figure:1.2 The Significance of Energy in Our Lives

a) **Types of Energy and its Definition**

- **Kinetic Energy:** Kinetic energy is the energy that an item contains because of its motion. It is given by the equation,

$$KE = \frac{1}{2}mv^2 \qquad 1.1$$

  Where, m=Mass and v=Velocity of the Object

  Example: Car and Airplane

- **Potential Energy:** Potential energy is the stored energy in an item because of its location or condition. The types of potential energy included in this category are gravitational potential energy, elastic potential energy, and chemical potential energy. Examples of potential energy include a boulder at the highest point of a hill due to gravitational forces, a spring that is squeezed and stores elastic potential energy, and a battery that stores chemical potential energy.

- **Thermal (Heat) Energy:** The internal energy of an item is a result of the kinetic energy possessed by its molecules or atoms. It is often transmitted between bodies because of a disparity in temperature. Example: Boiling water, heating a room with a radiator
- **Chemical Energy:** Chemical substances have stored energy inside their molecular bonds. Energy is either released or absorbed during chemical processes. Example: Energy stored in food, batteries, gasoline.
- **Electrical Energy:** Electric current is the energy generated by the movement of electric charge. It is linked to the presence of electric fields and the motion of electrons. Example: bulb, electric motor.
- **Radiant (Light) Energy:** Electromagnetic waves transport energy. These include visible light, ultraviolet light, infrared radiation, microwaves, radio waves, and X-rays. Example: Sunlight, x-rays, microwave ovens.
- **Nuclear Energy:** Nuclear energy refers to the potential energy held inside the nucleus of an atom. Nuclear events, such as fission (atom splitting) and fusion (atom combining), may result in its release. Example: Energy from nuclear power plants, the sun's energy.
- **Mechanical Energy:** The total energy of a physical system, which is the combination of kinetic and potential energy. Kinetic energy is the measure of the energy possessed by an item due to its motion and location. Example: A spinning flywheel, a moving car going up a hill.
- **Sound Energy:** Sound waves are a kind of energy that is generated by vibrating objects and transmitted via a medium like air, water, or solids. Example: Music, ringing bell.
- **Elastic Energy:** Elastic potential energy refers to the stored energy in things that have been compressed, stretched, or deformed. Example: A stretched rubber band, a compressed spring
- **Gravitational Energy:** Gravitational potential energy is a kind of potential energy that is determined by the location of an object inside a gravitational field. It refers to the energy that an item contains because to its vertical position above the ground. Example: Water stored in a reservoir at a height, a satellite orbiting Earth.

Energy may be classified mainly into the following categories

- Primary and secondary energy
- Commercial and non-commercial energy
- Renewable and Non-Renewable energy

1.2.1 Primary and Secondary Energy

The primary principal energy sources are coal, oil, natural gas, and biomass (such as wood). Additional important energy sources include nuclear energy derived from radioactive materials, geothermal energy stored inside the Earth's interior, and gravitational potential energy resulting from the Earth's gravity. Industrial utilities primarily transform primary energy sources, such as coal, oil, or gas, into secondary energy sources, such as steam and electricity. Primary energy may also be used in its raw form. Certain energy sources, such as coal or natural gas, may be used as feedstock in fertiliser factories, serving non-energy purposes. Figure 1.3 describes the primary and secondary energy sources.

a) **Primary Energy Examples**
- **Fossil Fuels**
    - Coal
    - Oil
    - Natural Gas
- **Renewable Sources**
    - Solar Energy
    - Wind Energy
    - Hydropower
    - Geothermal Energy
    - Biomass
- **Nuclear Energy**
    - Uranium

b) **Secondary Energy Examples**
- **Electricity**
- **Refined Fuels**
    - Gasoline
    - Diesel
    - Kerosene
- **Hydrogen**
- **Heat**
- **Biofuels**:
    - Ethanol
    - Biodiesel

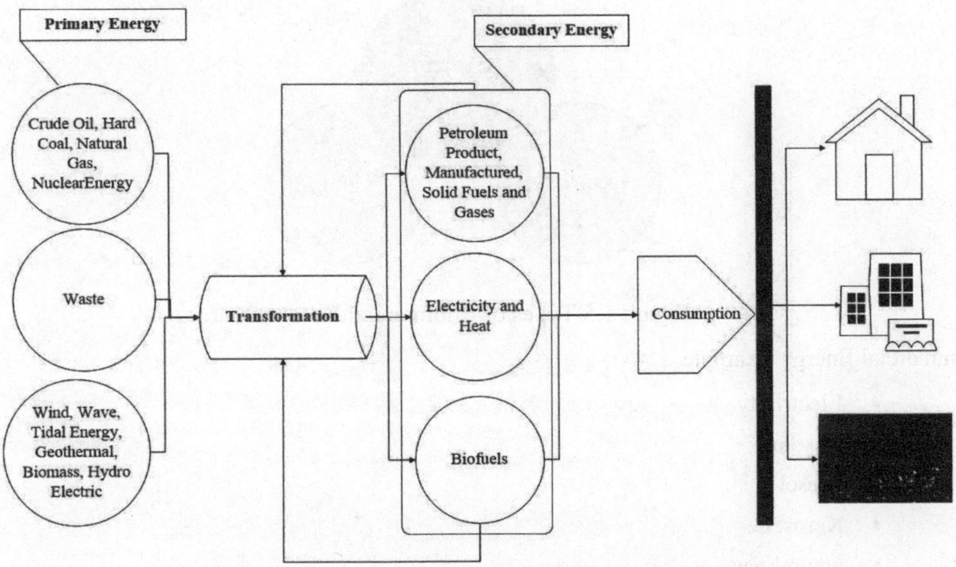

Figure 1.3 Primary and Secondary Sources of Energy

1.3 Commercial and Non-Commercial Energy

1.3.1 Commercial Energy

Commercial energy refers to the energy sources that are readily accessible in the market and may be purchased at a fixed price. The most significant types of commercial energy are electricity, coal, and refined petroleum products. Commercial energy is the fundamental source of growth and progress in industries, agriculture, transportation, and commerce in the contemporary world. In industrialised nations, commercialized fuels are the primary source of energy for economic output and home activities among the general population. Different types of Energy Sources shown in Figure 1.4. The types of commercial energy sources are given in Figure 1.5.

Figure 1.4 Types of Energy Sources

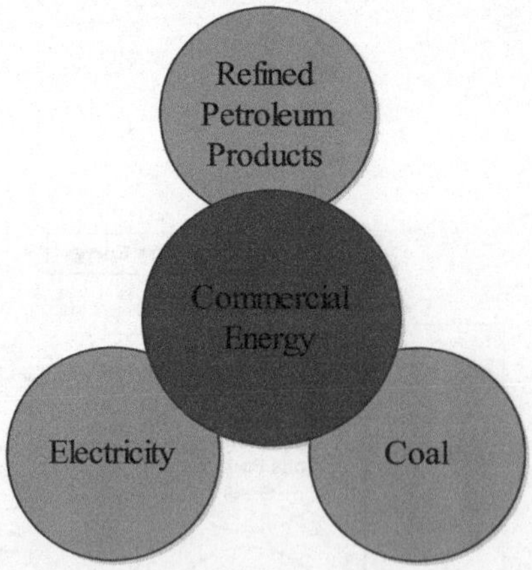

Figure 1.5 Types of Commercial Energy Sources

Commercial Energy Example

- Electricity
- Gasoline
- Diesel
- Kerosene
- natural gas

- Coal
- LPG
- Ethanol
- Biodiesel.

1.3.2 Non-Commercial Energy

Non-commercial energy refers to energy sources that are not commercially accessible for purchase. Non-commercial energy sources include fuels such as firewood, cow dung, and agricultural wastes, which are traditionally collected rather than purchased and mostly used in rural communities. These fuels are often referred to as conventional fuels. Non-commercial energy is often overlooked in energy bookkeeping. Different types of Non-Commercial Energy Sources shown in Figure 1.6.

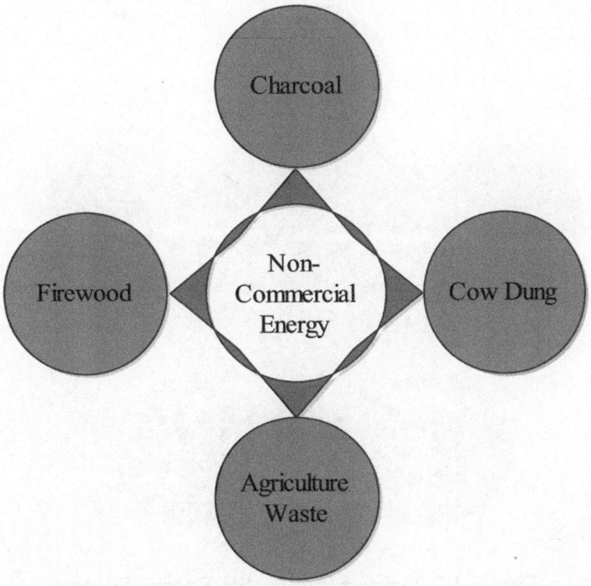

Figure 1.6 Types of Non- Commercial Energy Sources

Non-Commercial Energy Examples

- Firewood
- Agricultural residues
- Animal dung
- Unprocessed biomass
- Solar energy for domestic use
- Human and animal muscle power.

1.3.3 Renewable and Non-Renewable Energy

Renewable Energy

Resources that are naturally renewed within a human timeframe are the source of renewable energy. These energy sources include solar, wind, biomass, geothermal heat, tides, and waves. The sustainability of renewable energy and its lower environmental impact compared to non-renewable options are two of its main benefits. Hydropower produces electricity from flowing water, biomass uses organic materials to produce energy, wind energy collects the power of the wind, and solar energy harnesses the energy of the sun. Renewable energy sources are regarded as sustainable because they are constantly replenished, reduce reliance on scarce resources, and help to prevent environmental damage. Important types of renewable energy sources are described Figure 1.7.

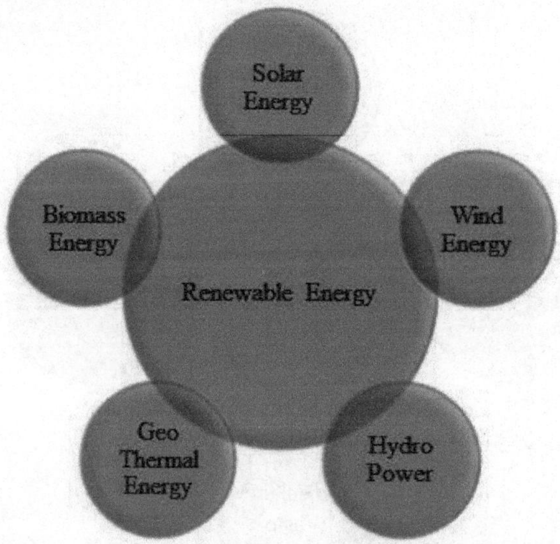

Figure 1.7 Type of Renewable Energy Sources

Example of Renewable Energy

- Solar Energy
- Wind Energy
- Hydro Power (Hydro Electric Energy)
- Geothermal Energy
- Biomass Energy

Non-renewable energy on the other hand, comes from limited resources that. cannot be replenished during a human lifetime. The most widely used non-renewable energy sources are natural gas, oil, and coal, which are examples of fossil fuels. Although these resources have played a pivotal role in driving industrialization and technological progress, their limitations include greenhouse gas emissions, environmental degradation, and limited supplies. The exploitation of these resources becomes increasingly difficult and harmful to the environment when they are exhausted. Figure 1.8 shows the different types of non-renewable energy sources.

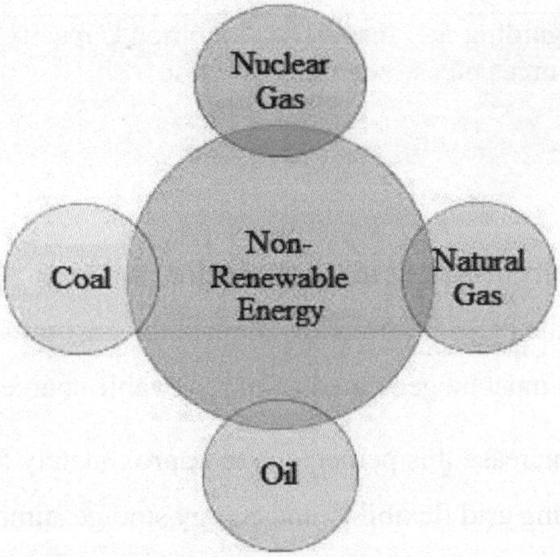

Figure 1.8 Types of Non-Renewable Energy Sources

Example of Non-Renewable Energy

- Oil and Petroleum.
- Coal.
- Natural gas.
- Fossil Fuels.
- Nuclear Fuels.
- Minerals.
- Water.
- Metal ores.

The realization of how non-renewable energy sources affect the environment and the desire to build a more sustainable energy future are driving the worldwide transition towards renewable energy.

To reduce carbon footprints and solve the issues brought on by climate change, governments, businesses, and people are spending more money on and implementing renewable energy solutions.

The installed capacity and share of various renewable energy sources is given in Table 1.1.

Table: 1.1 Total Installed Capacity of Renewable Energy Resources as on June, 30-2024
(Data source: Ministry of Power)

Renewable Energy Resources	Installed Capacity (MW)	Share in Total Installed Capacity (%)
Solar	85,474 MW	19.2 %
Wind	46,656 MW	10.5 %
Biomass	10,355 MW	2.3%
Small Hydro	5,005 MW	1.1%

For more information regarding the: Installed Generation Capacity of Renewable Energy Resources please scan the QR code

1.3.4 National Scenario

India's energy sector is primarily dedicated to the expansion of renewable energy sources, with a specific goal. According to the Press Information Bureau, the government has set a target that about 30% of the total energy must be generated from renewable sources by 2024-25.

The government's goal is to increase this percentage to approximately 50% by the year 2030. Efforts are focused on enhancing grid flexibility and energy storage, aiming for India to possess the greatest battery capacity worldwide by 2040 according to the International Energy Agency (IEA). The nation's objective is to decrease emissions intensity by 45% by the year 2030 and attain a state of net-zero emissions by the year 2070, according to S&P Global.

1.3.5 Energy Scenario in India

The country's power consumption has been seeing tremendous growth and is projected to continue increasing in the future. The power industry in India is very varied, distinguishing it from other emerging nations where crude oil, natural gas, and renewable energy sources are predominant. The sources of power production in India include a variety of options, including traditional sources such as coal, lignite, natural gas, oil, hydro, and nuclear power, as well as other feasible non-conventional sources including wind, solar, agricultural, and household waste. The nation is facing energy shortages due to inadequate fuel supply and limitations in power generating and transmission capacity. The details of installed capacity id described in Figure 1.9.

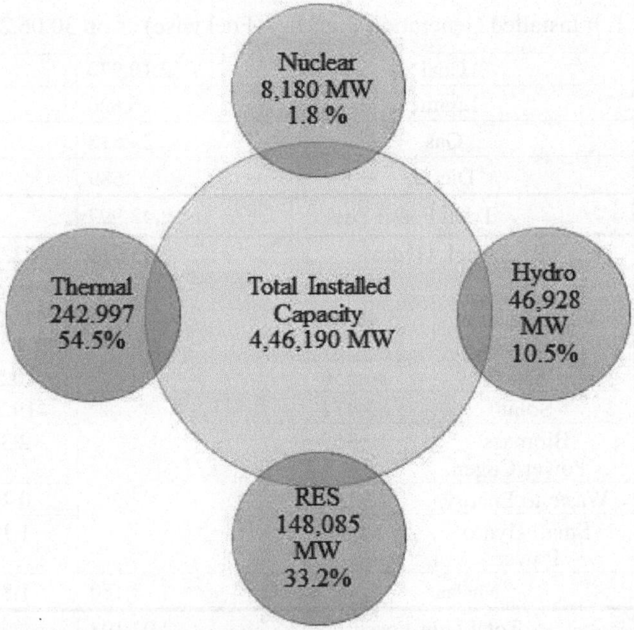

Figure: 1.9 Total Installed Capacity as on 30.06.2024 (Data source: Ministry of Power)

India is a developing nation, as seen by its energy production and consumption. The energy produced from various sources provides information on how resources are used to fulfil the demand. The sector wise installed capacity is presented in Table 1.2. The power generation from various sources is provided in Table 1.3.

Table 1.2: Installed Generation Capacity (Sector wise) as on 30.06.2024 (Data source: Ministry of Power)

Sector	Installed Generation Capacity (MW)	% Share in Total
Central Sector	1,04,453	23.4%
State Sector	1,07,671	24.1%
Private Sector	2,34,065	52.5%
Total Installed Capacity	4,46,190	

For more information regarding the: Installed Generation Capacity (Sector wise) please scan the QR code

Table 1.3: Installed Generation Capacity (Fuel wise) as on 30.06.2024

Category	Source	Sub-capacity	Capacity	Share
Fossil Fuel	Coal		2,10,970	47.3%
	Lignite		6,620	1.5%
	Gas		24,818	5.6%
	Diesel		589	0.1%
	Total Fossil Fuel:		2,42,997	54.5%
Non-Fossil Fuel	RES (Incl. Hydro)		1,95,013	43.7%
	Hydro	46,928		10.5%
	Wind, Solar & Other RE	1,48,085		33.2%
	Wind	46,656		10.5%
	Solar	85,474		19.2%
	Biomass Power/Cogen.	10,355		2.3%
	Waste to Energy	593		0.1%
	Small Hydro Power	5,005		1.1%
	Nuclear		8,180	1.8%
	Total Non-Fossil Fuel:		2,03,193	45.5%
	Total Installed Capacity (Fossil Fuel & Non-Fossil Fuel)		4,46,190	100%

For more information regarding the: Installed Generation Capacity (Fuel wise) please scan the QR code

1.3.6 Overview of Global Energy Consumption Trends

In the changing climate of the 21st century, the problem of worldwide energy use is a crucial concern that demands urgent attention and collaborative endeavors.

With the rapid growth of the global population and the increasing pace of industrialization worldwide, there is an unparalleled need for energy. The complex interaction between economic expansion, technological breakthroughs, and rapid urbanization has moved the globe into a period when energy is not just a product but also a crucial factor in determining socioeconomic success. Figure 1.10 shows the global power generation from different sources of energy.

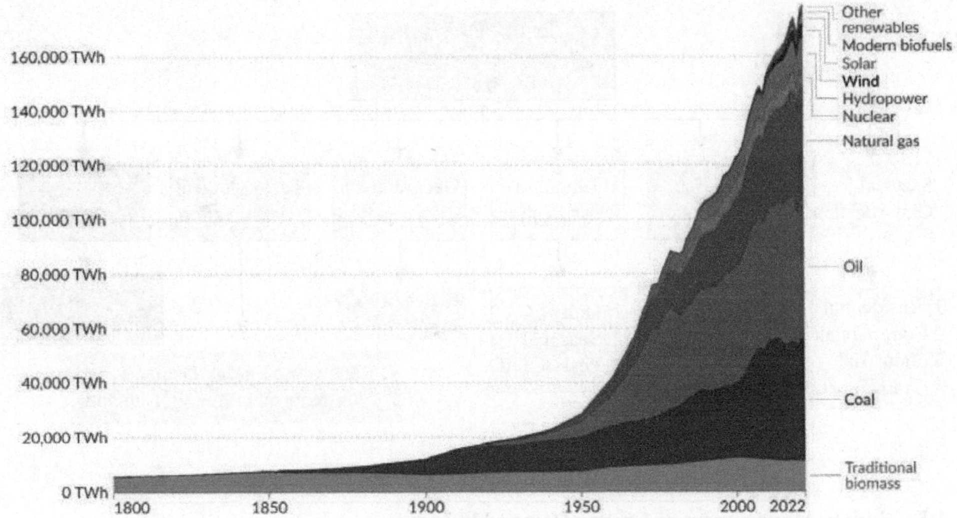

Figure: 1.10 Global Primary Energy Consumption by Source (Data source: Energy Institute's Statistical Review of World Energy (2023)).

For more information regarding the: Global Primary Energy Consumption by source please scan the QR code

1.4 Energy Demand and supply

Any kind of energy needed to meet a person's or a sector's energy demands is often referred to as "energy demand".

The term "individual energy demand" refers to the energy needed for a variety of tasks, such as heating, cooling, and cooking.

The energy needs of various sectors, including transportation, residential, and industrial ones, are referred to as sectoral energy demand.

Energy demand may be divided into two categories: (a) primary energy demand, which is the quantity of energy needed by a nation; and (b) final energy demand, which is the quantity of energy given to customers. At any given time, the entire energy demand should be met by the power supplying agencies. Energy demand in different sectors is shown in Figure 1.11.

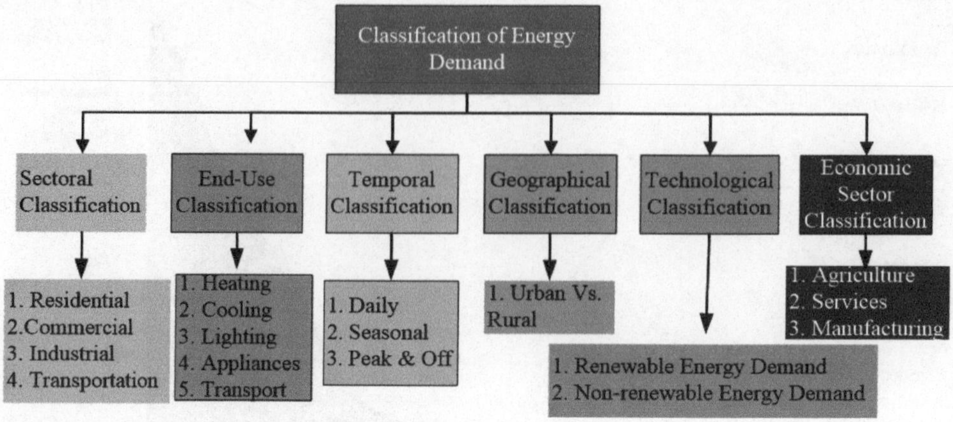

Figure 1.11 Classification of Energy Demand

1.4.1 Supply Management of Energy Demand in India

The amount of a product that manufacturers have on hand for sale is known as the supply. The amount of energy available for end users to get from suppliers or resources is known as the energy supply. India's fast increasing population, urbanisation, and industry provide a difficult task for the country in managing its energy needs. Environmental issues are exacerbated by the nation's heavy reliance on coal to produce power. India is focusing on renewable energy sources like solar and wind power to diversify its energy mix to solve this.

Improving grid connection, encouraging energy-saving initiatives, and making infrastructure investments are all necessary for effective supply management of sustainable energy. Growth of solar photovoltaic in India increased day by day, this data shown in Figure 1.12.

The National Solar Mission and the Ujwal DISCOM Assurance Yojana are two examples of government programmes that aim to increase the use of renewable energy sources and strengthen the financial standing of power distribution firms.

Demand-side management, energy storage options, and smart grid technologies are essential for maintaining supply and demand equilibrium.

Further enhancing India's energy security may be achieved via promoting global partnerships for investment and technology transfer.

India must take a comprehensive strategy to ensure a dependable, reasonably priced, and ecologically conscious energy supply. This includes enacting regulatory changes, fostering technological advancements, and raising public awareness.

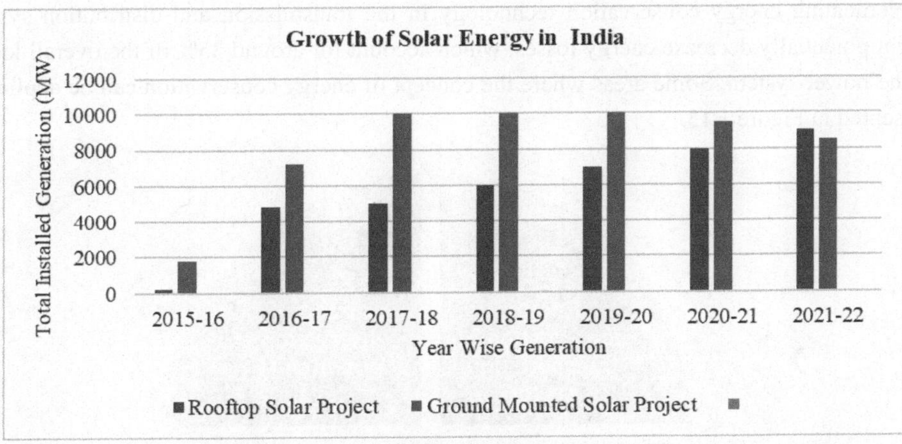

Figure 1.12 Growth Solar India (Source:https://hareda.gov.in/intoduction-jnnsm/)

For more information regarding the: Jawaharlal Nehru Solar Mission please scan the QR code

Example 1.1: *Calculate the energy consumed in one month by an equipment of 200 Watts rating and used for 5 hrs in a day. (Assume that there are 30 days in that month)*

Solution: Given Data, Power P = 200 W,

Total number of hours = 5 hrs

Energy = Power × Time

$$E = P \times t$$

$$E = \frac{200}{1000} \times 5 \times 30$$

$$Total\ Energy\ Consumption\ (E) = 30\ kWh$$

1.5 Energy Conservation

Energy conservation is the effort to reduce wasteful energy consumption by using fewer energy services. This could be achieved through efficient energy use or changing one's behavior to use less service. There are certain advantages of energy conservation, such as reduction in greenhouse gas emissions, less carbon footprint, less cost, and energy savings.

Energy conservation may lead to enhanced economic resources, improved ecological conditions, strengthened national defence, heightened personal safety, and greater human well-being.

The areas where energy conservation may be used include power generating stations, transmission & distribution systems, and consumers' premises.

Implementing energy conservation technology in the transmission and distribution system might potentially decrease energy losses, which account for around 35% of the overall losses in the power system. Some areas where the concept of energy conservation can be applied is presented in Figure 1.13.

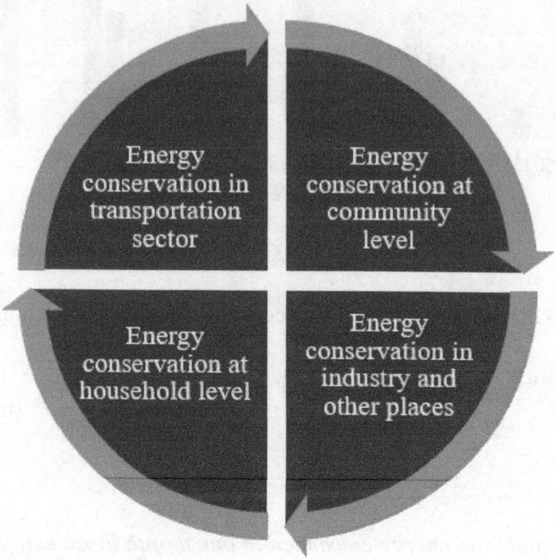

Figure: 1.13 Various Levels of Energy Conservation

1.5.1 Need of Energy Conservation

An energy study done by the Ministry of Power in 1992 revealed that the need for improvements in energy generating efficiency, energy transportation (transmission and distribution networks), and the performance efficiency of end-use equipment.

The study of 'Energy strategies for the Future' encompasses two main aspects: the effective utilisation of energy, including energy conservation, and the use of renewable energy sources. Energy conservation is particularly crucial for developing nations in the third world, as they face increasing energy prices and the need to adopt efficient energy technologies, which are of great importance to both the industry and the utility sector.

Environment Aspects of Energy Conservation

Increasing use of energy is seriously affecting our environment. Fossil fuels, such as coal and oil, which have undergone a lengthy formation process, are rapidly approaching depletion. Over the last two centuries, humanity has depleted about 60% of the total available resources. To achieve sustainable development, it is imperative that we implement energy efficiency measures and use more and more renewable energy sources for various applications.

These reserves are augmenting demand and will endure for future years.

- Fossil fuels, despite their previous widespread use, are now closely associated with environmental deterioration and the phenomenon of climate change.
- The burning of coal, oil, and natural gas emits greenhouse gases, namely carbon dioxide, into the atmosphere, plays a crucial role in the global warming phenomenon.

Efforts to Protect Environment

To protect environment, there is a need to replace fossil fuels with sustainable and renewable energy sources.

- Renewable energy, which includes solar, wind, hydro power, and geothermal sources, has become a symbol of optimism in the pursuit of a sustainable energy future.
- The use of renewable energy sources not only addresses environmental issues but also enhances energy security by decreasing reliance on limited resources and unstable global markets.
- The importance of energy efficiency is paramount when striving for sustainable consumption habits.
- Cutting-edge energy storage systems and intelligent grid technologies are becoming essential elements of the shift, guaranteeing a dependable and robust energy supply.
- Technological improvements are crucial in optimizing energy use across several industries, ranging from energy-efficient appliances to green building designs.
- Both governments and corporations are increasingly acknowledging the economic and environmental advantages of implementing energy-efficient methods. This has resulted in a significant change in consumer behavior and industrial operations.

1.5.2. Energy Efficiency

Energy efficiency refers to the practice of reducing energy use while maintaining the same level of service. For example, replace an ineffective incandescent light bulb with LED lamp.

1.5.2.1. Energy elasticity

Energy elasticity refers to the proportional change in energy consumption that occurs in response to a one percent change in a country's national GDP over a certain period.

1.5.2.2. Energy Policy

Energy Policy defines the overall guidelines for the efforts to achieve greater energy efficiency. It is established and maintained by the top management of the company.

1.5.2.3. Energy Planning

Energy Planning entails establishing specific energy objectives in accordance with the overarching energy strategy and developing detailed strategies to accomplish these objectives within a certain timeframe. The planning of multiple activities include the anticipation, allocation of funds, establishment of necessary facilities, procurement of materials and equipment, implementation of advanced technologies, management of financial resources, recruitment of personnel, and research and development planning.

1.5.2.4. Energy Management

Energy management can be defined in many ways. One way of defining it is: "The judicious and effective use of energy to maximize profit and enhance competitive positions".

Another comprehensive definition is "The strategy of adjusting and optimizing energy, using systems and procedures so as to reduce energy requirements per unit of output while holding constant or reducing total cost of producing the output from these systems".

The objective of energy management is to achieve and maintain optimum energy procurement and utilization throughout the organization and to: (i) minimize energy cost/energy waste without affecting production and quality, (ii) minimize environmental effects.

1.6. Energy Conservation and Energy Efficiency: Concepts and Difference

- Energy conservation and efficiency are interconnected concepts; however, they possess separate meanings within the realm of energy.
- Energy conservation entails reducing energy use by modifying one's actions and routines.
- Energy efficiency refers to the use of technology that consumes less energy while yet achieving the same level of performance.

1.6.1. Energy Efficiency: Crucial Elements

A direct influence on the economy, the environment, and the long-term availability of non-renewable energy sources may be achieved via the conservation of usable energy, which would otherwise be squandered.

A decrease in energy consumption is what is meant by the term "energy conservation." This is accomplished by minimising energy losses and waste via the use of energy-efficient methods of energy production and utilisation. To save energy, there are three essential aspects to consider:

1.6.2. Economic Aspect

- **Product Cost Reduction**

Energy conservation eventually results in economic advantages due to the reduction in manufacturing costs. The cost of energy is a substantial portion of the overall cost of products in energy-intensive sectors such as steel, aluminium, cement, fertiliser, pulp, and paper.

We must endeavour to achieve optimal energy efficiency by using energy-efficient technology. This will result in a decrease in the manufacturing expenses and thus enable the manufacture of more affordable and superior quality items. It is crucial to maintain competitiveness with our business adversaries.

- **Potentially better employment prospects**

To reduce energy consumption, it is common practice to invest in new, more efficient machinery to replace older, less efficient models, track energy use, educate employees, etc. So, new work possibilities may arise because of energy saving.

- **Aspect of the Environment**

There is no energy production or consumption method that does not have some kind of indirect or direct impact on the natural world. The major energy source largely determines the level of environmental deterioration. Heat is another kind of energy that may be released into the environment at any phase of energy conversion. Therefore, energy is produced and used with negative consequences for the environment. To lessen the impact of this, energy-saving measures should be used.

1.6.3. Environment Aspect

Every kind of energy creation or utilisation process has an impact on the environment, whether it is via direct or indirect means. The degree of environmental deterioration is mostly determined by the kind of primary energy source. Furthermore, throughout every step of energy conversion, a fraction of the energy is lost. Transfers to the surrounding environment and manifests as thermal energy. Consequently, energy is produced and used, but this comes at the cost of detrimental effects on the environment. Implementing energy saving measures may reduce the extent of this harm.

1.6.4. Conservation of Non-Renewable Energy Assets

The predominant source of energy used in the contemporary world is derived from non-renewable fossil fuels. These resources were deposited millions of years ago and are no longer being replenished. This limited, exhaustible resource is being depleted rapidly. The global community consumes fossil fuels at a rate that surpasses the time it took the Earth to produce them by a factor of a thousand. Consequently, their prices are inevitably poised to increase in comparison to all other items. We must discontinue inefficient methods in energy use and preserve this valuable resource at all costs for future generations.

Energy Audit

- An energy audit is a comprehensive examination, assessment, and evaluation of energy use in a structure, process, or system with the goal of conserving energy.
- The purpose is to identify ways to decrease the amount of energy required for operation without compromising the desired results.
- An energy audit is the first stage in commercial and industrial sector to find out the potential ways to decrease energy costs.
- It serves as a baseline for managing energy inside an organization and lays the foundation for planning a more efficient use of energy throughout the organization.
- The necessity of energy audit is provided in Figure 1.14.

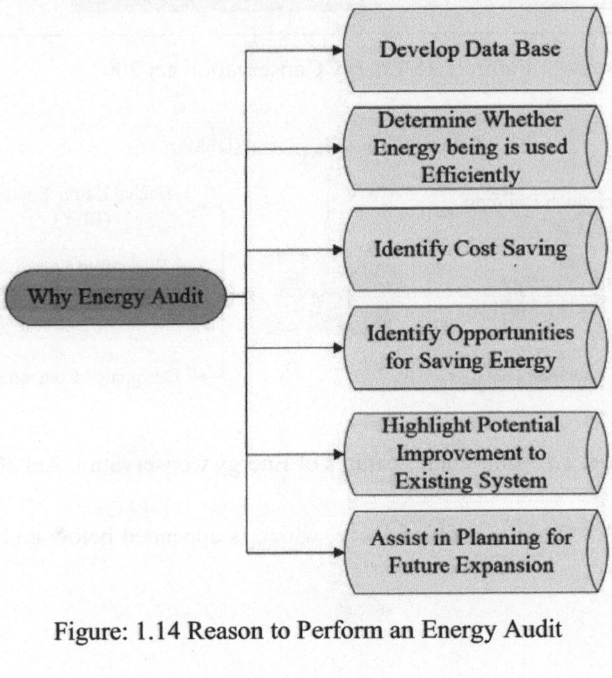

Figure: 1.14 Reason to Perform an Energy Audit

1.7. Indian Electricity Act 2001

The Government of India adopted the Energy Conservation Act in 2001 to provide a legislative framework and institutional mechanisms to improve energy efficiency. The implementation of this act resulted in the establishment of the Bureau of Energy Efficiency (BEE) as the central agency and State Designated Agencies (SDAs) at the state level to enforce the terms of the Act. The Act's implementation involves significant participation from the Central Government, State Government, and BEE.

The objective of BEE is to establish policies and methods grounded on self-regulation and market principles, aimed at decreasing the energy intensity of the Indian economy.

This objective will be accomplished by the active involvement of all parties involved, leading to swift and enduring implementation of energy saving measures across all industries.

The details of energy conservation act 2001 along with important features are described in Figure 1.15 and Figure 1.16 respectively.

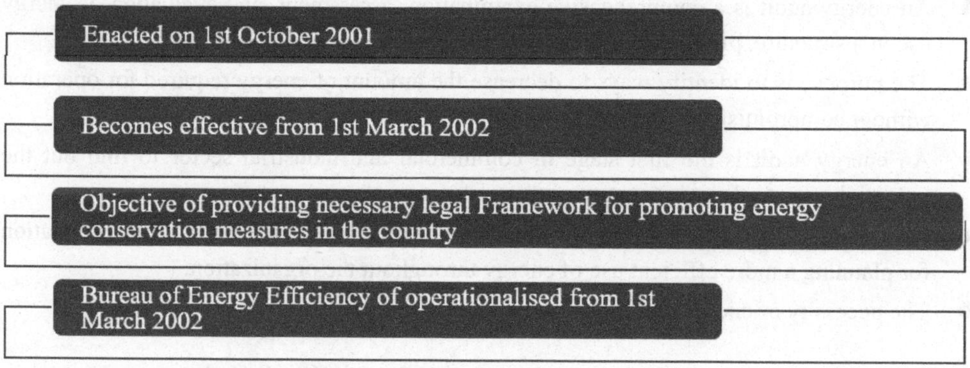

Figure:1.15 Energy Conservation act 2001

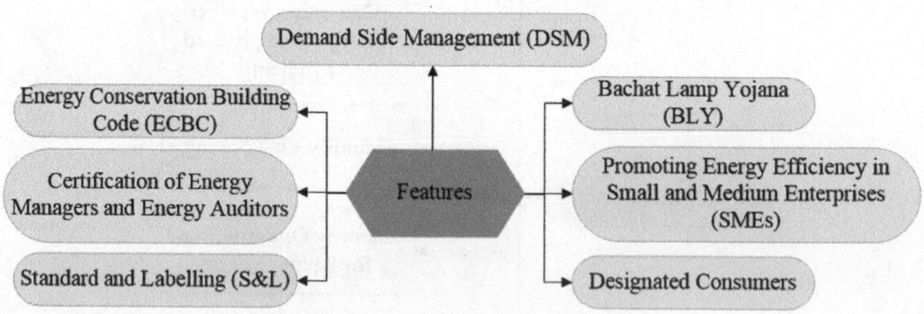

Figure: 1.16 Important Features of Energy Conservation Act 2001

This act provides a long-range consequence, which is appended below and shown in Figure 1.17.

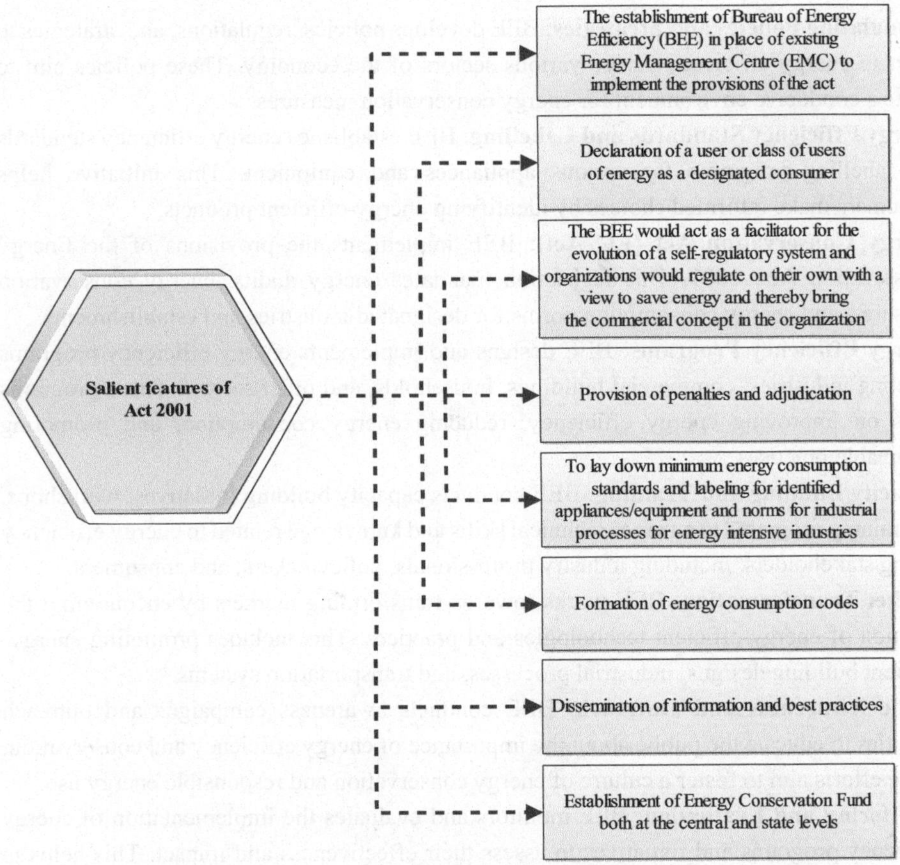

Figure:1.17 Description of Energy Conservation Act 2001

1.8. Bureau of Energy Efficiency (BEE) and its Roles

The Bureau of Energy Efficiency (BEE) was established by the Government of India on March 1, 2002, in accordance with the Energy Conservation Act of 2001.

The Bureau of Energy Efficiency's objective is to support the development of policies and initiatives that prioritise self-regulation and market principles, within the broader context of energy management.

The Conservation Act of 2001 was enacted with the main goal of decreasing the energy intensity of the Indian economy.

The primary objective of the Bureau of Energy Efficiency is to establish and integrate energy efficiency services, facilitate effective delivery mechanisms nationwide, and assume a leadership role in promoting energy efficiency across all sectors of the country.

The main goal is to decrease the energy intensity in the economy.

1.8.1 Role of Bureau of Energy Efficiency (BEE)

The Bureau of Energy Efficiency (BEE) plays a significant role in promoting energy efficiency and conservation in India. Some of the key roles and functions of BEE include:

a) **Formulating Policies and Strategies**: BEE develops policies, regulations, and strategies to promote energy efficiency across various sectors of the economy. These policies aim to create a conducive environment for energy conservation measures.
b) **Energy Efficiency Standards and Labelling**: BEE establishes energy efficiency standards and labelling programs for various appliances and equipment. This initiative helps consumers make informed choices by identifying energy-efficient products.
c) **Energy Conservation Act (EC Act)**: BEE implements the provisions of the Energy Conservation Act, 2001. This legislation mandates energy audits, energy conservation measures, and energy consumption norms for designated industries and establishments.
d) **Energy Efficiency Programs:** BEE designs and implements energy efficiency programs targeting industries, commercial buildings, households, and other sectors. These programs focus on improving energy efficiency, reducing energy consumption, and promoting sustainable practices.
e) **Capacity Building and Training**: BEE conducts capacity building initiatives, workshops, and training programs to enhance technical skills and knowledge related to energy efficiency among stakeholders, including industry professionals, policymakers, and consumers.
f) **Market Transformation**: BEE works towards transforming markets by encouraging the adoption of energy-efficient technologies and practices. This includes promoting energy-efficient building designs, industrial processes, and transportation systems.
g) **Public Awareness and Outreach**: BEE conducts awareness campaigns and outreach activities to educate the public about the importance of energy efficiency and conservation. These efforts aim to foster a culture of energy conservation and responsible energy use.
h) **Monitoring and Evaluation**: BEE monitors and evaluates the implementation of energy efficiency programs and initiatives to assess their effectiveness and impact. This helps in identifying areas for improvement and refining strategies to achieve energy conservation goals.

1.8.2 Functions of Bureau of Energy Efficiency (BEE)

The Bureau of Energy Efficiency (BEE) in India plays a crucial role in various aspects related to energy conservation and efficiency. Here are some of its key functions:

- The primary regulatory functions of BEE encompass
- Develop and establish minimal energy performance requirements and build a labelling system for equipment and appliance
- Establish precise energy conservation building codes
- Activities that specifically target a certain group of customers
- Establish precise standards for energy use.
- Accredit individuals as energy managers and energy auditors
- Certify energy auditors
- Specify the method and frequency of compulsory energy audits
- Create standardised reporting formats to document energy use and the implementation of energy auditors' recommendations
- Promote awareness and provide information on energy efficiency and conservation

- ➢ Coordinate and structure the training of individuals and experts in the methodologies for optimising energy use and promoting its preservation
- ➢ Enhance the provision of consultation services in energy saving
- ➢ Facilitate and encourage the advancement of research and development
- ➢ Create and establish protocols for testing and certification, as well as actively advocate for the use of testing facilities.
- ➢ Create and oversee the development and execution of pilot projects and demonstration projects
- ➢ Encourage the use of energy-efficient methods, machinery, gadgets, and systems
- ➢ Implement measures to promote the prioritisation of energy-efficient equipment or appliances
- ➢ Encourage the use of creative methods to fund energy efficiency initiatives
- ➢ Provide financial aid to institutions to support the promotion of energy efficiency and conservation
- ➢ Create an educational programme focused on the optimisation of energy use and the preservation of energy resources
- ➢ Establish and execute worldwide collaboration initiatives focused on the effective utilisation and preservation of energy resources

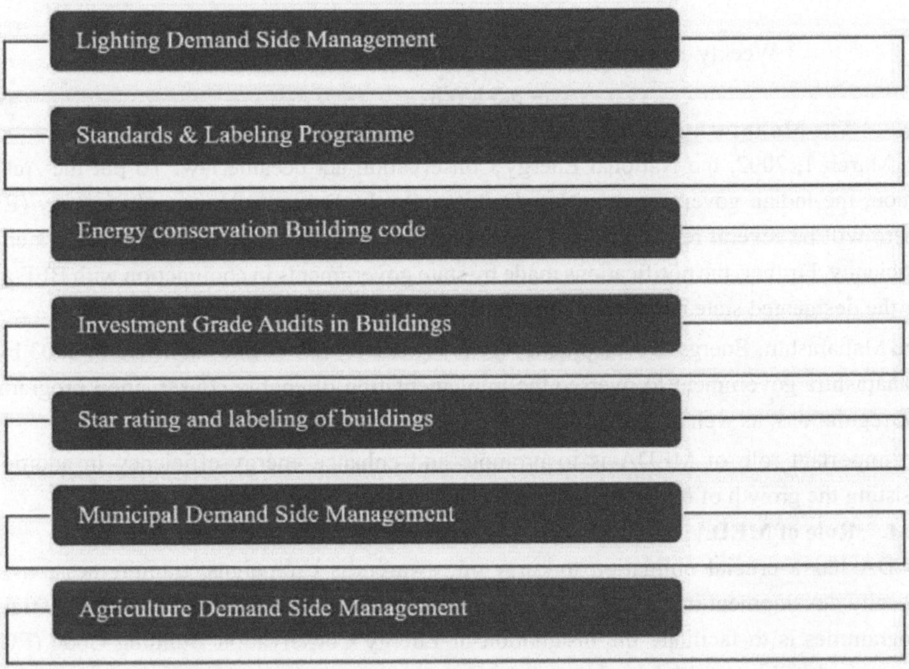

Figure: 1.18 Schemes Under Bureau of Energy Efficiency (BEE)

Example 1.2: An electric motor used in a factory having rating of 20 kW. It runs for a period of 8 hrs/day. Calculate the total energy consumption in one month.

Solution: The daily energy consumption:

$$\text{Energy (daily)} = \text{Power} \times \text{Time}$$

Where:

Power P = 20 kW

Time t = 8 hours

$$\text{Energy (daily)} = 20\times 8 = \mathbf{160\ kWh}$$

Monthly energy consumption:

$$\text{Energy (monthly)} = \text{Energy (daily)} \times \text{Number of days}$$

Energy (monthly) = 160 × 30

= 4800 kWh

Example 1.3: *A lamp is used for 10 hrs per day. The rating of lamp is 50 W. Determine the energy consumption by lamp in a week.*

Solution: *Given data*

Power P = 50 W

Time t = 10 hours

The daily energy consumption:

$$\text{Energy} = \text{Power} \times \text{Time}$$

$$= \frac{50 \times 10}{1000}$$

$$= 0.5\ \text{kWh}$$

$$\text{Weekly energy consumption: } 0.5 \times 7$$

$$= \mathbf{3.5\ kWh}$$

1.9. The Maharashtra Energy Development Agency (MEDA)

On March 1, 2002, the National Energy Conservation act became law. To put the Act into action, the Indian government in New Delhi set up the Bureau of Energy Efficiency (BEE). There will be several regulatory and promotional tools used to increase the country's energy efficiency. Further, the notifications made by state governments in conjunction with BEE allow for the designated state nodal agencies to carry out the Act's implementation.

The Maharashtra Energy Development Agency (MEDA) has been established in 2003 by the Maharashtra government to oversee the implementation of energy conservation programmes and regulations, as well as to coordinate and enforce the Energy Conservation Act.

An important role of MEDA is to promote and enhance energy efficiency in addition to assisting the growth of renewable energy sources.

1.9.1. Role of MEDA

MEDA has a crucial obligation to carry out awareness campaigns, training sessions, and capacity development initiatives for different stakeholders. The primary goal of these training programmes is to facilitate the installation of Energy Conservation Building Code (ECBC) compliant buildings in Maharashtra.

In addition to the process of modifying and enforcing the regulations in the state, the capacity development training activity is crucial in raising knowledge of the energy conservation development code throughout the state.

1.9.2. Responsibilities of MEDA

The Maharashtra Energy Development Agency (MEDA) is a government agency in the state of Maharashtra, India, dedicated to the promotion and development of renewable energy and energy conservation. The major responsibilities of MEDA are provided in Figure 1.19.

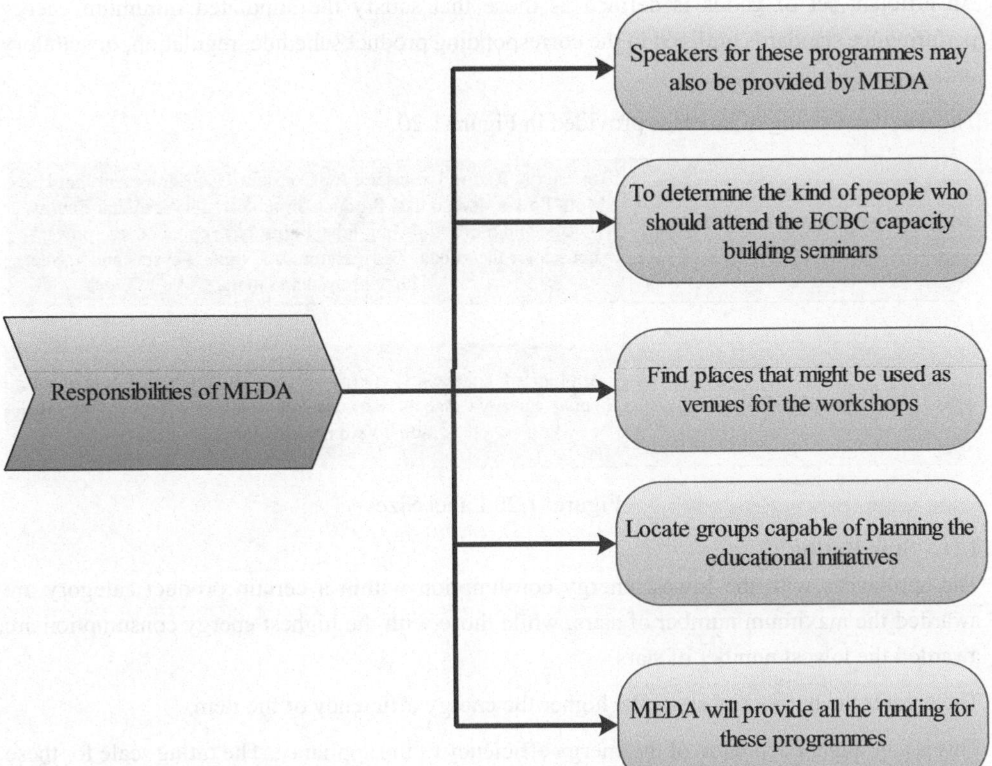

Figure: 1.19 Responsibilities of MEDA

1.10. Star Labelling

Objectives of star labelling

- To provide information on energy performance so that consumers can make informed decisions while purchasing appliances.
- To make aware the consumer about the energy saving potential among the available products.
- To create a demand in the market for energy efficient equipments.

1.10.1. Labelling

Energy efficiency labels on items highlight energy performance (typically energy usage, efficiency, or cost) to help buyers make educated selections. Two main types of labelling are as follows:

a) Comparative label:

Enable customers to assess the efficiency of all product models to facilitate an educated decision-making process. It displays the comparative energy consumption of a product in relation to other models currently on the market.

b) Endorsement label:

An efficient set of goods is defined as those that satisfy the stipulated minimum energy performance standards outlined in the corresponding product schedule, regulation, or statutory order.

The details of sizing of labels is provided in Figure 1.20.

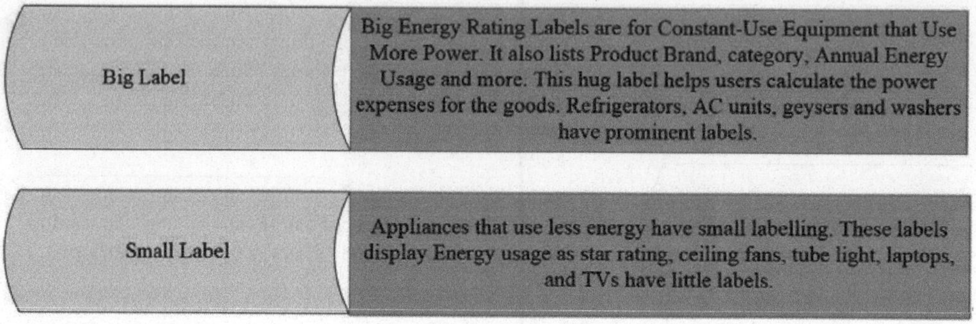

Figure: 1.20 Label Sizes

1.11. Star Rating

The appliances with the lowest energy consumption within a certain product category are awarded the maximum number of stars, while those with the highest energy consumption are awarded the lowest number of stars.

The greater the number of stars, the higher the energy efficiency of the item.

This is a graphical depiction of the energy efficiency of the appliance. The rating scale for these stars often spans from one, representing the least efficient, to five, representing the most efficient product within its category.

1.11.1. Advantages of Star Labelling

Star labelling is essential to promote energy-efficient products, addressing the increasing need for sustainable consumption.

It empowers consumers to make informed choices, fostering energy conservation and reducing environmental impact.

This standardized approach encourages manufacturers to innovate, complying with regulations and achieving market competitiveness.

Overall, star labelling benefits consumers by lowering energy costs, contributes to global sustainability goals, and enhances environmental well-being through reduced energy consumption and improved efficiency.

Need: With growing concerns about energy consumption and environmental impact, there is a need to encourage the use of energy-efficient appliances and products.

Benefits: Star labelling helps in promoting energy conservation by guiding consumers toward products that consume less energy, contributing to overall energy efficiency.

Star Labelling of Equipment's

Star labels have been created to standardize the energy efficiency ratings of different electrical appliances and indicate energy consumption under standard test conditions.

The following equipment have been star rated

- Frost Free (No-Frost) refrigerator
- Tubular Fluorescent Lamps
- Room Air Conditioners
- Direct Cool Refrigerator
- Distribution Transformer
- Induction Motors
- Pump Sets
- Ceiling Fans
- LPG Stoves
- Electric Geysers
- Colour TV

The details of energy consumption and annual energy savings is provided in Table 1.4.

Table 1.4 Star Labelling

Equipment	Star Rating	Energy Consumption (kWh/year)	Annual Energy Savings (kWh)	Remarks
Refrigerator	1 Star	600	0	Baseline non-rated model
	2 Stars	520	80	13% energy savings
	3 Stars	440	160	27% energy savings
	4 Stars	360	240	40% energy savings
	5 Stars	280	320	53% energy savings
Air Conditioner	1 Star	2000	0	Baseline non-rated model
	2 Stars	1800	200	10% energy savings
	3 Stars	1600	400	20% energy savings
	4 Stars	1400	600	30% energy savings
	5 Stars	1200	800	40% energy savings

Washing Machine	1 Star	300	0	Baseline non-rated model
	2 Stars	270	30	10% energy savings
	3 Stars	240	60	20% energy savings
	4 Stars	210	90	30% energy savings
	5 Stars	180	120	40% energy savings

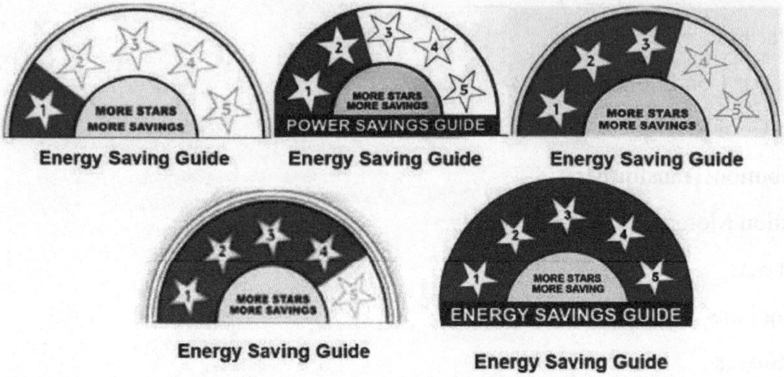

Figure 1.21 Star Labelling Diagram

BEE Star Label is now mandatory for this equipment from 7th January 2010

- The stars highlighted in colour indicate the relative efficiency of the equipment.
- The more number of stars, more the savings in energy and money. This is the average amount of electricity used by the equipment in a year in KWh/year. Star labelling or equipment, unit consumption/year shown in Figure 1.21.
- Manufacturers of equipment can participate in the scheme by registering with the BEE.
- A separate application will be made by the Manufacture for each equipment/ model, along with non – refundable registration charges and labelling fee.
- An agreement will be made with the Bureau of Energy Efficiency.
- After receiving the complete application for an equipment and model the bureau will scrutinize the of application, and seek further information, if required, within a month from the date of receipt.
- The user of label will print and affix the labels as per the label design, manner of display and the rating plan prescribed for the particular equipment.
- A list of labeled equipment (and information on the label) will be maintained by the Bureau and made available to the public through publications and its web site.

Star Labelling of Buildings:

The Bureau of Energy Efficiency has developed a scheme for energy efficiency labeling of buildings, in February 2009.

- Energy audit studies in buildings have shown large potential for energy savings both in government and commercial office buildings.
- Study of the available data has shown that there is an urgent need for improved energy efficiency of buildings. The move is aimed at accelerating the energy efficiency activities in commercial buildings across the country.
- This programme would rate the buildings on a 1-5 Star scale with 5 Star labeled buildings being the most efficient.
- Five categories of buildings - office buildings, hotels, hospitals, retail malls, and IT Parks in five climate zones in the country have been identified for this programme.
- The scheme is currently invoked for two categories – Office buildings and BPO Building.
- Initially, the programme targets the following 3 climatic zones for air-conditioned and non-air-conditioned office buildings:
- Warm and Humid
- Composite
- Hot and Dry

It will be subsequently extended to other climatic zones

- To apply for rating of office buildings, a standardized format is developed for collection of actual energy consumption: data required includes building's built up area, conditioned and non-conditioned area, type of building, hours of operation of the building in a day, climatic zone in which building is located, and other related information of the facility
- Those buildings having a connected load of 100 kW and above would be considered for BEE star rating scheme.
- Energy Performance Index (EPI) in kWh / sqm / year will be considered for rating the building.
- The star rating would provide public recognition to energy efficient buildings, thus create a demand for such buildings.

1.11.2. Informed Consumer Choices

Need: Consumers often lack clear information about the energy efficiency of products, making it challenging to make environmentally conscious choices.

Benefits: Star labelling provides a simple and standardized way for consumers to compare products and make informed decisions based on energy efficiency, leading to more sustainable choices.

a) Environmental Impact Reduction

Need: High energy consumption contributes to environmental degradation and climate change, necessitating measures to reduce the carbon footprint.

Benefits: Star labelling facilitates the purchase of energy-efficient products, which, in turn, reduces overall energy consumption and mitigates environmental impact.

b) Regulatory Compliance

Need: Governments and regulatory bodies seek ways to enforce and incentivize energy efficiency standards among manufacturers.

Benefits: Star labelling serves as a regulatory tool, encouraging manufacturers to produce energy-efficient products to comply with standards and potentially benefit from incentives.

c) Cost Savings for Consumers

Need: Consumers may desire to reduce their energy bills and operating costs associated with using appliances and devices.

Benefits: Energy-efficient products, identified through star labels, often result in cost savings for consumers over the product's lifecycle due to lower energy consumption.

d) Market Transformation

Need: Transitioning to a more energy-efficient market is crucial for long-term sustainability and resource conservation.

Benefits: Star labelling drives market transformation by creating demand for energy-efficient products, encouraging manufacturers to innovate and improve the overall efficiency of their offerings.

e) Global Consistency

Need: In a globalized market, a standardized system for energy efficiency is required to facilitate international trade and cooperation.

Benefits: Star labelling provides a consistent and easily understandable method for communicating energy efficiency, aiding global efforts to promote sustainability and reduce energy consumption.

f) Health and Well-being

Need: The environmental impact of energy consumption can affect public health and well-being.

Benefits: By promoting the use of energy-efficient products, star labelling indirectly contributes to better air quality, reduced pollution, and improved overall environmental health, benefiting communities.

SUMMERY

In this unit, the general idea about renewable and non-renewable energy resources, energy scenario in India, the gap between energy demand and supply are presented in the beginning. Basic concepts of energy conservation and its necessity is described. The government's initiative for energy conservation, the Indian Electricity Act-2001, and the importance of star labelling in energy conservation for electrical appliances are also discussed at the end of the unit, along with some practical examples and simple numerical exercises.

EXERCISE

Short Answer Type Questions

1. How can energy resources be classified?
2. What are the different forms of energy?
3. Differentiate between energy audit and energy conservation.
4. What is star labelling? Discuss its need and benefits.
5. What is the basic difference between renewable energy and sustainable energy?
6. Explain MEDA and its role.
7. Discuss BEE and its role.
8. List any two functions of BEE related to energy conservation.
9. What are the benefits of the Star Labelling program?
10. Explain the significance of the Indian Electricity Act 2001 for energy conservation.

Long Answer Type Questions

1. Discuss the need for energy conservation and its measurements.
2. Discuss the merits and demerits of various renewable energy sources.
3. Discuss the Government of India's initiatives to promote energy conservation.
4. How have scientific innovations and inventions impacted society and the environment?
5. Explain the role of MEDA and BEE to promote energy conservation programme.
6. Distinguish between Energy conservation and Energy audit based on activities.
7. Analyze the relevant clauses of the Indian Electricity Act 2001 that pertain to energy conservation and their impact on energy management practices.
8. Compare and contrast the concepts of energy conservation and energy audit, providing examples of each.
9. Discuss the current energy demand and supply scenario in India and its implications for future energy policy.
10. Evaluate the role of the Maharashtra Energy Development Agency (MEDA) in promoting energy conservation and renewable energy in the state of Maharashtra.

Multiple Choice Questions

1. What is primary energy?
   A. Energy that is directly harvested from natural resources
   B. Energy derived from secondary sources

C. Energy that is stored in batteries
D. None of the above
2. Which of the following is a primary source of energy?
A. Coal
B. Electricity
C. Diesel
D. None of the above
3. What factors influence energy demand?
A. Population growth
B. Economic development
C. Technological advancements
D. All the above
4. What does the national energy scenario refer to?
A. The energy situation within a particular region
B. The overall energy situation of a country
C. The global energy consumption patterns
D. None of the above
5. What is the primary goal of energy conservation?
A. To reduce energy bills
B. To minimize environmental impact
C. To increase energy production
D. None of the above
6. What is an energy audit?
A. A systematic process of assessing energy usage
B. A method to generate energy from renewable sources
C. A way to store energy for later use
D. None of the above
7. What is the main difference between energy conservation and energy audit?
A. Energy conservation focuses on reducing energy usage, while energy audit evaluates energy consumption.
B. Energy audit focuses on reducing energy usage, while energy conservation evaluates energy consumption.
C. There is no difference between the two concepts.
D. None of the above
8. Which of the following is covered under the Indian Electricity Act 2001?
A. Energy generation
B. Energy transmission
C. Energy conservation
D. All of the above
9. What is the significance of energy conservation clauses in the Indian Electricity Act 2001?
A. To promote sustainable energy practices
B. To regulate energy consumption
C. To minimize energy wastage
D. All of the above
10. What does BEE stand for?
A. Bureau of Environmental Energy

B. Bureau of Energy Efficiency
C. Bureau of Electrical Engineering
D. None of the above

11. What are the primary roles of BEE?
A. Developing energy conservation policies
B. Implementing energy efficiency programs
C. Conducting energy audits
D. All of the above

12. What does MEDA stand for?
A. Maharashtra Energy Development Agency
B. Ministry of Energy and Development Agency
C. Madhya Pradesh Energy Distribution Authority
D. None of the above

13. What are the primary roles of MEDA?
A. Promoting renewable energy projects
B. Implementing energy efficiency measures
C. Providing financial incentives for energy conservation
D. All of the above

14. Why is star labeling implemented?
A. To identify energy-efficient products
B. To promote consumer awareness about energy consumption
C. To encourage manufacturers to produce energy-efficient appliances
D. All of the above

15. What are the benefits of star labeling?
A. Helps consumers make informed choices
B. Encourages manufacturers to improve energy efficiency
C. Reduces energy consumption
D. All of the above

16. The energy sources, that are either found or stored in nature are _________.
A. Secondary Energy Sources
B. Primary energy sources
C. both (a) and (b)
D. none of the above

17. Which of the following is commercial energy source?
A. Electricity
B. Coal
C. Oil
D. All the above

18. Inexhaustible energy sources are known as_________.
A. Commercial Energy
B. Renewable Energy
C. Primary energy
D. Secondary energy

19. Which of the following terms does not refer to specific energy consumption
A. kWh/ton
B. kCal/ton

C. kJ/kg
D. kg/kCal

20. Which of the following GHGs has the longest atmospheric life time
    A. CO_2
    B. Sulfur Hexafluoride (SF6)
    C. CFC
    D. Per FluoroCarbon (PFC)
21. Energy Intensity is the ratio of
    A. Fuel Consumption / GDP
    B. GDP/Fuel Consumption
    C. GDP/ Energy Consumption
    D. Energy Consumption / GDP
22. Which of the following is an energy security measure?
    A. fully exploiting domestic energy resources
    B. diversifying energy supply source
    C. substitution of imported fuels for domestic fuels to the extent possible
    D. all of the above
23. The objective of energy management is
    A. To minimize energy costs
    B. To minimize environmental effects
    C. a & b
    D. None of the above
24. Providing information to BEE is the role of energy manager as per
    A. Energy Conservation Act 2003
    B. Energy Conservation Act 2004
    C. Energy Conservation Act 2002
    D. Energy Conservation Act 2001

Answer of Multiple-Choice Questions

1	A	2	A	3	D	4	B	5	B	6	A
7	A	8	D	9	D	10	B	11	D	12	A
13	D	14	D	15	D	16	B	17	D	18	B
19	D	20	D	21	A	22	D	23	C	24	D

REFERENCES AND SUGGESTED READINGS

1. BEE. "Energy Efficiency in Electrical Utilities" New Delhi, India: BEE; 2015.
2. BEE. "General Aspects of Energy Management and Energy Audit" New Delhi, India: BEE; 2015.
3. BEE. "Energy Efficiency in Thermal Utilities" New Delhi, India: BEE; 2015.
4. BEE. "Energy Performance Assessment For Equipment and Utility Systems" New Delhi, India: BEE; 2015.
5. A. Kumar, "Energy Generation Through Vedas," International Journal of Science Technology and Management, 5, pp. 294-304, 2016.

6. C. Smith, "The Science of Energy – a Cultural History of Energy Physics in Victorian Britain," The University of Chicago Press, 1998.
7. A.M. Helmenstine, "How Does Electrical Energy Work?", Thought Co, 2020, URL: www.thoughtco.com/electrical-energy-definition-and-examples-4119325.
8. Britannica, The Editors of Encyclopedia, "energy," Encyclopedia Britannica, 2021, https://www.britannica.com/science/energy. Accessed 28 May 2022.
9. M. Walker, "Chapter 2: Concept of Energy," Centre of Daily Times, 1986 URL: https://personal.ems.psu.edu/~radovic/Chapter2.pdf
10. NCERT Experts, "Chapter 11: Work and Energy," Physics Book, NCERT, 2021
11. M. Kumar, "Social, Economic, and Environmental Impacts of Renewable Energy Resources," Wind Solar Hybrid Renewable Energy System, Intech Open Press, 2019.
12. IRENA, "Renewable capacity statistics 2021," International Renewable Energy Agency, Abu Dhabi, 2021.
13. United Nations, "Paris Agreement," United Nations, Paris, 2016.
14. IBEF, "Renewable Energy Industry in India Report," India Brand Equity Foundation, 2021.
15. Ministry of Renewable Energy, "Development of Solar Parks and Ultra Mega Solar Power Projects," Government of India, New Delhi, 2017.
16. Ministry of Renewable Energy, "Scheme for setting up of over 5000 MW grid connected SPV power projects under IV of JNNSM PHASE II," Government of India, New Delhi, 2019.
17. Ministry of Renewable Energy, "Grid Connected Solar Rooftop Programme," Government of India, New Delhi, 2019.
18. M. J. Rogoff, F. Screve, "Waste-To-Energy: Technologies and Project Implementation," Elsevier, Amsterdam, Netherlands, 2019.
19. United Nations, "Global Environment Outlook 6 (GEO6) – 2019," New York, USA, 2019.

****

2 Energy Conservation in Electrical Machines

UNIT SPECIFICS

In this unit, the following topics have been discussed to understand the applications of energy conservation in electrical machines.

- Why is energy conservation needed in electrical machines?
- Energy conservation in induction machines and transformers
- Solution to the problems of energy conservation in electrical machines.

Energy conservation is an important aspect of utilizing electrical energy for economic growth, prosperity, and technical, industrial, and sustainable development. Electrical machines are the most power consuming devices. Therefore, electrical machines should be highly energy efficient. Here, in this unit, the focus is to propose the solutions of energy conservation in electrical machines and transformers. Different energy conversation techniques used in electrical machines and transformers are described here in this unit. An integrated and system-based approach to energy conservation is described and recommended for practice in industries in daily life.

RATIONALE

Since electrical machines consume major part of electrical energy, therefore energy conservation is of utmost important in electrical machines to achieve the objectives of green energy for the sustainable growth and development of the nation.

PRE-REQUISITES

Basic Knowledge of Electrical Machines.

UNIT OUTCOMES

The outcomes of this unit are as follows

U2-O1: To understand the concepts of energy conservation and energy auditing.

U2-O2: Why energy conservation is important for electrical machines and transformers?

U2-O3: Techniques used for energy conservation in electrical machines and transformers.

U2-O4: To apply the concept of energy conservation in electrical equipments.

U2-O5: Energy efficient machines and transformers.

Unit outcomes	EXPECTED MAPPING WITH COURSE OUTCOMES (1- Weak Correlation; 2- Medium correlation; 3- Strong Correlation)				
	CO-1	CO-2	CO-3	CO-4	CO-5
U2-O1	3	2	-	-	-
U2-O2	1	3	-	-	1
U2-O3	1	3	3	-	2

U2-O4	-	3	2	-	2
U2-O5	-	3	3	-	3

2.1. Introduction

Energy conservation is a critical practice that involves reducing the amount of energy used while achieving the same level of productivity or services.

Energy conservation in electrical machines refers to the practice of reducing energy consumption while maintaining or improving the performance of electrical machines.

It involves employing various techniques, technologies, and practices to minimize energy losses and maximize efficiency in the operation of electrical machines such as motors, generators, transformers, and other devices.

It plays a pivotal role in addressing environmental concerns, promoting sustainability, and mitigating the impacts of climate change.

Electrical energy conservation is a worldwide priority.

Along with economic scheduling in power production and modem equipment in transmission and distribution networks, optimising electric load energy requirements is crucial.

Increasing the efficiency of electrical equipment is a cost-effective alternative to building new power plants to fulfil rising demand for energy services in many nations.

Today, industry are the primary users of electricity in any nation. Even a minor energy savings in electrical motors, the most often utilised energy converters in industries, is significant in current industrial driving applications.

In the previous unit, a general idea of energy conservation, its importance in the management of electricity and related electricity regulations and acts are presented. Here in this chapter, focus is on energy conservation in electrical machines, exploring specific strategies and technologies crucial for effective energy conservation in machines.

2.1.1.Need for Energy Conservation

The importance of energy saving in electrical equipment cannot be overstated due to several reasons. Firstly, it decreases operating expenses by reducing power use, which is especially important in businesses with continuous machine running. Furthermore, the conservation of energy improves the effectiveness of electrical machinery, resulting in extended equipment lifespan and decreased maintenance expenses. Additionally, it helps alleviate environmental consequences by minimising the need for fossil fuels, thereby lowering greenhouse gas emissions and supporting sustainability objectives.

In addition, energy-efficient devices often adhere to more stringent regulatory requirements, so avoiding possible penalties and bolstering the company's market image.

By incorporating energy-saving techniques and technology, such as high-efficiency motors and variable frequency drives, companies may not only save energy but also foster technical developments and innovation in the sector.

Hence, the preservation of energy in electrical devices is crucial for achieving economic, environmental, and regulatory advantages, leading to immediate and long-term benefits.

2.2. Need of Energy Conservation in Induction Motor

Energy conservation in induction motors is of paramount importance due to their extensive use in various industrial and commercial applications. Induction motors are employed in many applications such as pumps, fans, and other essential systems. One primary driver for energy conservation in induction motors is the imperative to enhance overall energy efficiency.

- There are certain losses in induction motors and these losses occur in the form of heat dissipation, friction, and other resistive elements within the motor.
- These motors, while widely adopted, are not 100% efficient, meaning a portion of the electrical energy they consume is wasted.
- By addressing these inefficiencies, energy conservation not only reduces operational costs but also contributes significantly to broader environmental and sustainability goals.
- Energy conservation in these motors is a direct strategy to reduce the overall demand for electricity, mitigating the environmental consequences associated with power generation.
- Industries that actively engage in energy-efficient practices not only contribute to a more sustainable future but also enhance their reputation, attract environmentally conscious consumers, and align with global efforts to combat climate change.

In essence, the need for energy conservation in induction motors extends beyond immediate economic considerations, encompassing environmental stewardship, regulatory compliance, and a commitment to sustainable business practices. When all industrial applications are taken into consideration, only electric motors powered equipment accounts for 70% of the total electrical energy utilised.

2.2.1. The Importance of Energy Conservation in Induction Motors

- Electric motors are essential in several sectors, including industrial, commercial, agricultural, and residential, and they need significant quantities of energy. Approximately 70% of the total industrial load consists of electric motors.
- The rising cost of electrical power necessitates the need for motors to operate at better efficiency to achieve maximum savings.
- To lower production costs, it is necessary to decrease the running expenses of the machinery being employed, without compromising the quality.
- Most of the energy generated and used to power electric motors is derived from the combustion of valuable fuels or the use of natural resources such as coal and oil.
- Inefficient motors need a significant amount of power to function, leading to the rapid loss of valuable fuels and resources.
- Therefore, it is essential to use energy conservation methods in induction motors to avoid the depletion and squandering of energy supplies.

2.3. Energy Conservation Techniques in Induction Motor

For induction motors to have the least possible environmental effect and to save operating expenses, energy saving is essential. Because of their efficiency and dependability, induction motors are extensively utilized in many different sectors. They may, however, use a substantial amount of energy. Energy consumption can be greatly decreased by putting energy conservation techniques into practice. These include using motors that are the right size and efficiency, installing variable frequency drives (VFDs) for precise speed control, doing routine maintenance to ensure optimal performance, and using power factor correction to increase energy efficiency. These tactics support ecologically beneficial and sustainable industrial processes in addition to lowering power costs. In this section discussed the various types of energy conservation techniques in induction motor.

2.3.1. Improving power Quality

By ensuring that the voltage level is maintained within the standard norms, which are defined as having a tolerance of +/-6%, and the frequency is maintained with a tolerance of +/-3%. Some issues related to power quality are described in Figure 2.1.

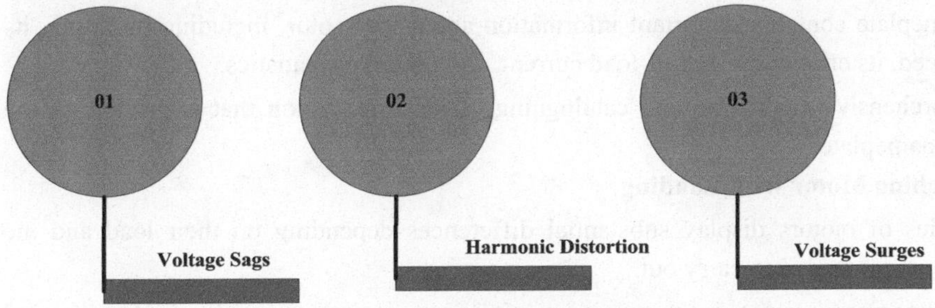

Figure: 2.1 Common Power Quality Issue

2.3.1.1. Enhancing Power Quality to Conserve Energy in Induction Motors:

- **Voltage:** Ensuring that the voltage remains at the specified value for motors leads to the desired torque-speed characteristics necessary to operate the load.
  Reducing the voltage results in an increase in the current drawn, leading to higher line losses, increased copper losses in the machine, and an increase in line voltage drops.
  Although the voltage may be above the acceptable amount, a greater flux density in motors will still result in increased iron losses. These factors result in a reduction in efficiency. Therefore, it is necessary to maintain the appropriate voltage.
- **Frequency:** It controls the losses associated with speed and iron. If the value exceeds the rated value, these losses will grow since the speed is directly proportional to the frequency. Consequently, the speed-dependent friction and windage losses will also increase, leading to a drop in efficiency. A decrease in frequency results in a decrease in speed, which in turn impacts the output power. Therefore, it is necessary to keep the frequency at its rated value.
- When the supply waveform is fully sinusoidal, the presence of harmonics is eliminated, resulting in the absence of iron and copper losses caused by harmonic voltage and currents. In addition, even minuscule harmonics result in the generation of undesirable harmonic torques in motors, necessitating the expenditure of energy to counteract them. This energy consumption is inefficient and wasteful.

2.3.2. Motor Survey

An essential component of energy conservation is the execution of a motor survey, particularly when determining the appropriate size for a replacement of a motor.

- This is because motors function most effectively when they are near full load.
- Operating below this threshold results in a significant decrease in efficiency.

- Efficiency reaches its highest point when it is more than 80% of full load torque.

Consequently, to save energy and pick a new motor that is of an acceptable size, it is necessary to conduct a thorough motor survey, beginning with an exhaustive review of the data on the nameplate.

This is necessary to guarantee the highest possible level of efficiency and performance.

2.3.2.1. Motor Survey Steps

- Precisely assessment of load.
- Name plate statistics are quite helpful in picking the replacement motor that is of the suitable size to provide an ideal level of performance.
- The nameplate contains important information about the motor, including its rating, its rated speed, its efficiency, its full-load current, and other key statistics.
- A comprehensive evaluation and cataloguing of the information that is printed on the motor's nameplate.

2.3.3. Matching Motor with Loading

The properties of motors display substantial differences depending on their load and the function they are intended to carry out.

- When choosing a motor for a certain use, it is important to carefully analyse several elements including constant speed, constant torque, variable speed, abrupt or rapid starting, continuous or intermittent operation, frequent starting and stopping, and other relevant considerations.
- Ensuring the appropriate alignment between the motor type and the specific need of the application is of utmost importance, since it directly impacts the amount of power used.
- Choosing a motor that is efficient and specifically suited to the load requirements will significantly decrease the total amount of power used.
- It is crucial to acknowledge that motors that operate at loads below 40% have subpar efficiency. In such instances, energy conservation may be achieved by either replacing these motors with suitably dimensioned ones or by exchanging them with alternative loads.
- Choosing the wrong motor may cause a range of problems, such as early motor breakdown, which can result in significant losses in output. To address these issues effectively, it is crucial to give priority to accurately determining the appropriate dimensions and choosing motors that are specifically suited to the distinctive features of the given application.

Moreover, the crucial aspect of energy conservation is in reducing the occurrence of idle and unnecessary operation of motors. To prevent extended periods of inactivity in machine tools, conveyors, exhaust fans, and lights, it is important to accurately align the motor specifications with the individual operational needs. It is important to avoid the unnecessary use of auxiliary equipment such as cooling towers, air compressors, and pumps while manufacturing machines are not in use for a prolonged period. Adopting this comprehensive method for choosing and operating motors not only improves energy efficiency but also extends the lifespan of equipment, therefore decreasing maintenance expenses and supporting sustainable industrial methods.

2.3.4. Minimizing the Idle and Redundant Running of Motor

It is possible to minimize lengthy idle running of machine tools, conveyors, exhaust fans, lighting, and other components by reducing the amount of idle and redundant motor running throughout the process. When manufacturing machines are stopped for an extended period, it is possible to prevent the idle operation of auxiliary machinery such as cooling towers, air compressors, pumps, and so on.

2.3.5. Operating in Star Mode

In situations when the load is running at less than 30% of its maximum capacity, especially when the load is light, the practice of operating a "Delta"-connected motor in "Star" connection may result in decreased energy consumption.

It is particularly advantageous to use this setup when a motor is large and is loaded at a level that is consistently lower than 30 % of its rated shaft load.

Under these circumstances, it is possible to realise energy savings by permanently connecting the motor in the "Star" configuration.

The installation of automated Star-Delta changeover switches becomes essential in circumstances in which the load is below 30% for most of the time but periodically reaches 50%. This adaptive method to motor connection has the potential to result in energy savings that range from 5 to 15% of the power consumption that is now being used.

Star (Wye) Connection: A star connection, often referred to as a wye (Y) connection, is a technique used to link the windings of a three-phase system. In this configuration, one end of each winding is connected to a shared neutral point, resulting in a Y-shaped arrangement. It is shown in Figure 2.2.

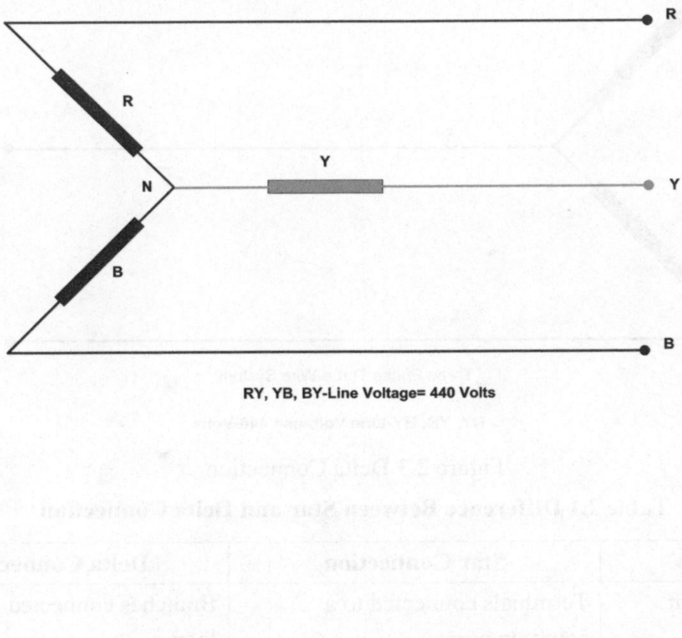

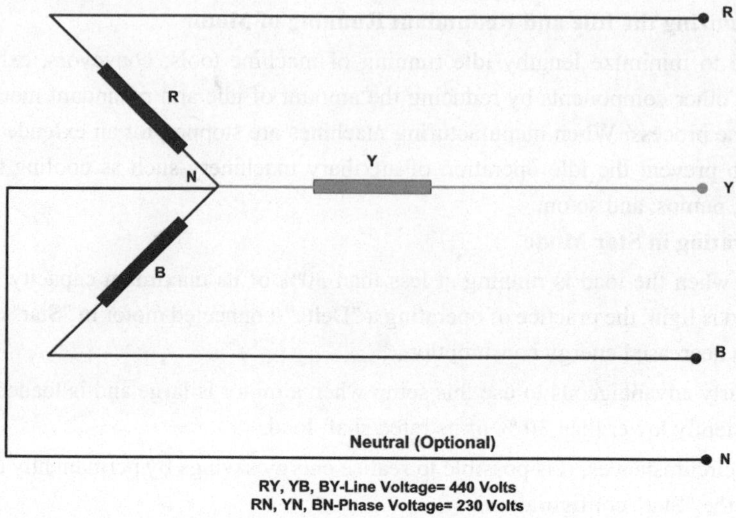

Figure 2.2 Star Connection

Delta (Δ) Connection: A delta connection is a technique used to interconnect the windings of a three-phase system in a manner that the terminal of each winding is linked to the start of the subsequent winding, creating a closed loop or triangular configuration. The description of delta connection is shown in Figure 2.3. The basic difference between star and delta connections are shown in Table 2.1.

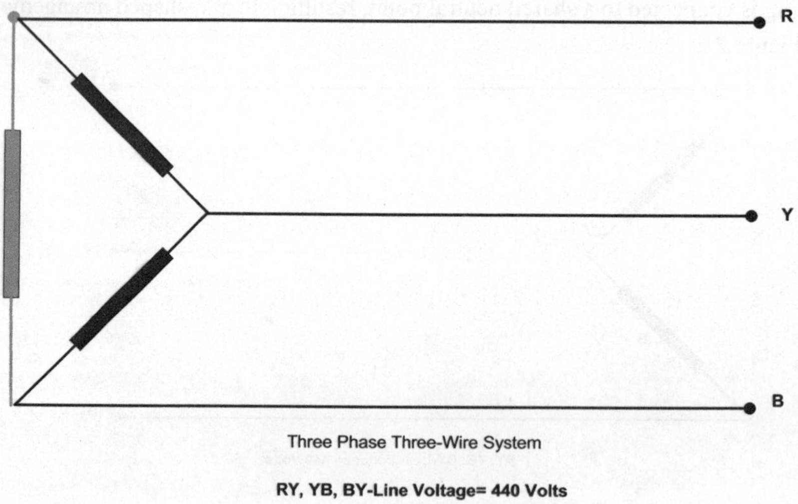

Figure 2.3 Delta Connection

Table 2.1 Difference Between Star and Delta Connection

Property	Star Connection	Delta Connection
Basic definition	Terminals connected to a common point	Branches connected in a closed loop

AICTE'S LIST OF PRESCRIBED TEXTBOOKS

As Per Model Curriculum & Outcome Based Education

aligned with

NATIONAL EDUCATION POLICY 2020

UNDERGRADUATE COURSE BOOKS

S.No.	ISBN	Book Name	Author
1	9789355382160	Advanced Electrical Machines: Theory and Practicals	Bharat Singh Rajpurohit
2	9789355382139	Analog Electronic Circuits: Theory and Practical	Venu Sonti, Sachin Jain
3	9789355383808	Analog Electronic Devices: Theory and Practicals	N. B Balamurugan
4	9789391505158	Basic Electrical Engineering (with Lab Manual)	S.K. Sahdev
5	9789355388087	Basic of Electronics	Brijesh Iyer
6	9789355387127	Basics of Electrical Machines: Theory and Practicals	D. K. Palwalia, U. K. Kalla, R. K. Kumawat
7	9789355389381	Basics of Mechanics	Shubhankar Bhowmick, N. Venkata Swamy Naidu
8	9789355386250	Basics of Thermodynamics	Parmod Kumar, Atul Dhar
9	9789355386984	Biology for Engineers	Annamma Odaneth
10	9789391505141	Chemistry-I	Manisha Agarwal
11	9789355384843	Civil Engineering Societal and Global Impact	Shakuntala Acharya
12	9789355382184	Computer Aided Civil Engineering Drawing	D. Chandra Mouli, B. Swathi
13	9789355382580	Computer Aided Design & Analysis	Hari Kumar Voruganti
14	9789355387592	Computer Architecture	D. Vaithiyanathan
15	9789355385093	Computer Networks	Hari Prabhat Gupta
16	9789355385307	Construction Engineering & Management	Sparsh Johari
17	9789355388728	Control Systems	S.N. Deepa
18	9789355385420	Data Structure and Algorithms	Ranbir Singh Sanasam
19	9789355386700	Design and Analysis of Algorithms	Hari P. Gupta, Rahul Mishra
20	9789355388872	Digital Electronics and System	Abhishek Bhatt
21	9789355386571	Digital Signal Processing	Sanjeev Sharma
22	9789355383396	Disaster management	Pradeep K. Goyal, Anil K. Gupta
23	9789355385222	Discrete Mathematical Structures	Narendra S. Chaudhari, Sharmila S. P.
24	9789355387868	Effective Technical Communication	Pritee Sharma, Sanchita Verma
25	9789355383389	Electrical Circuit Analysis and Network Theory	Shouri Chatterjee
26	9789355388957	Electromagnetic Waves	Uttam M. Pal, Srijith K.
27	9789355384652	Electronic Communication	Vimal Bhatia
28	9789355388711	Embedded Systems	Santanu Chattopadhyay
29	9789355385147	Energy Science and Engineering	M. Rizwan, Majid Jamil
30	9789355387929	Engineering Economics, Estimation & Costing	Yogesh C. Joshi
31	9789355384669	Engineering Geology	R. N. Khare, Ketan Chourasia
32	9789391505066	Engineering Graphics & Design	Pradeep Jain
33	9789391505097	English (with Lab Manual)	Kulbhushan Kumar
34	9789355385963	Environmental Engineering	Chandra Sekhar Matli
35	9789355388117	Fluid Mechanics	Shreenivas N. Londhe, Pradnya R. Dixit
36	9789355388377	Fluid Mechanics & Fluid Machines	R.P. Saini
37	9789355387103	Geotechnical Engineering	Paramita Bhattacharya

UNDERGRADUATE COURSE BOOKS

S.No.	ISBN	Book Name	Author
38	9789355385130	Hydraulic Engineering	Sayantan Ganguly
39	9789355385550	Hydrology & Water Resources Engineering	Mitthan Lal Kansal, P.K. Agarwal
40	9789355389688	Information Technology Workshop in MATLAB	Hari Prabhat Gupta
41	9789355383235	Instrumentation for Civil Engineering Applications	Ashim Kanti Dey, Manita Das
42	9789355387042	Introduction to Civil Engineering	Manabendra Saharia, Nagendra R. Velaga
43	9789355384805	Introduction to Database Systems	Vikram Singh
44	9789355387509	Machine Element & System Design	Sabah Khan
45	9789355385383	Machine Learning	Himanshu Mittal
46	9789355388414	Manufacturing Automation	Chitragupt Swaroop Chitransh
47	9789355387233	Manufacturing Processes	Dheerendra Kumar Dwivedi
48	9789355389886	Materials Engineering	Dheerendra Kumar Dwivedi
49	9789391505172	Mathematics - I Calculus and Linear Algebra [For Non-Computer Science Engineering Branches]	Reena Garg
50	9789391505271	Mathematics - I Calculus and Linear Algebra [For Computer Science Engineering Branches]	Reena Garg
51	9789355384607	Measurements & Metrology	V.P. Chandramohan
52	9789355383730	Mechanics of Materials	Arvind Vyavahare
53	9789355383358	Mechatronics, Robotics & Control	J. Srinivas
54	9789355385116	Microprocessor and Microcontroller	Saurabh Chaudhury, Risha Mal
55	9789355386083	Microprocessors	Yogendra Kumar Gupta
56	9789355389169	Mobile Communication and Networks	Vimal Bhatia
57	9789355385475	Operating Systems	Sukomal Pal
58	9789355385604	Operating Systems	Sanjaya Kumar Panda
59	9789391505134	Physics (Oscillations, Waves and Optics) With lab manual	A.B. Bhattacharya, Atanu Nag
60	9789391505257	Physics (Quantum Mechanics for Engineers) With lab manual	A.B. Bhattacharya, Atanu Nag
61	9789391505165	Physics (Introduction to Electromagnetic Theory) (with Lab Manual)	A.B. Bhattacharya, Atanu Nag
62	9789391505059	Physics (Introduction to Mechanics) (with Lab Manual)	A.B. Bhattacharya, Atanu Nag
63	9789355385956	Power Electronics: Theory and Practicals	Lalit Chandra Saikia
64	9789355384942	Power Systems-I	Suresh Mikkili
65	9789355386236	Power Systems-II	Arun Rahul S, Manas K. Jena
66	9789355383754	Product Innovation & Entrepreneurship	Vigneswaran C
67	9789355384584	Production & Operation Management	Navin Kumar Dev
68	9789391505219	Programming for Problem Solving (with Lab Manual)	R.S. Salaria
69	9789355385451	Signals and Systems	Sanjay L. Nalbalwar
70	9789355386021	Strength of Materials	Uday Shanker Dixit, Nelson Muthu, S. M. Kamal
71	9789355383792	Structural Engineering	T.D. Gunneswara Rao, D. Ravi Prasad
72	9789355387004	Surveying and Geomatics	P. K. Garg
73	9789355384317	Testing & Evaluation of Civil Engineering Materials	Sandeep Chaudhary, Kashyap A Patel
74	9789355382306	Theory of Computation	Debi Prasanna Acharjya
75	9789355384928	Transportation Engineering	A.K. Raji
76	9789355385208	VLSI Design	Mahendra Sakare, Shonal Chouksey
77	9789391505332	Workshop / Manufacturing Practices (with Lab Manual)	Veeranna D.K.

DIPLOMA COURSE BOOKS

S.No.	ISBN	Book Name	Author
1	9789355382481	Aanandam An Act of Community Service	Shuchi Sharma
2	9789355385567	Advanced Manufacturing Processes	Ranjeet Kumar Sahu, Devendra Laxman Kamble
3	9789355385109	Advanced Surveying: Theory & Practice	Ramakant Agrawal, Parshottam Sarathe
4	9789355384546	Algorithms	Piyoosh P, Arnab Sarkar
5	9789391505448	Applied Chemistry (with Lab Manual)	Anju Rawlley, Devdatta Vinayakrao Saraf
6	9789391505431	Applied Physics-I (with Lab Manual)	Vinod Kumar Yadav, Mina Talati
7	9789391505578	Applied Physics-II (with Lab Manual)	Hussain Jeevakhan
8	9789355387530	Basic Mechanical Engineering	Dharmendra Singh, Chandra Shekhar Rajoria
9	9789355387394	Building Construction	Rinku Kumar, Sandeep Panchal
10	9789355383280	Building Electrification	Arnab Ghosh
11	9789355384379	Building Planning and Drawing	Aparna Dwivedi
12	9789391505493	Communication Skills in English	Anjana Tiwari
13	9789355383570	Computer Aided Machine Drawing Practice	Kanak Kalita
14	9789355388964	Computer Networking and Data Communication	Sanjaya Shankar Tripathy
15	9789355382986	Computer Networks: Theory & Practicals	Brijendra Pratap Singh, Manoj Madhava Gore
16	9789355382672	Computer Programming: Theory and Practicals	Satyendra Singh Chouhan
17	9789355387714	Computer System Organization	Sonal Yadav
18	9789355382658	Concrete Technology: Theory and Practice	Sasankasekhar Mandal, Vishwajit Anand, Sushil K. Agarwala
19	9789355383334	Construction Materials and Testing	Vanita Aggarwal
20	9789355383501	Consumer Electronics	Amit M. Joshi, Maulin M. Joshi, Urvashi Prakash Shukla
21	9789355387684	Data Structures: Theory & Practicals	NB Venkateswarlu
22	9789355388513	Design of Machine Elements	A. Kumaravel, M. Kathirselvam
23	9789355388360	Design of Steel and RCC Structure	Sparsh Johari
24	9789355383303	Digital Communication	Muralidhar Kulkarni, K. S. Shivaprakasha
25	9789355387295	Digital Electronics	Menka Yadav
26	9789355389435	Electric Circuits and Networks	Jamuna K., Nilanjan Tewari
27	9789355388452	Electric Motors and Transformers (Theory and Practicals)	Sanjay B. Bodkhe
28	9789355385901	Electric Power Transmission and Distribution	Sudhir Sharma
29	9789355389466	Electrical & Electronics Measurements and Instrumentation	Sudarsan Sahoo, Vipin Chandra Pal, Sudipta Chakraborty
30	9789355382696	Electronic Communication	M. D. Selvaraj, P. Nagaradjane
31	9789355387202	Electronic Devices and Circuits	Ankesh Jain
32	9789355386373	Electronic Equipment Maintenance	Chanchal Sharma
33	9789355384690	Embedded Systems	Deepa M, G. Santhanamari, Susithra. N
34	9789355384867	Energy Conservation and Audit	M. Rizwan, Majid Jamil
35	9789391505509	Engineering Graphics	Sharad K. Pradhan, K.K. Jain
36	9789391505608	Engineering Mechanics (with Lab Manual)	Bhankhar Bharat, Gokaldas Vandana Somkuwar

DIPLOMA COURSE BOOKS

S.No.	ISBN	Book Name	Author
37	9789391505516	Engineering Workshop Practice	A. K. Sarathe
38	9789391505653	Environmental Science	Subrat Roy
39	9789355384966	Estimating, Costing and valuation	Sandeep Panchal
40	9789355389510	Fluid Mechanics & Hydraulic Machinery	Suman Chakraborty, Sourav Mitra, Aditya Bandopadhyay
41	9789391505592	Fundamentals of Electrical and Electronics Engineering (with Lab Manual)	Susan S. Mathew, Saji T. Chacko
42	9789355387240	Fundamentals of Power Electronics	Soumitra Kumar Mandal
43	9789355389602	Geotechnical Engineering (Theory & Practicals)	Neelima Satyam
44	9789355386137	Induction, Synchronous, and Special Electrical Machines	K. Selvajyothi, S. Tamilselvi, Sarat Kumar Sahoo
45	9789355382290	Industrial Engineering & Management	A. Manimaran
46	9789355384959	Internet of Things	Sujata Pal
47	9789355388650	Introduction to DBMS: Theory & Practicals	Myneni Madhu Bala
48	9789355384294	Introduction to e-Governance	Kamal Kant Verma
49	9789355386564	Introduction to Electric Generation Systems	Lalit Chandra Saikia, Nalin Behari, Deb Choudhury
50	9789391505585	Introduction to IT Systems (with Lab Manual)	Prashant Joshi
51	9789355382900	Linear Integrated Circuit	B. T. Krishna
52	9789355388148	Manufacturing Engineering	Santosh Kumar
53	9789355383877	Material Science & Engineering	Vinod Kumar, Nisheeth k. Prasad
54	9789391505424	Mathematics-I	Deepak Singh
55	9789391505523	Mathematics-II	Garima Singh
56	9789355385994	Measurements and Metrology	A. Gnanavelbabu, M. Santhana kumar, R. Saranraj
57	9789355388131	Mechanics of Materials and their Testing	R. Velmurugan, Pragathi
58	9789355385048	Microcontroller Applications	Ritula Thakur
59	9789355385062	Microcontrollers and Applications	Santanu Chattopadhyay
60	9789355388100	Mobile and Wireless Communication	Maulin Joshi, Urvashi P. Shukla
61	9789355387790	Production & Operations Management	Mayank Kumar Agrawal
62	9789355388704	Public Health Engineering	Rinku Kumar
63	9789355387455	Python Programming	Rupesh Nasre
64	9789355387189	Renewable Energy Technologies	Sanjay Agrawal, Rajeev K. Mishra
65	9789355387479	Software Engineering	Salman Abdul Moiz
66	9789355389749	Theory of Machines & Mechanisms	G. C. Mohan Kumar
67	9789355387332	Theory of Structures	Arunachalam Subramanian Balu
68	9789355389015	Thermal Engineering - I	V. Raghavan
69	9789355389831	Thermal Engineering - II	Parvesh Antil
70	9789355386779	Transportation Engineering (Theory & Practice)	A.K. Raji, K.K. Babu
71	9789355384287	Water Resource Engineering (Theory & Practice)	Prakash C. Swain, Dillip K. Ghose
72	9789355383051	Web Technologies: Theory & Practical	Raman Dugyala

Property	Star Connection	Delta Connection
Terminal connection	Similar ends of the three coils connected	Opposite terminals of the coils connected
Neutral point	Neutral point exists	Neutral point does not exist
Line/phase current	Line current equals phase current	Line current equals root three times phase current
Line/phase voltage	Line voltage equals root three times phase voltage	Line voltage equals phase voltage
Motor speed	Slow (receives $1/\sqrt{3}$ of the voltage)	Fast (each phase receives full line voltage)
Phase voltage	Low ($1/\sqrt{3}$ times line voltage)	Equal to line voltage
Number of turns	Fewer turns required	More turns required
Insulation level	Low	High
Network type	Power transmission networks	Power distribution networks
Voltage received by each winding	230 volts	414 volts
Type of system	3 phase 4 wire, 3 phase 3 wire	3 phase 3 wire

2.3.6. Rewinding of Motor

If electric motors fail, rewinding them might be an alternative that is cost-effective in many ways. Although it is anticipated that the rewinding process would be comprehensive and capable of restoring the motor to a state that is comparable to that of a brand-new instrument, there is sometimes a lack of accuracy in following each step, which influences the effectiveness of the rewound motor.

Rewinding often results in a drop in efficiency of between two and five percent in most motors. However, technological improvements have made it possible to find methods that reduce losses in rewound motors. After a motor burn out, new winding is filled in it which is shown in the Figure 2.4. In certain very rare instances, there have been situations in which the efficiency of a motor has risen after it has been subjected to the rewinding process.

- By keeping the original winding qualities, such as material quality, design, and structure, it is feasible to preserve the original operational characteristics throughout the rewinding process.
- By using conductors with a greater cross-sectional area and improved insulation, the copper losses may be minimized.
- Rewinding the system to get the desired torque and power or speed reduces losses, leading to improved efficiency and energy savings.
- The extension of coils beyond the slot insulation should be minimized to limit the quantity of copper consumed, which in turn decreases the copper losses.

Figure 2.4 Rewinding 3-Phase Motor (Source: https://www.instructables.com/Rewinding-3-Phase-Motor/)

A problem that often occurs during the process of applying heat to strip old windings is the possibility of the insulation between the laminations being destroyed, which results in an increase in the amount of eddy current that is lost.

Furthermore, any change in the air gap may influence the power factor as well as the output torque of the motor.

It is possible to enhance efficiency by modifying the winding design to meet these issues; however, this would have the potential to influence the power factor of the process.

The use of wires that have a bigger cross-section is still another approach that may be utilised. This strategy helps to decrease stator losses, which eventually leads to a gain in efficiency. Even if there is a possibility that the efficiency of the rewinding process may decline, the use of these new technologies and the cultivation of cautious rewinding techniques can lead to enhanced motor performance as well as savings in energy consumption.

2.3.7. Replacement by Energy Efficient Motor

- Energy efficient motors replace conventional motors while maintaining the same shaft output power.
- Energy efficient motors consume less input power compared to standard motors.
- Energy efficient motors are designed with enhancements aimed at reducing intrinsic motor losses. These enhancements include the use of lower-loss silicon steel and thicker wires to minimize resistance.
- Energy efficient motors also utilize thinner laminations and maintain smaller air gaps between the stator and rotor.
- Copper is often preferred over aluminium bars in the rotor for increased efficiency.
- Superior bearings and smaller fans are incorporated to further enhance efficiency.
- Energy efficient motors typically have efficiencies three to four percentage points higher than standard motors.

- Despite their increased availability, energy efficient motors are becoming more accessible in India.
- Energy efficient motors adoption aligns with global initiatives promoting energy efficiency and sustainability.

2.3.8. Periodic Maintenance

Cleaning the machine is necessary to provide adequate ventilation and motor cooling, both of which contribute to the machine's best operation. When it comes to ensuring that belt drives and couplings are configured correctly, the setup and alignment of the machine are also considered to be very important factors. To ensure that bearings are appropriately lubricated and sealed, it is required to perform bearing lubrication inspections on a regular basis. This prevents excessive wear and friction from occurring.

The inspection of the system's condition, which includes the monitoring of vibration, and the identification of temperature increases that are not typical, acts as an early signal of possible issues within the system. It is essential to conduct performance evaluations by continually measuring the fluctuations in supply voltage. Voltage imbalances may result in greater energy losses; thus, it is important to monitor these variations.

2.4. Need for Energy Conservation in Transformer

- Transformers are essential components in a power system, serving a crucial function in the generation, transmission, and distribution of electrical energy.
- The efficiency of a transformer has a direct impact on the costs and advantages of the overall power system.
- Transformer power loss typically accounts for around 10-20% of the overall transmission and distribution losses in a standard power distribution system.
- Due to the high demand for distribution transformers, the power loss they create might be significant because of their substantial transportation energy and extended operation periods.
- Statistics indicate that transformers may cause power losses up to around 10% of the overall generating capacity. Hence, it is important to investigate the energy conservation of transformers to minimise losses and optimise the overall efficiency of the power system.

2.4.1. Energy Conservation in Transformer

Energy conservation in transformers is of paramount importance due to its direct impact on both economic and environmental considerations.

- Transformers play a crucial role in electrical power transmission and distribution systems by facilitating the efficient transfer of electricity between different voltage levels. However, these devices are not perfectly efficient, and a significant amount of energy is lost in the form of heat during the transformation process. This energy loss not only results in increased operational costs but also contributes to environmental concerns as it necessitates the generation of additional power to compensate for the losses.
- One primary reason for energy conservation in transformers is the economic aspect. Energy losses translate directly into increased operational expenses for power utilities and end-users. As the demand for electricity continues to rise globally, optimizing the

efficiency of transformers becomes essential to minimize the overall cost of power generation and distribution. Energy conservation measures in transformers can lead to substantial savings over the operational lifespan of these devices, making them more economically viable and sustainable in the long run.

- Additionally, environmental considerations underscore the need for energy conservation in transformers. The generation of electricity often involves the combustion of fossil fuels or the use of other non-renewable resources, contributing to greenhouse gas emissions and climate change. By reducing energy losses in transformers, the overall demand for electricity can be mitigated, resulting in decreased environmental impact. This aligns with global efforts to transition towards cleaner and more sustainable energy sources, promoting a greener and more environmentally friendly power infrastructure.
- Energy conservation in transformers is imperative for both economic and environmental reasons.
- By implementing measures to minimize energy losses in these crucial components of electrical systems, we can enhance the overall efficiency of power transmission and distribution, reduce operational costs, and contribute to a more sustainable and eco-friendly energy landscape.

2.5. Energy Conservation Techniques in Transformer

It is important to use energy conservation methods in transformers to enhance overall efficiency and reduce energy wastage. An effective technique is using low-loss materials, such as amorphous metal cores, to minimise core losses. In addition, the use of sophisticated insulating materials and design improvements aids in reducing losses in the winding. Efficiency may be optimised by using load control measures, such as running transformers near their rated capacity.

By implementing voltage control devices and tap changers, the transformer can function within an ideal voltage range.

Performing routine maintenance, such as oil analysis and preventative measures, aids in the detection and resolution of possible problems, thereby maintaining the optimal performance of the transformer.

Energy-efficient transformers not only result in financial savings but also adhere to sustainable energy principles, therefore minimising their ecological footprint.

By using these methodologies, enterprises may optimise the effectiveness and durability of transformers, hence fostering energy preservation and conscientious energy use.

2.5.1. Load sharing

The coordinated distribution of the electrical load across many transformers running in parallel is referred to as load sharing in transformers.

By ensuring that the load is evenly distributed across the transformers, this method maximises efficiency, reduces losses, and improves the stability and dependability of the power supply system.

The transformers can prevent overloading, lower the chance of failure, and increase the length of time they can operate by sharing the load.

There is a general prevalence of issues with transformers, including overloading, voltage fluctuation, and heating, which necessitates a substantial amount of time and capital for repairs and maintenance.

Overloading may result in lower efficiency, which can lead to the secondary winding overheating or even burning owing to being exposed to an excessive amount of heat.

To protect transformers from these problems, load sharing becomes an extremely important strategy.

A secondary transformer that is operated in parallel with the primary transformer may help to ease the additional load, hence minimising the likelihood of damage occurring.

In situations when the loads on the transformer remain constant, the total active power loss and reactive power consumption will change depending on the distribution of the loads.

As a result, the total active power loss and reactive power consumption may be minimised via the use of economic dispatch to optimise load distribution amongst transformers. This, in turn, promotes energy saving in transformers.

- Load sharing in transformers refers to the distribution of power among multiple transformers connected in parallel.
- Transformers connected in parallel share the total load based on their respective ratings and impedance characteristics.
- The load sharing process ensures that each transformer operates within its specified capacity and efficiency range.
- Transformers with similar ratings and parameters share the load more evenly.
- Load sharing is achieved through the automatic voltage and reactive power control mechanisms in modern power systems.
- It helps in optimizing the utilization of each transformer in the parallel configuration.
- Load sharing also enhances system reliability by providing redundancy and backup in case of a failure of one transformer.
- Proper synchronization and control mechanisms ensure smooth load sharing and prevent overloading of any individual transformer.
- Advanced monitoring and control systems continuously monitor the load sharing and adjust parameters to maintain stability and efficiency.
- Load sharing configurations are commonly employed in power distribution networks to ensure reliable and efficient operation.

2.5.2. Parallel Operation

When the main windings of two or more transformers are linked to a shared voltage source and their secondary windings are connected to a shared load. Subsequently, it is said that the transformers are linked in parallel, meaning that they are operating in parallel.

Transformers that operate in parallel have their main windings connected to a shared voltage source, while their secondary windings are connected to a shared load, as shown in Figure 2.5. This configuration allows the transformers to operate in parallel. The capacity of the transformer is the most important factor to consider while choosing one. In power transformers, optimal efficiency is attained when the transformer is operating at full load. Selecting a transformer with a capacity that is more than the required results in larger investment and higher losses while the transformer is not operating. It is recommended to run transformers in parallel in a selected manner to have the highest possible efficiency. By activating just those transformers that together fulfil the present demand and function near their full-load ratings, one can manage the system in an efficient manner. As the load grows, more transformers that are linked in parallel may be successively turned on to match the rising demand. This ensures that the system runs with the highest possible efficiency.

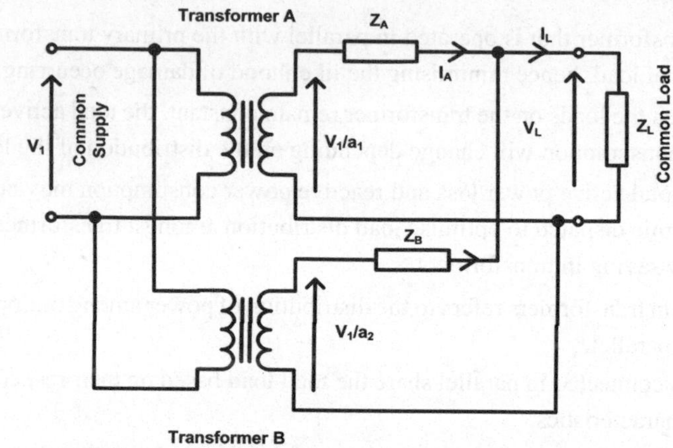

Figure 2.5: a) Parallel Operation of Single-Phase Transformer

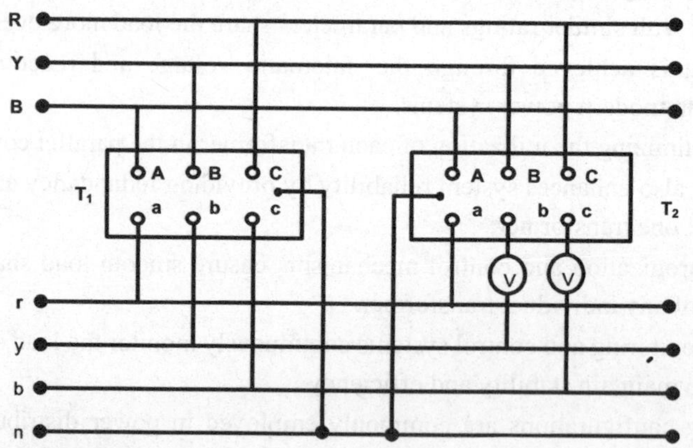

Figure 2.5: b) Parallel Operation of Three-Phase Transformer

- The design of the Power Control Centre (PCC) and the Motor Control Centre (MCC) of any new plant should have the provision for operating two or more transformers in parallel. Additional switchgears and bus couplers should be provided at the design stage.
- Whenever two transformers are operating in parallel, both should be technically identical in all aspects and more importantly should have the same impedance level. This minimises the circulating current between transformers.

- Where the load is fluctuating in nature, it is preferable to have more than one transformer running in parallel, so that the load can be optimised by sharing it between transformers. The transformers can be operated close to the maximum efficiency range by this operation.

2.5.2.1. Condition for Parallel Operation of Transformer

To establish a parallel connection between transformers, the main windings of the transformers are linked to the source busbars, while the secondary windings are connected to the load busbars. The effective parallel functioning of transformers requires the fulfilment of many requirements.

- Same voltage ratio and turns ratio (both primary and secondary voltage rating is same).
  i. Same percentage impedance and X/R ratio.
- Identical position of tap changer
- Same KVA ratings
- Same phase angle shift (vector group are same)
- Same frequency rating
- Same polarity
- Same phase sequence

Certain criteria are optional while others are obligatory. The conveniences include same voltage ratio and turns ratio, identical % impedance, identical kVA rating, and identical location of the tap changer. The required requirements are same phase angle shift, consistent polarity, matching phase sequence, and identical frequency. Parallel operation is feasible but sub-optimal when the necessary criteria are not satisfied.

- **Same voltage Ratio & Turns Ratio (on each tap)**

If the transformers connected in parallel have slightly different voltage ratios, an inequality in the induced emfs in the secondary windings will result in a circulating current in the loop formed by the secondary windings under no-load conditions. This circulating current may exceed the normal no-load current. The current will be significantly elevated due to the low leakage impedance. When the secondary windings are under load, the circulating current will create an imbalance in the load distribution between the two transformers. since a result, it may not be feasible to fully use the combined capacity of these two parallel transformers, since one of them may become overloaded.

When two transformers with different voltage ratios are connected in parallel using the same main supply voltage, there will be a discrepancy in the secondary voltages. When the secondaries of these transformers are connected to the same bus, a circulating current will flow between the secondaries and, as a result, between the primary as well. Due to the low internal impedance of the transformer, even a tiny voltage change might result in a significant circulating current, leading to avoidable additional I2R loss. The ratings of both primary and secondary elements should be the same. Put simply, the transformers must possess identical turn ratios, also known as transformation ratios.

i. Same Percentage Impedance and X/R Ratio

When two transformers with comparable per unit impedances are coupled in parallel, they will mostly divide the load in proportion to their KVA ratings. In this case, the load is mostly balanced since it is feasible to have two transformers with equivalent per unit impedances but varying X/R ratios. Under these circumstances, the magnitude of the line current will be lower than the total of the currents in the transformers, resulting in a proportional decrease in the overall capacity. The difference in the ratio of reactance to resistance in the per unit impedance causes a variation in the phase angle of the currents carried by the two paralleled transformers. As a result, one transformer operates with a higher power factor while the other operates with a lower power factor compared to the combined output. Therefore, the transformers will not distribute power proportionately.

The current flowing through two transformers operating in parallel should be directly proportionate to their MVA ratings. The current flowing through these transformers is inversely proportional to their internal impedance.

Based on the two assertions provided, it can be concluded that the impedance of transformers operating in parallel is inversely proportional to their MVA ratings. Put simply, the percentage impedance or per unit values of impedance must be the same for all transformers operating in parallel.

Proper impedance matching is of increased importance when linking single-phase transformers in three-phase banks. Furthermore, it is advisable to strive for matching the X/R ratios of the three series impedances to maintain balanced three-phase output voltages, in addition to adhering to the three requirements for parallel operation.

Impedance mismatches in Y-connected single-phase transformers with identical KVA ratings might result in a substantial imbalance in load distribution among the transformers.

Let us analyse the many types of cases involving impedance, ratio, and KVA.

In the case of connecting single-phase transformers in a Y-Y configuration with an isolated neutral, it is necessary for the magnetising impedance to be equal in terms of ohmic measurement. Alternatively, the transformer with the greatest magnetising impedance may experience a higher proportion of exciting voltage, leading to increased core losses and perhaps causing saturation of its core.

1. **Case 1: There is no difference in impedance, ratios, or kVA**

To link transformers in parallel, it is customary to ensure that they have identical turn ratios, % impedances, and kVA ratings. When transformers with identical characteristics are connected in parallel, the load is evenly distributed between them and there are no circulating currents in the windings of the transformers.

2. **Case 2: Equal Impedances, Ratios and Different kVA**

It is uncommon to use this parameter in new installations. Occasionally, two transformers with different kVAs and the same % impedances are linked to a shared bus. Under these circumstances, the existing division of current ensures that each transformer is carrying its designated load. Circulating currents will not occur because to the equal voltages (turn ratios).

3. **Case 3: Unequal Impedance but Same Ratios & kVA**

Primarily, this feature is used to augment the power capacity of plants by linking together pre-existing transformers in parallel that possess the same kVA rating, however with varying % impedances. This is a frequent occurrence when financial limitations restrict the acquisition of a new transformer with identical specifications. It is crucial to comprehend that the current is distributed in inverse proportion to the impedances, meaning that higher current will flow via lower impedances. Therefore, the transformer with a lower percentage of impedance might experience overloading when exposed to severe loads, whereas the transformer with a greater percentage of impedance will be subjected to lighter loads.

4. **Case 4: Unequal Impedance & kVA Same Ratios**

This specific kind of transformers is seldom used in industrial and commercial establishments when they are linked to a shared bus. These transformers have varying kilovolt-ampere (kVA) ratings and differing percentage impedances. However, there may arise a specific scenario where two single-ended substations may be interconnected by busing or cables in order to enhance voltage support during the initiation of a substantial load. while the % impedance and kVA ratings of transformers vary, it is important to exercise caution while loading them.

5. **Case 5: Equal Impedance & kVA Unequal Ratios**

Minor disparities in voltage result in a substantial flow of electric current. It is crucial to emphasise that paralleled transformers must always be connected to the same tap. The circulating current is entirely unaffected by the load and the distribution of the load. When transformers are operating at maximum capacity, a significant degree of overheating occurs because of the circulating currents. It is important to note that circulating currents do not flow on the line. Therefore, they cannot be observed if monitoring equipment is located either upstream or downstream of the common connecting points.

6. **Case 6: Unequal Impedance, kVA & Different Ratios**

This parameter would be quite improbable in practical scenarios. To get the total current in each transformer unit, the circulating current resulting from the uneven ratio, along with each transformer's portion of the load current, should be summed if both the ratios and the impedance are different.

A circulating current of 10 percent, caused by mismatched turn ratios, contributes only 0.5 percent to the total current to achieve a unity power factor.

At decreasing power factors, the circulating current will undergo significant changes.

- **Same Polarity**
  - Polarity of a transformer refers to the instantaneous direction of induced electromotive force (emf) in its secondary winding.
  - When the instantaneous directions of induced secondary emf in two transformers are opposite to each other with the same input power, the transformers are said to be in opposite polarity.
  - Proper connection about polarity is crucial to prevent short circuits caused by the induced emfs acting together in the secondary circuit.
  - If transformers relate to incorrect polarities, induced emfs in parallel secondary windings will produce a short circuit.
  - Transformers running in parallel should have the same polarity to prevent huge circulating currents without feeding any load.

- Two transformers are in the same polarity if their generated secondary emf have the same instantaneous directions and they have the same input power.

- **Same Phase Sequence**

Phase Sequence refers to the sequential sequence in which the voltages in a three-phase system reach their maximum positive value. In a three-phase system, there are three voltages or electromotive forces (EMFs) that have the same magnitude. However, their frequencies are electrically displaced by an angle of 120 degrees.

To operate three-phase transformers in parallel, it is essential that the phase sequence of the line voltages of both transformers is the same. If the phase sequence is wrong, there will be short-circuits between each pair of phases in every cycle. Strict adherence to this criterion is necessary for the parallel functioning of transformers. Phase sequence of 120° of each phase shown in figure 2.6.

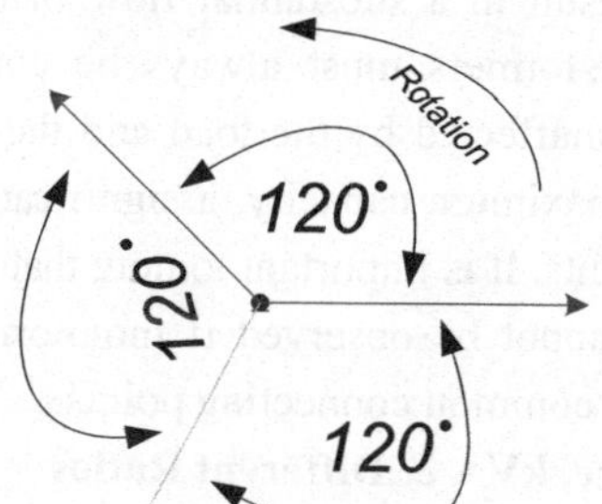

Figure:2.6 Phase Sequence

For instance, if the phases of a coil are labelled as R, Y, B, the positive phase sequence would be RYB, YBR, BRY, which is also referred to as the clockwise sequence. Similarly, the negative phase sequence will be RBY, BYR, YRB, which is known as the anti-clockwise pattern. Positive-Negative Sequence of Phase Sequence of winding are shown in figure 2.7.

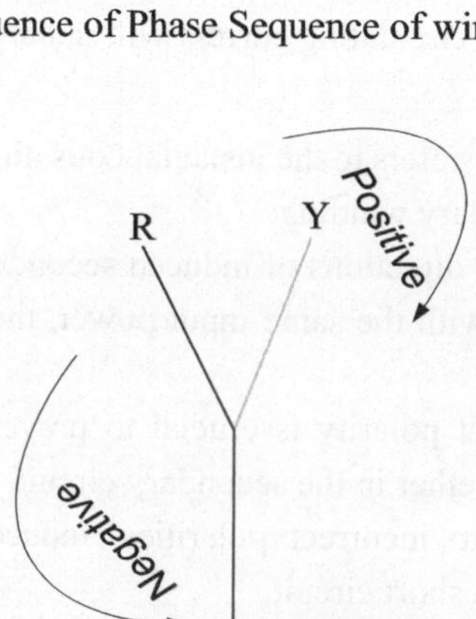

Figure:2.7 Positive-Negative Sequence of Phase Sequence

The following are some of the reasons why it is necessary:

1. The concurrent functioning of the three-phase transformer or alternator can only occur when its phase sequence is determined.
2. The rotational direction of a three-phase induction motor is determined by the sequence of phases in the three-phase power supply. To reverse the direction of the motor, the phase sequence of the supplied power must be altered.

1. Same Phase Angle Shift: (zero relative phase displacement between the secondary line voltages)

Various configurations may be used to link the windings of a transformer, resulting in varied levels of secondary voltage magnitude and phase displacement. Transformer connections may be categorised by certain vector groupings.

Group 1 consists of three types of phase displacement: Yy0, Dd0, and Dz0.

Group 2 exhibits a 180° phase displacement, which is represented by the symbols Yy6, Dd6, and Dz6.

Group 3 consists of three elements: Yd1, Dy1, and Yz1, which have a phase displacement of -30°.

Group 4 consists of transformers with a phase displacement of +30°. The specific transformer models in this group are Yd11, Dy11, and Yz11.

Paralleling transformers from the same group allows for the elimination of any relative phase shift in the secondary side line voltages. For instance, it is possible to parallel two transformers that have Yd1 and Dy1 connections.

Transformers belonging to groups 1 and 2 may only be connected in parallel with transformers from their respective groups. However, the transformers belonging to groups 3 and 4 may be connected in parallel by reversing the phase sequence of one of them. For instance, a transformer with a Yd1 1 connection (group 4) may be connected in parallel with a transformer with a Dy1 connection (group 3) by reversing the phase sequence of both the main and secondary terminals of the Dy1 transformer.

To parallel Dy1 and Dy11 transformers, one must cross the two incoming phases and the same two outgoing phases on one of the transformers. Therefore, if someone has a DY11 transformer, they can cross the B&C phases on both the primary and secondary sides to convert the +30-degree phase shift into a -30-degree shift. This will allow it to parallel with the Dy1 transformer, provided that all other conditions are met.

- **Same kVA Ratings**

When two or more transformers are connected in parallel, the distribution of the load between them is determined by their respective ratings. If all individuals have identical ratings, they will distribute the workload evenly among themselves.

Transformers with different kVA ratings will distribute the load approximately in proportion to their ratings, if their voltage ratios are the same and their percentage impedances (at their respective kVA ratings) are nearly identical. In such cases, a total of more than 90 percent of the combined ratings is typically accessible. It is advised against operating transformers with kVA ratings that vary by greater than a 2:1 ratio in parallel on a permanent basis.

Transformers with varying kVA ratings may be used in parallel, where the load is divided in such a way that each transformer bears its proportional part of the total load. To accomplish precise load distribution, it is essential that the transformers be wrapped with identical turn ratios and that the % impedance of all transformers is equivalent, with each percentage represented in relation to the kVA base of its corresponding transformer. It is essential that the ratio of resistance to reactance in all transformers be same. To ensure optimal performance, it is advisable to keep the circulating current below ten percent of the entire load rated current of the smaller unit, regardless of the ratios and impedances involved.

2.5.2.2. Advantages of Transformer Parallel Operation

- **Maximize Electrical System Efficiency**
    - o Typically, electrical power transformers achieve their highest efficiency while operating at full load. By operating many transformers in parallel, it is possible to selectively activate just those transformers that can meet the overall demand by operating closer to their maximum load rating at that moment.
    - o When the load grows, one may switch to another transformer linked in parallel to meet the complete demand. By using this approach, one may operate the system with optimal efficiency.

➢ **Explanation:**

Efficiency Transformers that are functioning at or close to their ideal load conditions have reduced losses, leading to improved energy efficiency. Parallel operation enables transformers to distribute the workload, ensuring that each unit functions optimally and minimising total system losses.

- **Maximize electrical system availability**
    - o If many transformers are operating in parallel, it is possible to shut down any one of them for maintenance purposes. The other parallel transformers in the system will continue to provide electricity to the load without any complete stoppage.

➢ **Explanation**

Availability In a parallel configuration, the malfunction of one transformer does not cause disruption to the whole system. The remaining transformers can function, serving as a fail-safe mechanism that improves system availability and minimises the likelihood of power outages.

- **Maximize power system reliability**
    - o If any one of the transformers operating in parallel has a fault and trips, the other parallel transformers in the system will distribute the load among themselves. As a result, the power supply may not be disrupted until the shared loads cause the other transformers to become overloaded.

➢ **Explanation**

Reliability: Implementing load sharing across several transformers ensures that no one unit becomes a single point of failure. The dispersion of the load improves the longevity and dependability of the power system since the strain is distributed across several components rather than focused on one.

- **Maximize electrical system flexibility**
  - o There is a possibility of future fluctuations in the demand for electricity in the system, which might either increase or decrease. If there is a prediction of increased power demand in the future, it is necessary to connect transformers in parallel to meet the additional demand. This is because it is not cost-effective to install a larger single transformer based on the forecasted increase in future demand, as it would be an unnecessary investment of money.
  - o In the future, if there is a decline in demand, transformers that are operating in parallel may be taken out of the system to balance the capital investment and its return.

➢ **Explanation**

Flexibility: Parallel operation enables seamless scalability and adaptation. Additional transformers may be activated or deactivated as necessary to accommodate fluctuations in power needs. This allows for a flexible reaction to variations in load and enhances the performance of the system without the need for substantial reconfiguration.

2.5.2.3. Disadvantages of Transformer Parallel Operation

- The short-circuit currents are increasing, which requires an increase in the capacity of the breaker.
- The danger of inter-transformer circulating currents. Circulating currents reduce the load capacity and increase losses.
- The bus ratings may be excessively elevated.
- Paralleling transformers result in a large reduction in transformer impedance, leading to the possibility of having parallel transformers with extremely low impedance. This, in turn, causes the generation of high short circuit currents.
- Consequently, it is necessary to have some devices that restrict the flow of current, such as reactors, fuses, and high impedance buses. Managing and safeguarding three units operating in tandem is a more complex task.
- This industry does not often engage in this technique.

2.5.3. Isolating Techniques

Transformer isolation techniques refer to ways of keeping the primary and secondary windings from coming into direct electrical contact with one another. This is accomplished via physical separation with the use of electromagnetic induction, insulating materials, and occasionally shielding to reduce interference.

Along with improving isolation, proper grounding ensures safe and effective energy transfer without an electrical connection—an essential safety feature that also lowers interference in a variety of electrical applications.

Isolation is an essential operation that involves switching off the electrical supply to guarantee the safeguarding of personnel who are working on machinery by de-energizing live components. It is possible to open or close a circuit off-load with the assistance of an isolator, which is a mechanical device that is operated manually. The isolator switch, which is located close to the supply point, makes it possible to perform transformer repair in a secure manner. Circuit-breakers, fuse connections, and isolation switches are all examples of devices that are suitable for isolation functions. Three-phase LT supplies are equipped with a triple-pole switch that is equipped with a neutral link for the purpose of isolation. This switch ensures that the live conductors are severed while the neutral link is maintained during the operation of the switch. When transformers are operating in parallel to share a particular load, it is necessary to isolate some transformers during times of low demand to improve the overall efficiency of the equipment. The secondary load must first be disconnected before a transformer may be removed. This is accomplished by tripping the circuit breaker and opening the load switches that are equipped with high rupturing capacity fuses (CTP). After that, the isolator switch on the main side is opened, which guarantees that the transformer is totally separated from the busbar. For reasons of safety, the isolator is locked and earthed while it is in this condition. To reconnect the transformer in parallel, the earthing of the isolator switch must be removed, the isolator must be closed, and then either the circuit breaker or the load switch must be closed. This will enable the transformer to begin sharing the load in accordance with its kVA capacity.

- Isolation refers to the deliberate disconnection of electrical power to a system to guarantee the safety of anyone working on the equipment. This is achieved by deactivating the components that are normally energised.
- An isolator is a manually controlled mechanical device used to disconnect or connect a circuit while it is not under load.
- When transformers are working in parallel to distribute a certain load, it is essential to disconnect and isolate some transformers when the load demand is lower. This allows other transformers to deliver energy at their optimal efficiency.
- When removing the transformer from the circuit, start by disconnecting the load on the secondary side. This is done by tripping the circuit breaker and opening the load switches (Iron Clad Triple Pole-ICTP) that have high rupturing capacity fuses.
- Currently, the transformer will stay connected to the bus without transferring any load. Nevertheless, even when there is no load, the primary of the transformer remains connected to the line. This may lead to the absence of primary copper losses under no load conditions, caused by the absence of current, as well as magnetic core losses resulting from the rated voltage applied across the primary. This leads to inefficiency in energy use.
- To avoid the energy wasting indicated above, the circuit breaker and isolator switch on the main side are opened, thereby isolating the transformer, and totally disconnecting it from the busbar.
- Therefore, the act of isolating method serves to avoid the needless dissipation of energy and encourages the preservation of energy.

2.5.4. Energy-Efficient Transformer Replacement

Transformers that are efficient in terms of energy consumption play a crucial part in lowering transmission and distribution losses, which in turn contributes to a more environmentally friendly electrical system.

A decrease in transformer losses has been made possible because of developments in the characteristics of silicon steel. Efficiency levels are further increased using novel magnetic materials, such as amorphous metal transformers, which are an example. They provide several compelling advantages, including decreased peak loads, decreased power expenditures, and improved supply stability. The energy efficiency of a transformer may be improved by doing things like altering the geometric layout of the core and winding assemblies, as well as improving the materials that are used in the building process, such as employing high-quality core steel or winding material. To achieve this improvement, a compromise must be made between the use of more costly materials and designs that have lower loss rates and the importance that consumers have on minimising losses.

No-load losses and load losses are often inversely connected to one another, which means that lowering one typically results in an increase in the other. This is the case for any given efficiency level. The use of energy-efficient transformers, for example, has the potential to enhance efficiency from 95% to 97%, while the utilisation of amorphous transformers has the potential to further enhance efficiency to 98.5%. In a similar vein, the use of epoxy resin cast/encapsulated dry-type transformers has the potential to increase efficiency from 93% to 97%. Important Features of energy efficient transformers are shown in figure 2.8.

- The primary cause of energy loss in traditional transformers is heat or vibration generated by the core.
- The newly developed high-efficiency transformers significantly reduce these losses.
- The traditional transformer consists of a core constructed of silicon alloyed iron, specifically grain-oriented iron. These transformers are susceptible to losses, since the amount of iron loss in a transformer is determined by the kind of core used.
- However, the most recent technological advancement involves using amorphous material or epoxy resin as the core. Transformers that use such materials are referred to as energy efficient transformers.
- The anticipated decrease in energy loss compared to traditional transformers with silicon and iron cores is around 70%, which is a substantial improvement.
- Such transformers have remarkable efficiencies even under modest loads, achieving an efficiency of 98.5% with a load of 35%.

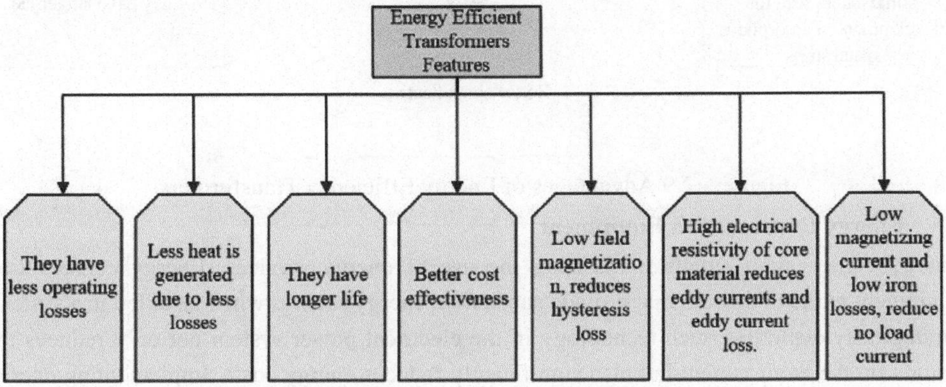

Figure: 2.8 Features of Energy Efficient Transformers

2.5.5. Periodic Maintenance of Transformer

Maintenance at regular intervals is an essential component of loss control efforts, particularly in transformers. The frequency of losses is decreased because of this periodic maintenance, which monitors degradation, identifies, or predicts problems with insulating equipment and systems, and so on. Because they are static devices that do not have any moving components, transformers are very dependable and, with the right kind of maintenance, may survive for more than forty years. On the other hand, they are often exposed to overloading and operating strain that exceeds their capability, which ultimately results in degradation. Alterations to the load, adjustments to the circuit, wrongly chosen protective devices, and variations in voltage are all factors that might lead to deterioration. When it comes to minimising the risk of equipment failure, addressing latent defects, and making troubleshooting easier, it is necessary to implement a regular periodic maintenance programme. Not only does this proactive strategy guarantee the dependability of the system, but it also makes a substantial contribution to the achievement of energy efficiency in transformers. There are so many advantages of Advantages of energy efficiency transformers are shown in figure 2.9.

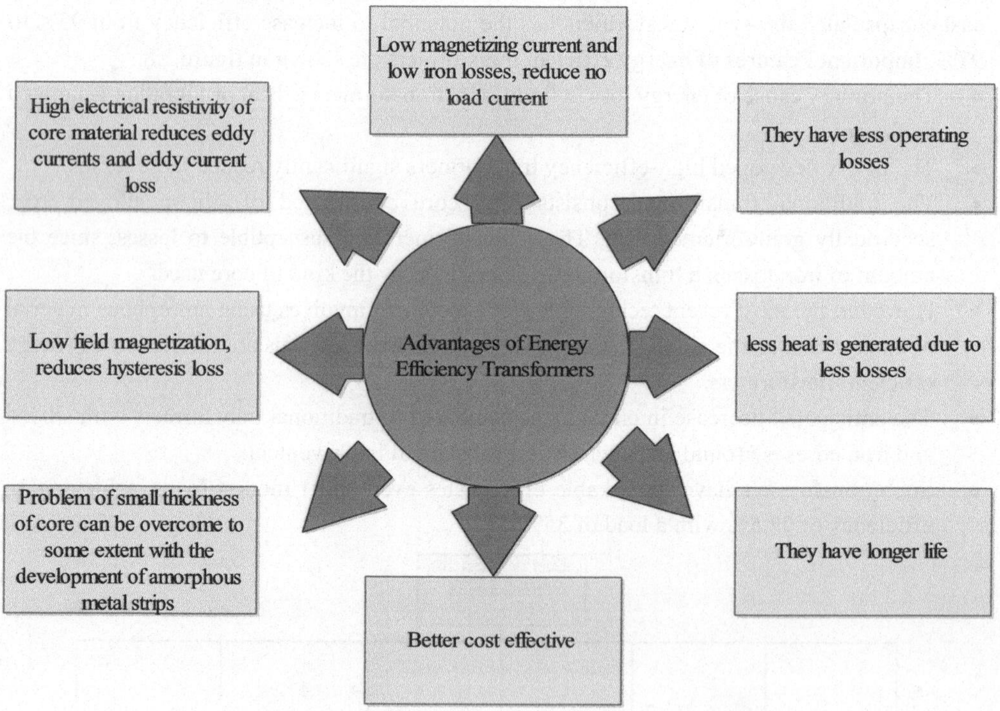

Figure: - 2.9 Advantages of Energy Efficiency Transformers

2.6 Energy Conservation Equipment

Energy conservation entails minimising the use of energy services. Energy conservation equipment refers to devices that provide substantial energy savings when installed in a system. Strategically deploying such technology in the electrical power system not only reduces the burden on the environment but also significantly reduces energy costs. Implementing energy saving techniques is crucial for advancing sustainability and achieving cost-effectiveness in power use. These endeavours enhance the efficiency and eco-friendliness of electrical systems, in line with worldwide efforts to conserve resources and decrease carbon emissions.

Energy conservation equipment encompasses items specifically engineered to minimise energy use and optimise efficiency across a wide range of applications. These devices are essential for reducing energy use, decreasing operating expenses, and supporting sustainability. Various forms of energy conservation technology are available, each designed to target distinct elements of energy use in various systems. Illustrative instances comprise:

2.6.1 Soft Starter

An electrical device called a soft starter is used to progressively raise the voltage applied to an electric motor, allowing for a regulated and seamless startup. This improves system dependability and lengthens the motor's lifetime by lowering the inrush current and mechanical stress on the motor and related equipment.

During the first startup of an AC induction motor, it produces a torque that exceeds the necessary amount for operating at maximum speed. This results in mechanical strain on the gearbox system. The tension experienced causes accelerated deterioration, leading to early malfunction of crucial parts such as chains, belts, and gears. In addition, the abrupt acceleration results in a substantial effect on the input power source, leading to large inrush currents that surpass 600% of the standard current. While the use of Star Delta offers a partial remedy, it fails to completely resolve the problem.

To address these issues efficiently, soft starts provide a dependable and cost-effective solution by giving a regulated discharge of power to the motor. This guarantees seamless and continuous acceleration and deceleration, reducing mechanical strain on the gearbox system. Soft starters are equipped with soft start and soft stop capabilities, which are incorporated into 3-phase units. These features enable regulated beginning and stopping, with the ability to customise ramp periods and current limit settings. Soft starters function as stator voltage controllers, effectively limiting starting currents. This results in a regulated and seamless operation, which helps to prolong the lifespan of the motor by reducing potential harm to its windings and bearings. Offers a dependable and cost-effective solution to these issues by supplying a regulated amount of power to the motor. This results in a seamless and gradual increase or decrease in speed. The lifespan of the motor will be prolonged by minimizing damage to the windings and bearings. Soft Start & Soft Stop is incorporated into 3 phase devices, offering regulated initiation and termination with a range of ramp periods and current limit settings to accommodate all applications. The advantages of soft starter are provided in Figure 2.10.

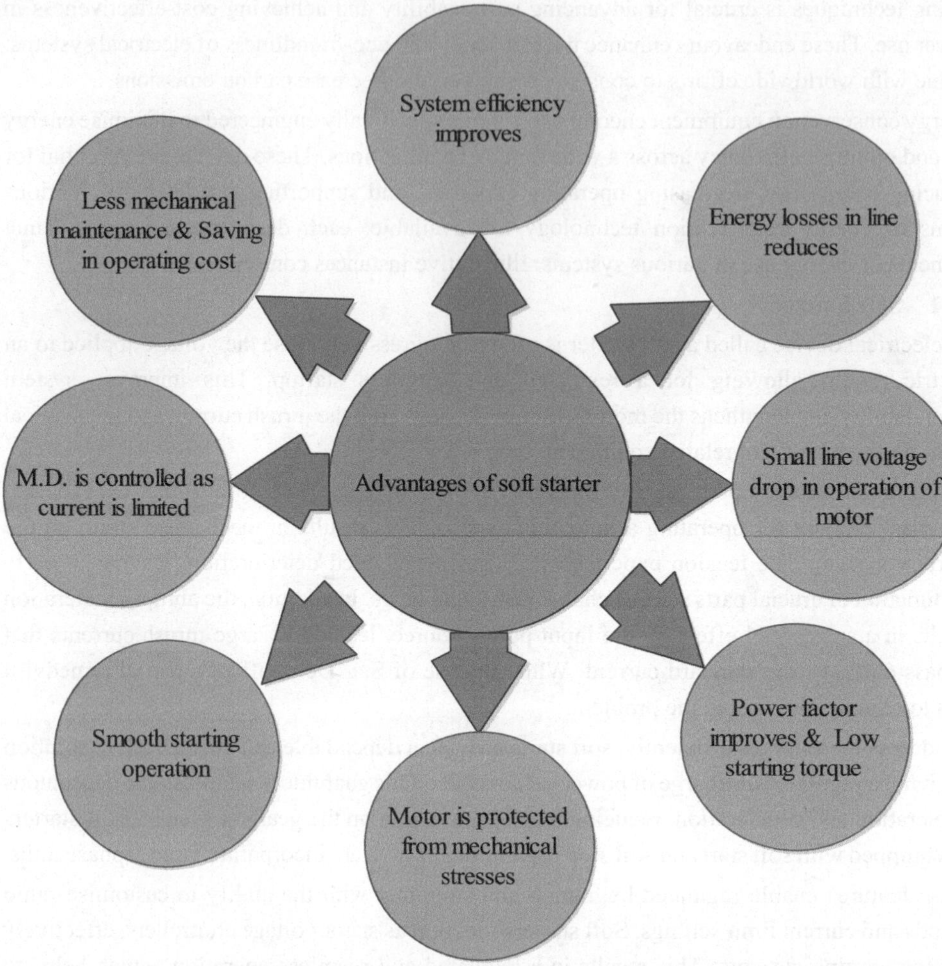

Figure: 2.10 Advantages of Soft Starter

2.6.2 Automatic Star Delta Convertor

Motor with greater capacity sometimes come fitted with star/delta windings to effectively handle the early starting process. During the first stage, the motor is linked in a star configuration to mitigate the surge of electric current. Upon reaching the specified velocity, the motor smoothly transitions into delta mode, enabling the loading process.

Automatic Delta-Load Switching (ADLS) takes use of the motor's ability to switch to star mode while operating at lesser loads (<40%). On the other hand, when the load exceeds 40%, it switches to delta mode. Implementing this approach leads to a decrease of one-third in the amount of electricity used by the motor while it works in star mode. Therefore, significant energy conservation is achieved, with savings ranging from 10% to 40%, depending on the motor's load and any variations in the load. Extended use of the motor at lower loads results in increased energy efficiency, with certain industrial uses showing savings of over 50%. Figure 2.11 showing circuit diagram of automatic star delta starter-power.

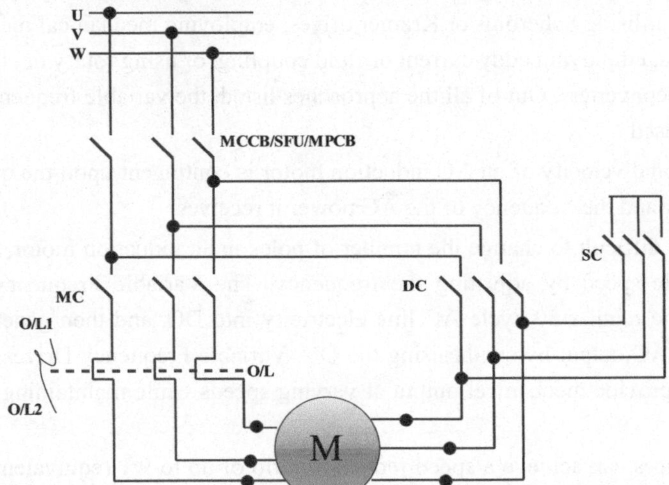

Figure 2.11 Circuit Diagram of Automatic Star Delta Starter-Power

2.6.3 Variable Frequency Drives

By varying the frequency of the supplied AC power, Variable Frequency Drives (VFDs) control the rotational speed of an AC induction motor using a simple principle of operation. Induction motors have a set number of poles, but they may have variable speeds thanks to frequency adjustments. This is accomplished by VFDs, which first convert conventional 50-cycle AC line power to DC before producing variable frequency AC output. VFD-connected motors provide a highly efficient mechanical output with variable speed, enabling up to 9:1 (11 percent of full speed) and 3:11 (300 percent of full speed) speed reductions and increases.

Speed and Frequency Relationship:

$$Ns = 120\ \frac{f}{P} \tag{2.1}$$

Where, Ns-Synchronous speed in rpm, F-Supply frequency in Herts(Hz) p- number of poles

Where $N \propto f$ and $N \propto \frac{1}{P}$

The development of VFDs has been greatly aided by recent technological developments, especially the use of high switching frequency Insulated Gate Bipolar Transistors (IGBTs) as power devices and digital microprocessor control. VFDs have become more efficient and compact in recent years because to the considerable cost, reliability, and physical size reductions brought about by this innovation.

- The induction motor is extensively used in several industries. It is cost-effective and has a good power-to-weight ratio.
- Due to the expensive nature and restrictions of DC systems, induction motors are favoured for variable speed applications. The speed of these motors may be adjusted by altering the supply frequency.

- The speed of the motor can be adjusted by manipulating various factors, such as altering the input voltage, adjusting the resistance of the rotor circuit, employing multi-speed windings, utilising Scherbius or Kramer drives, employing mechanical methods like gears and pulleys, employing eddy current or fluid coupling, or using rotary or static voltage and frequency converters. Out of all the approaches listed, the variable frequency drive (VFD) is widely used.
- The rotational velocity of an AC induction motor is contingent upon the quantity of poles in its stator and the frequency of the AC power it receives.
- While it is difficult to change the number of poles in an induction motor, it is possible to get variable speed by adjusting the frequency. The Variable Frequency Drive (VFD) converts the regular 50 cycle AC line electricity into DC, and then generates a variable frequency AC output by synthesising the DC. Variable Frequency Drives (VFDs) enable motors to provide mechanical output at varying speeds while maintaining a high level of efficiency.
- These devices can achieve a speed reduction ratio of up to 9:1 (equivalent to 11% of the maximum speed) and a speed increase ratio of 3:1 (equivalent to 300% of the maximum speed).
- Currently, the technology of AC variable frequency drives (VFD) has advanced to include advanced digital microprocessor control and high switching frequency IGBTs (Insulated Gate Bipolar Transistors) power devices.
- This has resulted in greatly enhanced capabilities, ranging from the simplicity of programming to the broadened scope of diagnostics.
- The primary advantages resulting from technological advancements are cost reduction, improved dependability, and a substantial decrease in physical dimensions.

2.6.4 Automatic Power Factor Controller (APFC)

"Power is the measure of how quickly energy is transported or transformed. Power is quantified in watts (W) and represents the quantity of labour performed or energy used per unit of time."

$$P = \frac{W}{\Delta t} \tag{2.2}$$

P= Power

W= Work

Δt=Elapsed time

A low power factor results in higher current, leading to increasing losses and negatively impacting voltage. Power Factor Controller or Automatic Power Factor Controller may be strategically placed near receiving substations, load centres, or loads.

"Power factor is a metric that quantifies the efficiency of electrical power use. The power factor is the ratio of the real power, which is the power that really accomplishes work, to the apparent power, which is the product of the current and voltage given to the circuit. A

greater power factor signifies a more effective utilisation of electrical power, whilst a lower power factor signifies a less effective utilisation."

$$Power\ Factor\ (Cos\phi) = \frac{Real\ Power\ (P)}{Apparent\ Power\ (S)} \qquad 2.3$$

Where, ϕ is the Phase angle refers to the angular difference between the voltage and current waveforms, figure 2.12 showing the circuit diagram of PF.

Real Power (P) is quantified in watts (W) and signifies the genuine power used by the load to accomplish tasks.

Apparent Power (S) is quantified in volt-amperes (VA) and denotes the multiplication of the voltage and current delivered to the circuit.

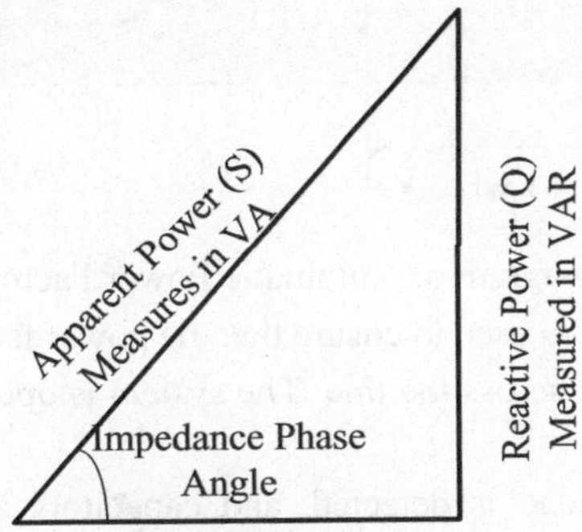

Figure 2.12 Power Factor

- ✓ P is the true power or real power, P = VI Cos ϕ Watt (W)
- ✓ Q is the reactive power,

  Q = VI Sin ϕ Volt Ampere Reactive (VAR)
- ✓ S is the apparent power,

  S = V I Volt Ampere (VA)

Power Factor Controller

A Power Factor Controller (PFC) is an electrical device used to regulate and enhance the power factor, defined as the ratio of actual power (useful power) to apparent power (total power), in electrical systems. Efficient energy utilisation relies on a fundamental quantity known as power factor. Keeping the power factor near to unity (1) is essential to minimise energy losses in the system. The PFC functions by regulating the connection and disconnection of capacitor banks in parallel with the load. Capacitors function to counterbalance the inductive reactive power present in the system, hence enhancing the power factor. The Power Factor Controller (PFC) constantly checks the power factor and, using the kVAR (kilo Volt-Ampere Reactive) demand of the load as a reference, regulates the capacitor banks to get the targeted power factor. Circuit diagram of automatic power factor controller (APFC) showing in Figure 2.13.

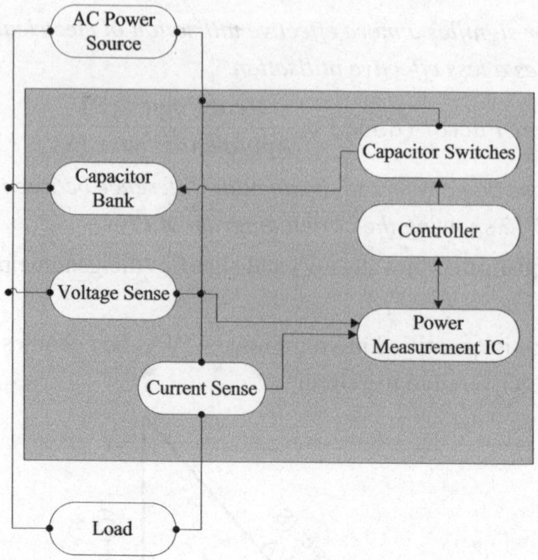

Figure 2.13 Circuit Diagram of Automatic Power Factor Controller (APFC)

- The power factor controller is used to ensure that the power factor remains at unity by using a capacitor bank connected across the line. The system is operated using a microcontroller and a contactor setup.
- The power factor of the load is detected, and capacitors are connected or disengaged according to the KVAR requirement.
- Maintaining the power factor at unity results in a decrease in the current flowing through the lines.

$$\text{Real power} = \text{apparent power} \times \text{power factor} \tag{2.4}$$

- The above figure displays the block diagram of the APFC. The supply main terminals are linked to the input of the Automatic Power Factor Correction (APFC) Panel. The power factor is detected by the current transformer (CT) and potential transformer (PT) located on the line side. The capacitor banks are controlled in accordance with the need to obtain the desired power factor using a microprocessor-based Automatic Power Factor Correction (APFC) relay. The capacitor bank that is suitable will function based on the needed kilovolt-ampere reactive (kVAR) to achieve the desired power factor (PF) as determined by the automatic power factor correction (APFC) panel. Following that, the CT and PT will assess the feedback obtained from the switching capacitors. At last, the desired power factor has been attained.

2.6.5 Intelligent Power Factor Controller (IPFC)

An Intelligent Power Factor Controller is a device designed to enhance the power factor of an electrical system.

An Intelligent Power Factor Controller (IPFC) is a complex device specifically designed to regulate the power factor dynamically and intelligently in electrical systems. An IPFC, in contrast to conventional power factor controllers, integrates sophisticated algorithms, microprocessor control, and real-time monitoring capabilities, enabling accurate and adaptable power factor adjustment.

The IPFC consistently evaluates the power factor and reactive power requirements of the electrical load. The system employs microcontroller-based intelligence to analyse the power factor dynamics and accordingly regulates the connection and disconnection of capacitor banks. This astute decision-making process relies on a comprehensive comprehension of the load characteristics, always guaranteeing the most efficient power factor adjustment.

An IPFC, equipped with sophisticated communication interfaces, may be seamlessly incorporated into supervisory control systems, allowing for remote monitoring and control. The inclusion of this capability improves the capacity to react to different levels of demand, thereby making the IPFC very versatile in dynamic industrial and commercial settings. The dynamic operation of the IPFC guarantees effective power factor adjustment under various load conditions, resulting in decreased energy losses and enhanced system dependability. Furthermore, the gadget enhances overall energy efficiency by dynamically adjusting to fluctuations in the electrical network, so ensuring that the power factor remains near to unity.

- The controller calculates the capacitance rating for each step during the first hour of operation and saves them in memory.
- Based on this assessment, the IPFC activates the most suitable actions, hence resolving the hunting issues often linked to capacitor switching.

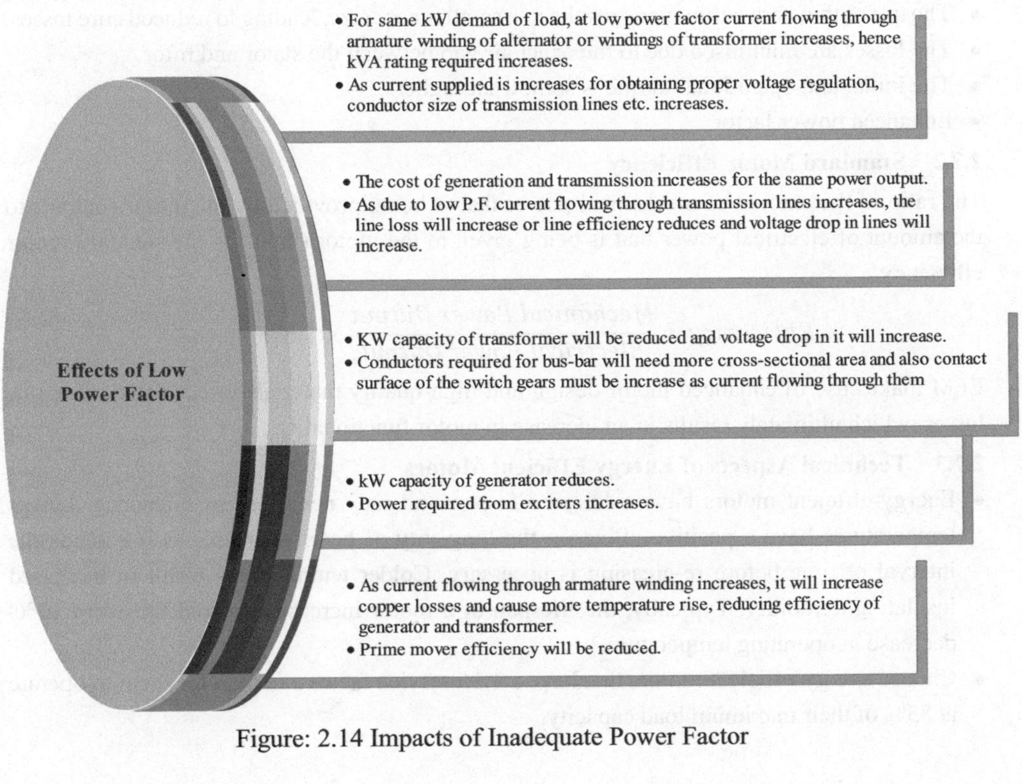

Figure: 2.14 Impacts of Inadequate Power Factor

2.7 Energy Efficient Motor

An energy efficient motor (EEM) is a motor that continues to provide the same amount of output power while using a lower amount of electricity.

- Energy efficient motors (EEM) are motors that have been deliberately designed to boost operational efficiency compared to normal motors by using design changes.
- Design enhancements prioritise the reduction of inherent motor losses.
- Enhancements include the utilisation of silicon steel with reduced loss, an elongated core, thicker wire, thinner laminations, a diminished air gap between the stator and rotor, copper bars instead of aluminium in the rotor, better bearings, and a smaller fan, among others.

Even though EEM is Constructed Utilising the same chassis as a normal motor, there are a few fey distinctions between the two machines:

- Higher quality and thinner steel laminations in the stator
- more copper in the winding
- Optimized air gap between the rotor and the stator
- Reduced fan losses
- Closer machining tolerances
- High quality aluminium used in rotor frame.

2.7.1 Significant Features of Energy Efficient Motors

- The material used exhibits superior quality, leading to a high flux density and high current density.
- The use of thin core laminations results in a smaller core size, leading to reduced core losses.
- The losses are minimised due to the exact air gap between the stator and rotor.
- The initial and operational torque is somewhat higher.
- Enhanced power factor.

2.7.2 Standard Motor Efficiency

The ratio of the amount of mechanical power that is being provided by the motor (output) to the amount of electrical power that is being given to the motor (input) is the standard motor efficiency.

$$\% Efficiency = \frac{Mechanical\ Power\ Output}{Electrical\ Power\ Output} \times 100\% \qquad 2.5$$

EEM makes use of enhanced motor design and high-quality materials to cut down on motor losses, which ultimately results in an increase in motor functionality.

2.7.3 Technical Aspects of Energy Efficient Motors

- Energy-efficient motors have a longer lifespan and may need less maintenance. Lower temperatures have a positive effect on the longevity of bearing grease, as it extends the interval of time before re-greasing is necessary. Colder temperatures result in increased insulating durability. Typically, the lifespan of a motor increases twofold for every 10°C decrease in operating temperature.
- Choose energy-efficient motors that have a 1.15 service factor and plan for them to operate at 85% of their maximum load capacity.

- Electrical power issues, particularly inadequate incoming power quality, might impact the functioning of energy-efficient motors.
- Speed regulation is essential in some applications. Slip in polyphase induction motors quantifies the losses in the motor windings. Efficiency increases when slip decreases. Energy efficient motors have reduced slippage, leading to speeds that are about 1% higher compared to normal motors.
- The initial torque required for efficient motors may be lower compared to regular motors. Facility managers must exercise caution when using efficient motors for high torque applications.

Example 2.1: *A motor is Operating at 100 V and drawing a current of 15 A. If the output power of motor is 800 W, then determine the efficiency of motor.*

Solution: *Given data:*

Voltage, V=100V Current, I=15A

$$\text{Power is given by } P=V\times I$$

$$P=100\times 15$$

$$P=1{,}500\ W$$

Output power, P. = 800W

$$\text{Efficiency, } \eta=\frac{\text{Output Power}}{\text{Input Power}}\times 100\%$$

$$=\frac{800}{1{,}500}\times 100$$

$$\text{Efficiency, } \eta = 53\%$$

2.7.4 Need for Efficient Motors

Because of issues pertaining to the environment and the scarcity of resources, the cost of energy is expected to rise in the following years. A significant portion of the electric energy that is used in industrial settings is used by electric motors.

Therefore, the use of a motor that is energy efficient might cut down on a considerable quantity of power. It would also bring to a reduction in the production of greenhouse gases and a reduction in the overall environmental cost of the generating of electricity production. Additionally, the use of these motors may lower the costs of maintenance and enhance operations in the industrial sector. In most cases, the most effective way to achieve efficient energy consumption is not via changes in person behaviour but rather using more efficient technologies or processes.

An electrically excited synchronous motor (EEM) generates an equivalent amount of power at the output shaft, while using less power at the input compared to a motor with normal efficiency. A conventional motor is a trade-off between efficiency, durability, beginning torque, and initial cost. Typically, standard motors prioritise price above efficiency in their competition. In contrast, EEM's focus is on competing based on efficiency rather than price. In summary, EEM is required,

- When there is a new installation or modification to your plant
- When old motors are damaged and need rewinding

- When existing motors are underloaded or overloaded
- While protecting other devices

2.7.5 Advantages of Energy efficient Motor

- EEM motors feature a reduced slip, resulting in faster speeds compared to normal motors.
- Implementing EEM in industry may lead to cost savings in maintenance and improved operational efficiency, thanks to its resilience and dependability. It is less expensive than a normal motor.
- Enhancing productivity
- The efficiencies of these motors are 3% to 7% greater than those of ordinary motors.
- The design modifications aim to decrease the inherent motor losses.

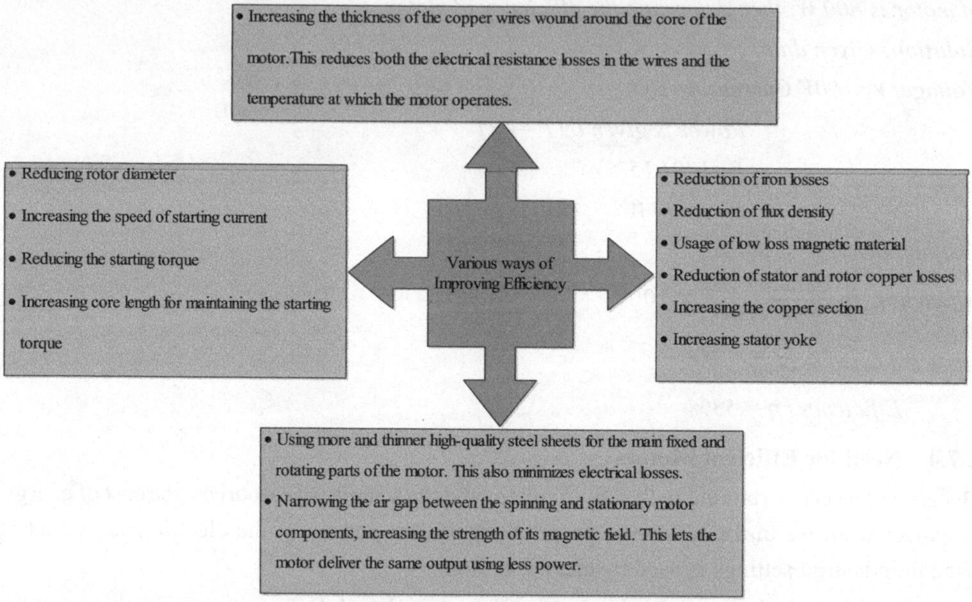

Figure: 2.15 Various Ways of Improving Efficiency

2.7.6 Applications of Energy Efficient Motor

- Energy efficient motors maintain their efficiency more effectively under partial loads, thereby improving their superiority over ordinary motors.
- The economic advantages of installing Energy Efficient Motors may be realised in three scenarios.
  - In a new application (Plant Expansion)
  - In Lieu of Rewinding of failed Motors
  - Proactive replacement for in-service standard motors
- Energy efficient motors are more economically advantageous than normal motors in the situations.
- The efficiency of EEMs is 4-6% more than the efficiency of Standard Motors.
- Energy Efficient Motors operate at lower temperatures, resulting in possibly extended lifespans compared to conventional efficiency motors.

2.7.7 Limitation of Energy Efficient Motors

- **Higher Initial Cost:** Energy-efficient motors can come with a higher price tag than normal motors, which may discourage enterprises or projects with limited funds.
- **Complexity in Design and Maintenance:** These motors often use sophisticated materials and technologies, necessitating specialised expertise for maintenance and repair. This might result in increased service expenses and a need for specialised experts.
- **Compatibility Issues**: Retrofitting energy-efficient motors into existing systems might pose challenges owing to compatibility concerns with older equipment or infrastructure, requiring further changes or upgrades.
- **Load Matching Requirements:** To optimise the efficiency advantages, it is essential to appropriately pair energy-efficient motors with the specific load demands. Inaccurate pairing may lead to less-than-ideal performance and diminished energy conservation.
- **Availability and Lead Time:** Availability of energy-efficient motors may be limited in some regions and may not always meet specified specifications, resulting in lengthier procurement lead times. This may cause a delay in projects and have an influence on deadlines.

2.8 Energy Efficient Transformers

Energy-efficient transformers play a *crucial role in achieving sustainable and ecologically* friendly electrical power distribution. The design of these transformers is primarily focused on minimising energy losses and optimising performance throughout the transmission and distribution operation. The primary objective is to optimise energy efficiency, minimise greenhouse gas emissions, and attain cost reductions in power systems.

Energy-efficient transformers use cutting-edge technology, superior materials, and inventive designs to exceed the efficiency benchmarks set by traditional transformers. They are designed to function with minimum inefficiencies, transforming electrical energy with enhanced accuracy and efficiency. Energy-efficient transformers provide a substantial contribution to conserving electrical energy by enhancing efficiency. This aligns with worldwide initiatives to encourage sustainable practices and minimise environmental effect.

There are two primary categories of transformers that are designed to save energy: We manufacture and provide resin cast dry-type transformers as well as amorphous metal transformers. Resin Cast Dry-Type Transformers use epoxy resin insulation, which eliminates the need for oil, making them ecologically sustainable and appropriate for indoor use. Amorphous Metal Transformers use a unique alloy with exceptional magnetic characteristics, resulting in a substantial decrease in core losses as compared to conventional transformers. Both categories of energy-efficient transformers have a vital function in the process of modernising power distribution networks and promoting a more sustainable and energy-conscious future.

- The primary cause of energy loss in dry type transformers is heat or vibration emanating from the core. The newly developed high-efficiency transformers significantly reduce these losses.

- The typical transformer consists of a core consisting of silicon alloyed iron, specifically grain oriented. The iron loss of a transformer is contingent upon the specific core material used.
- However, the most recent technological advancement involves the use of amorphous material, namely a metallic glass alloy, for the core.
- The anticipated decrease in energy loss compared to typical transformers with silicon and iron cores is around 70%, which is a substantial improvement.
- These novel transformers use an amorphous core with distinct physical and magnetic characteristics, resulting in improved efficiencies even while operating at low loads. Specifically, they achieve an efficiency of 98.5% at a load of 35%.
- Electrical distribution transformers constructed with amorphous metal cores provide a remarkable possibility to effectively preserve energy starting from the moment of installation.
- While these transformers may be more expensive than traditional iron core transformers, the long-term energy savings they provide will offset the higher initial cost.
- Currently, transformers with amorphous metal cores are available with a maximum capacity of 1600 kVA.

2.8.1 Advantages of Energy Efficient Transformers

- They have a lower number of operational losses.
- The generation of heat is reduced because of decreased losses.
- They have a longer lifespan.
- More cost-efficient.
- The issue of a thin core may be partially resolved with the advancement of amorphous metal strips.
- Low field magnetization decreases hysteresis loss.
- The high electrical resistivity of the core material decreases the occurrence of eddy currents and minimises eddy current loss.
- Minimal magnetising current and minimal iron losses result in a reduction of the no load current.

2.8.2 Amorphous Transformers

An amorphous transformer is a power distribution transformer that uses amorphous metal as the core material, rather than the conventional crystalline silicon steel.

The word "amorphous" refers to the non-crystalline or disordered arrangement of the metal, leading to distinctive magnetic characteristics.

This design has several benefits compared to traditional transformers in terms of energy efficiency, less environmental footprint, and overall performance.

The transformer's core is essential for enabling the efficient passage of electrical energy between the main and secondary windings.

The core of conventional transformers is often constructed using stacked layers of crystalline silicon steel sheets. Amorphous transformers use a unique alloy composed of iron, boron, and silicon, which is quickly cooled to create a non-crystalline or amorphous configuration.

Amorphous transformers provide significant advantages due to their exceptional magnetic characteristics, leading to reduced core losses.

The amorphous form minimises hysteresis losses and eddy current losses that are typically seen in crystalline steel cores. Consequently, amorphous transformers provide superior energy efficiency, leading to decreased energy use and reduced operational expenses.

The enhanced efficacy of amorphous transformers has substantial environmental ramifications. The decreased energy losses lead to decreased greenhouse gas emissions and aid in reaching energy conservation objectives.

Amorphous transformers are being rapidly embraced by governments and utility corporations globally as a component of their sustainable energy endeavours.

Amorphous transformers have many noticeable benefits, in addition to their energy efficiency. They have enhanced thermal stability, enabling greater overloading capabilities and enhanced dependability.

The transformers exhibit reduced noise emissions during operation, making them appropriate for installations in situations that are sensitive to noise.

The smaller size and reduced mass of amorphous transformers provide more convenient transportation, installation, and maintenance.

Although amorphous transformers provide certain advantages, they also present some difficulties.

Producing amorphous metal involves a more intricate and expensive manufacturing procedure compared to the production of standard transformer cores.

Nevertheless, the enduring energy cost reductions often rationalise the original capital outlay. Furthermore, amorphous metal exhibits greater brittleness compared to crystalline steel, necessitating meticulous handling throughout the production and shipping processes.

Continued technological advancements may result in more research and development in transformer design, perhaps leading to more inventive solutions for a sustainable and energy-efficient future.

2.8.3 Epoxy Resin Cast Transformer

A Cast Resin Transformer is a static transformer which means it doesn't have moving parts and because of this are often the transformer of choice for high-service reliability situations. They are designed to raise or lower voltage to the required level.

A dry type of transformer is a transformer that does not use any liquid substance for insulation or cooling of its windings or core. Conversely, the windings and core are contained inside a hermetically sealed container that is filled with pressurised air or gas. The use of dry type transformers is prevalent across many sectors and applications due to its inherent advantages in terms of safety, dependability, and environmental impact. These devices are capable of functioning well in challenging environments, including those with elevated levels of humidity, potential fire hazards, and seismic activity, without affecting their performance or creating any risks to people or property. The two primary categories of dry type transformers are cast resin dry type transformers (CRT) and vacuum pressure impregnated transformers (VPI).

2.8.4 Cast Resin Dry Type Transformer (CRT)

A cast resin dry type transformer (CRT) is a transformer that employs epoxy resin to encase its primary and secondary windings. This shields the windings from moisture, dust, rust, and other environmental elements that may impact their insulation and performance. A CRT is appropriate for environments with high humidity, interior installations, and regions prone to fire hazards because to its non-hygroscopic, non-inflammable, and maintenance-free properties. Additionally, it can endure excessive loads, partial discharges, and little losses, leading to exceptional efficiency and a prolonged lifespan.

The available ratings for a CRT range from 25 kVA to 12,500 kVA, with an insulating class of F and a temperature increase of 90°C.

2.8.5 Vacuum Pressure Impregnated Transformer (VPI)

A vacuum pressure impregnated transformer (VPI) is a transformer that employs vacuum and pressure to saturate its windings with class H polyester resin shown in Figure 2.16.

This process removes any spaces or empty areas in the insulation, which improves its physical strength, electrical strength, and capacity to withstand high temperatures.

A VPI (Vapour Phase Inhibition) is well-suited for outdoor installations, seismic events, and temperature variations because to its sturdy construction, moisture-resistant casing, and low thermal expansion coefficient.

Additionally, it has convenient upkeep, less susceptibility to fire hazards, and exceptional resilience to short circuit currents.

The VPI is offered in a range of rates, starting from 5 kVA, and going up to 30 MVA. It has an insulation class of either F, which can withstand temperatures up to 155°C, or H, which can withstand temperatures up to 180°C. Additionally, it provides protection up to IP56.

Figure: 2.16 Vacuum Pressure Impregnated Transformer (Source: https://www.indiamart.com/proddetail/vacuum-pressure-impregnated-transformer-24269264848.html?pos=7&pla=n)

SUMMARY

Since electrical machines are most power consuming devices in industries and transformers are extensively used in power systems, therefore, the focus of this unit is, the energy conservation in electrical machines and transformers. Need and necessity of energy conservation in electrical machines and transformers are explained in first part of this chapter.

After being familiar with the importance of energy conservation in electrical machines and transformers, different types of techniques used and their applications in electrical conservation in induction machines and transformers are discussed in details. Different energy efficient machines and their applications are also included in the unit.

EXERCISE

Short Answer Type Questions

1. How can electrical machines be made energy efficient?
2. What are the different methods used for energy conservation in transformers?
3. Explain, how variable frequency drives helps in energy conservation?
4. Differentiate between energy audit and energy conservation.
5. What is Cast Resin Dry Type Transformer (CRT)?
6. What is condition-based monitoring? How it helps in energy conservation?
7. State any four energy conservation techniques in Induction motor.
8. Outline any two features of energy efficient transformer.
9. What are the significant features of energy-efficient motors?
10. How does improving power quality contribute to energy conservation in induction motors?

Long Answer Type Questions

1. Discuss the need for energy conservation and its measurements in electrical machines.
2. Discuss the Government of India's initiatives to promote energy conservation.
3. Discuss any three energy efficient transformers.
4. How load sharing and parallel operation help in energy conservation?
5. Explain intelligent power factor controller (IPFC)
6. Explain the importance of minimizing the idle and redundant running of motors and operating them in star mode for energy conservation.
7. Analyze the impact of rewinding motors and replacing them with energy-efficient models on energy conservation.
8. Evaluate the role of periodic maintenance and loading sharing in energy conservation for transformers.
9. Discuss the applications, advantages, and limitations of energy-efficient motors and the use of energy conservation equipment like soft starters, automatic star-delta converters, and variable frequency drives.
10. Discuss various energy conservation techniques for induction motors, including improving power quality, motor surveys, and matching motor with loading.

Multiple Choice Questions

1. Why is energy conservation important in induction motors?
   A. To increase motor speed
   B. To reduce electricity costs and environmental impact
   C. To decrease motor size
   D. To increase motor weight
2. What percentage of electricity used in an industry is typically consumed by three-phase induction motors?
   A. 10%
   B. 30%
   C. 50%
   D. 70%
3. Why is energy conservation necessary in transformers?
   A. To reduce the physical size of transformers
   B. To minimize power losses and improve efficiency
   C. To increase the voltage levels
   D. To decrease the weight of transformers
4. Which technique involves analyzing and improving the quality of voltage and current supplied to the motor?
   A. Motor survey
   B. Rewinding of motor
   C. Improving power quality
   D. Operating in star mode
5. What is the purpose of conducting a motor survey?
   A. To increase motor speed
   B. To reduce motor weight
   C. To change motor type
   D. To identify energy-saving opportunities
6. Matching motor with loading ensures:
   A. Overloading the motor
   B. Operating the motor at optimal efficiency
   C. Reducing motor speed
   D. Increasing power factor
7. How can minimizing the idle and redundant running of motors save energy?
   A. By increasing motor voltage
   B. By increasing motor current
   C. By decreasing motor efficiency
   D. By reducing unnecessary power consumption

8. Operating an induction motor in star mode is useful for:
   A. High power applications
   B. Low load conditions
   C. Increasing motor size
   D. Decreasing motor voltage
9. Rewinding a motor can help in:
   A. Restoring its efficiency
   B. Decreasing the motor voltage
   C. Increasing the motor speed
   D. Increasing the motor weight
10. What is the benefit of replacing a standard motor with an energy-efficient motor?
    A. Increased energy consumption
    B. Reduced operational efficiency
    C. Lower energy costs and higher efficiency
    D. Increased maintenance costs
11. Periodic maintenance of motors helps in:
    A. Increasing motor weight
    B. Maintaining optimal performance and efficiency
    C. Reducing motor speed
    D. Increasing motor size
12. Load sharing in transformers aims to:
    A. Increase load on one transformer
    B. Decrease the overall load
    C. Distribute load evenly across multiple transformers
    D. Isolate one transformer from the system
13. What is the benefit of parallel operation of transformers?
    A. Reduced system flexibility
    B. Increased redundancy and reliability
    C. Increased power losses
    D. Decreased availability
14. Isolating techniques in transformer operation are used to:
    A. Increase transformer losses
    B. Decrease transformer efficiency
    C. Prevent unnecessary energy wastage
    D. Increase transformer voltage
15. Replacing a standard transformer with an energy-efficient transformer results in:
    A. Increased energy losses

B. Lower efficiency

C. Reduced energy consumption

D. Higher operational costs

16. Periodic maintenance of transformers helps in:

A. Reducing system efficiency

B. Ensuring reliable and efficient operation

C. Increasing power losses

D. Decreasing system availability

17. What is the function of a soft starter in motor control?

A. To increase motor speed instantly

B. To decrease motor efficiency

C. To increase power consumption

D. To gradually increase the motor speed

18. An Automatic Star-Delta Converter is used to:

A. Increase motor current

B. Switch motor windings from star to delta configuration

C. Decrease motor voltage

D. Increase motor weight

19. What is the role of Variable Frequency Drives (VFDs) in energy conservation?

A. To vary the motor speed according to load requirements

B. To decrease motor voltage

C. To increase motor weight

D. To maintain constant motor speed

20. An Automatic Power Factor Controller (APFC) is used to:

A. Decrease power factor

B. Increase power factor and improve efficiency

C. Decrease system voltage

D. Increase power consumption

21. Improvement of power factor helps in reduction of ________

A. Reactive power

B. Apparent power

C. Active power

D. Both reactive power and apparent power

Answer of Multiple Choice Questions

1	B	2	D	3	B	4	C	5	D
6	B	7	D	8	B	9	A	10	C
11	B	12	C	13	B	14	C	15	C
16	B	17	D	18	B	19	B	20	B
21	D								

REFERENCES AND SUGGESTED READINGS

1. BEE. "Energy Efficiency in Electrical Utilities" New Delhi, India: BEE; 2015.
2. BEE. "General Aspects of Energy Management and Energy Audit" New Delhi, India: BEE; 2015.
3. BEE. "Energy Efficiency in Thermal Utilities" New Delhi, India: BEE; 2015.
4. BEE. "Energy Performance Assessment For Equipment and Utility Systems" New Delhi, India: BEE; 2015.
5. O.P. Gupta, "Energy Technology" Khanna Publishing House, New Delhi
6. Henderson, P. D., "India - The Energy Sector", University Press, Delhi, 2016. ISBN: 978-0195606539.
7. Turner, W. C., "Energy Management" Handbook, Fairmount Press, 2012, ISBN 9781304520708
8. Sharma, K. V., Venkataseshaiah; P., "Energy Management and Conservation", I K International Publishing House Pvt. Ltd; 2011 ISBN 9789381141298
9. Mehta ,V. K., "Principles of Power System" S. Chand & Co.New Delhi, 2016, ISBN 9788121905947.
10. Singh, Sanjeev; Rathore, Umesh, "Energy Management" S K Kataria & Sons, New Delhi ISBN-13: 9789350141014.
11. Desai, B. G.; Rana, J. S.; A. Dinesh, V.; Paraman, R., "Efficient Use and Management of Electricity in Industry" Devki Energy Consultancy Pvt. Ltd.
12. Chakrabarti, Aman, "Energy Engineering And Management", e-books Kindle Edition, 2011, 978-8120342330.
13. A. Kumar, "Energy Generation Through Vedas," International Journal of Science Technology and Management, 5, pp. 294-304, 2016.
14. United Nations, "Global Environment Outlook 6 (GEO6) – 2019" New York, USA, 2019.

****

3 Energy Conservation in Electrical Installation Systems

UNIT SPECIFICS

In this unit, energy conservation in electrical installation systems is explained and covered the following topics.

- Importance of energy conservation in electrical installations
- Aggregated technical and commercial losses in power systems
- Energy conservation solutions in electrical installation systems
- Energy conversations in lighting

Power systems is one of the most complex geographically wide distributed systems. Power from the generating stations to the consumer end is transmitted through long transmission lines. Energy losses occur in the process of supplying electricity to consumers due to technical and commercial losses. The technical losses are due to energy dissipated in the conductors, transformers and other equipment used for transmission, sub-transmission, and distribution of power. These technical losses are inherent in a system and can be reduced to a certain level. However, pilferage by hooking, bypassing meters, defective meters, errors in meter reading and in estimating un-metered supply of energy are the main sources of the commercial losses. Hence, huge power and revenue losses in power delivery. Therefore, energy conservation in electrical installation systems is essential and addressed here in this unit. Energy conservation is an important aspect of utilizing electrical energy for economic growth, prosperity, and technical, industrial, and sustainable development.

RATIONALE

Energy conservation in electrical installations may reduce energy losses, which were in tune of about 35% of total losses in power system. Energy conservation technology will enhance the performance efficiency of electrical apparatus used by end users.

PRE-REQUISITES

Basic knowledge of electrical power systems.

UNIT OUTCOMES

The outcomes of this unit are as follows

U3-O1: To understand the concepts of energy conservation and energy auditing in electrical installations.

U3-O2: To identify the importance of energy conservation in respect of electrical installations.

U3-O3: To apply the techniques for energy conservation in electrical installations.

U3-O4: To study the equipment's used for energy conservation.

U3-O5: To apply the concept of energy conservation in lighting system.

Unit outcomes	EXPECTED MAPPING WITH COURSE OUTCOMES (1- Weak Correlation; 2- Medium correlation; 3- Strong Correlation)				
	CO-1	CO-2	CO-3	CO-4	CO-5
U3-O1	3	2	1	-	2
U3-O2	3	1	1	-	1
U3-O3	-	3	3	1	1
U3-O4	-	2	3	-	2
U3-O5	3	2	3	1	2

3.1 Introduction

Power system is one of the most complex, geographically wide spread system connected with grids at different levels like, national, regional, state and local. Losses either technical or commercial in any part of the power systems cannot be ruled out. In India more than 25% losses take place in the power system resulting huge revenue loss as well as power loss. It is said that one unit loss is equal to two units generated. Steps are to be taken to enhance the performance efficiency of generating stations and energy conservation technology adopted in transmission and distribution system. Implementation of energy conservation technology will lead to energy saving which means increasing generation of energy with available sources. Here in this unit measures of energy conservation in power installations, equipment used and energy conservation in lighting system is described.

3.1.1 Aggregated Technical and Commercial Losses (ATC)

ATC is crucial in evaluating the effectiveness, financial stability, and adherence to regulations of electricity distribution networks. Technical and commercial losses take place in transmission and distribution system. Losses of transmission and distribution system are broadly classified as technical losses and non-technical losses as shown in Figure 3.1.

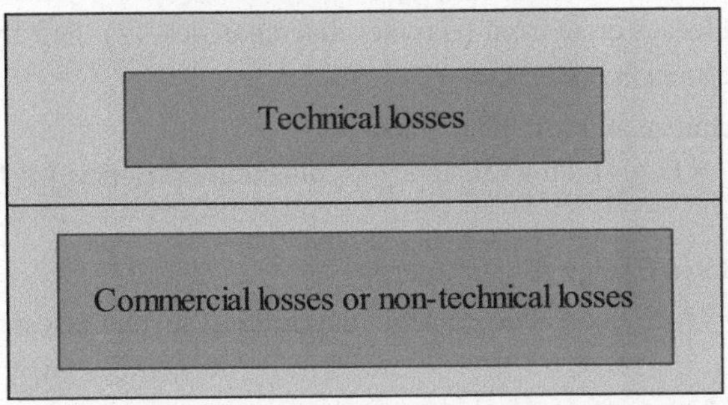

Figure:3.1 Losses of Transmission and Distribution System

However, these losses occur at various stages in the transmission and distribution part of power system and shown in Figure 3.2.

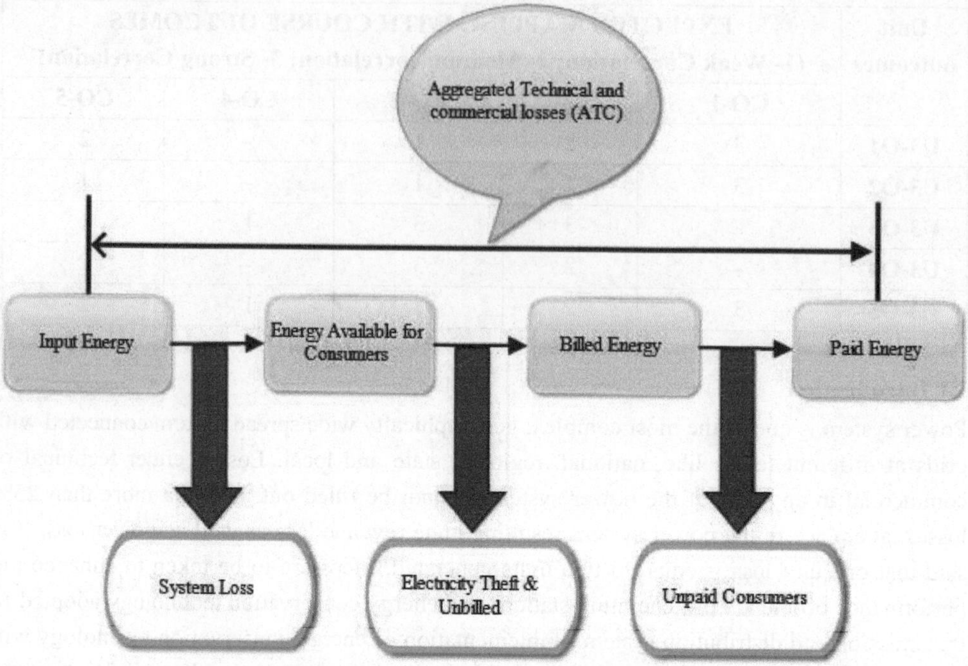

Figure:3.2 Aggregated Technical and Commercial Losses (ATC)

The aggregate technical and commercial losses, often known as AT&C losses, are made up of two components:

a) Technical losses occur largely because of (i) losses during the transformation process at different stages of transformation, and (ii) excessive losses on distribution lines owing to the inherent resistance and inadequate power factor in the electrical network.

b) Commercial losses occur when electrical energy is used illegally without proper metering, billing, and revenue collection, resulting in financial losses for the utilities. Commercial losses arise from (i) meter discrepancies, (ii) theft by direct hooking, and (iii) inefficiencies in collection.

Aggregated technical and commercial losses

$$= \{1 - (\text{Billing Efficiency} \times \text{Collection Efficiency})\} \times 100 \qquad 3.1$$

Where,

Billing Efficiency = Billed Energy / Input Energy

Collection Efficiency = Revenue Collected / Billed Amount (Current Assessment)

3.1.2 Billing Efficiency

Billing Efficiency is a metric that measures the ratio of energy billed (including both metered and unmetered sales) to customers, relative to the energy provided to a certain location.

$$\text{Billing Efficiency} = \frac{\text{Total Billed Unit (kWh)}}{\text{Total Input Energy (kWh)}} \qquad 3.2$$

3.2 Electrifying Horizons: Unveiling Power Systems from Local to Global

Power system includes power generation, transmission, and distribution. Whole electric installation is connected to grids at state, regions, national and global level to ensure continuous, reliable, uninterrupted, economical, maximum possible share of sustainable and green energy supply to the consumer ends. Different levels of power system installations are shown in Figure 3.3. Power systems serve as the fundamental framework of contemporary society, supplying the necessary energy infrastructure that supports economic endeavours, improves quality of life, and drives technological progress. Power systems are crucial at many levels of hierarchy - state, regional, national, and global to fulfil the growing electricity demand and address the problems posed by limited resources, environmental issues, and the changing energy technology landscape.

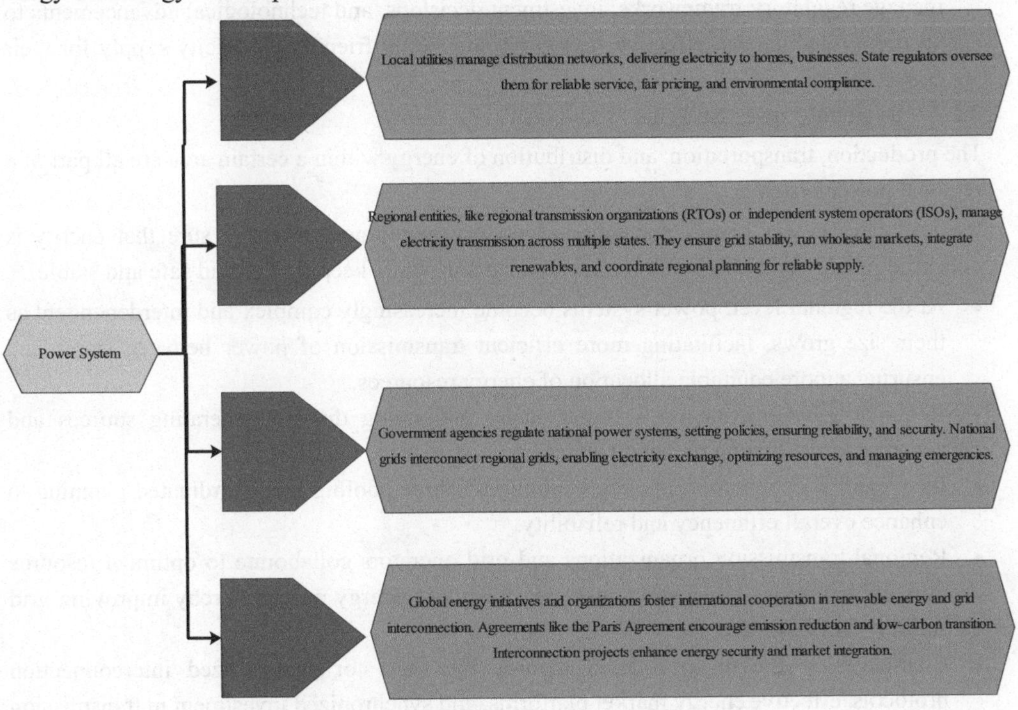

Figure 3.3 Different Lavel of Power System

3.2.1 State-Level Power Systems

A power system state is the exact way an electrical power grid is working at a certain point in time. It is made up of factors like voltages, currents, power flows, and system frequency. It decides how stable, efficient, and reliable the delivery of energy to homes and businesses is.

- State-level power systems serve as the backbone for distributing energy to residential, commercial, and industrial users within a specific geographic region.
- These systems ensure the reliable provision of energy, supporting everyday activities, businesses, and governmental functions.

- State power systems are interconnected with neighboring states and regions, enabling the transfer of surplus energy, and enhancing grid resilience.
- There's a notable shift towards cleaner and more sustainable energy sources in many jurisdictions, including solar, wind, and hydro power, to reduce carbon emissions and promote ecological sustainability.
- Uttar Pradesh Power Corporation Limited (https://www.uppcl.org/) implement regulations and incentives to encourage the adoption of green technology, fostering a greener power infrastructure.
- Challenges at the state level include balancing supply and demand, modernizing aging infrastructure, and meeting diverse energy needs across different areas.
- Uttar Pradesh Power Corporation Limited (https://www.uppcl.org/) must effectively manage regulatory frameworks, investment decisions, and technological advancements to ensure a reliable, cost-effective, and environmentally friendly electricity supply for their constituents.

3.2.2 Regional Power Systems

The production, transportation, and distribution of energy within a certain area are all part of a regional power system.

It coordinates power plants, substations, and grid equipment to make sure that energy is delivered reliably and efficiently to meet local needs while keeping the grid safe and stable.

- At the regional level, power systems become increasingly complex and interdependent as their size grows, facilitating more efficient transmission of power between states and ensuring a more equitable allocation of energy resources.
- Regional grids operate on a larger scale, integrating diverse generating sources and adapting to fluctuating demand patterns.
- Interregional cooperation is vital, enabling resource pooling and coordinated planning to enhance overall efficiency and reliability.
- Regional transmission organizations and grid operators collaborate to optimize resource utilization, manage congestion, and plan for future energy needs, thereby improving grid stability and resilience.
- Challenges at the regional level include the need for standardized interconnection protocols, effective energy market platforms, and synchronized investment in transmission infrastructure.
- Strategic planning is essential to ensure fair distribution of power, considering variations in energy demand and resource availability across regions.

3.2.3 National Power Systems

The network of power plants, transmission lines, and delivery systems that bring energy to homes and businesses across many countries and regions is called a global power system.

It requires countries to work together and coordinate to make sure that the energy supply is stable, efficient, and long-lasting.

To do this, different energy sources and cutting-edge technologies are used to meet the world's power needs.

- National power systems comprise multiple regional grids operating together to meet the energy needs of an entire country, incorporating a diverse mix of generating sources including fossil fuels, nuclear power, and an increasing proportion of renewables.
- The scale of national power systems requires advanced monitoring, control, and management methods to ensure smooth operation and effective response to changing electrical demand.
- National governments play a critical role in shaping energy policies, establishing regulatory frameworks, and overseeing the development of a robust and environmentally friendly power infrastructure.
- Integration of smart grid technologies, demand response programs, and energy storage systems is essential at the national level to enhance grid flexibility and adaptability.
- National power systems prioritize the transition to a low-carbon and sustainable energy future, with many nations investing in renewable energy initiatives, improving energy efficiency, and setting ambitious carbon reduction targets.
- A diverse energy mix enhances environmental sustainability, energy security, and resilience.
- Challenges at the national level include the need for significant investment in infrastructure, ensuring policy consistency, and striking a balance between affordable energy costs and environmental stewardship.
- Addressing energy inequality is paramount, with national power systems striving to ensure universal access to reliable and affordable electricity for all populations.

National power systems include the interconnected infrastructure inside a nation that produces, transports, and disseminates electrical energy. These systems are distinguished by the incorporation of many regional networks and a combination of energy sources. International power networks include the linking of national grids across borders to enable cross-border electricity trading, improve energy security, and encourage the worldwide use of renewable energy sources.

North America: Encompassing nations such as the United States and Canada, this region is recognised for its diverse energy portfolio, which comprises a combination of fossil fuels, nuclear power, and renewable energy sources.

Europe: Marked by a notable emphasis on renewable energy, with nations such as Germany and Denmark taking the lead.

Asia-Pacific: Includes major energy users such as China and India, characterised by a varied energy composition and rapidly expanding renewable industries.

Latin America: Countries such as Brazil are recognised for their heavy dependence on hydropower, resulting in a major portion of their energy being generated from renewable sources.

Middle East: Primarily focused on oil and gas extraction, but progressively allocating resources towards solar power investments.

Africa: Confronting distinct obstacles in achieving energy access, with an increasing focus on off-grid solar solutions and investments in renewable energy.

3.2.4 Global Power Systems

- On a global scale, the interconnection of electricity networks transcends individual country boundaries, with international cooperation, joint research, and development programs addressing common concerns like climate change and energy security.

- Geopolitical dynamics, technical innovations, and the pursuit of sustainable and universally accessible energy futures shape global power networks.
- International energy organizations and agreements, such as the International Energy Agency (IEA) and the Paris Agreement, play vital roles in fostering collaboration and establishing global standards for sustainable energy transitions.
- Sharing best practices, technological advancements, and establishing global transmission infrastructure are essential components of a globalized strategy for power systems.
- Global challenges include the need for standardized norms, equitable access to energy resources, and reducing environmental impacts that transcend national borders.
- Managing the complex dynamics of geopolitics, advocating for inclusive energy policies, and fostering innovation are critical for global power systems.
- Power systems operate across hierarchical tiers, each facing distinct challenges and opportunities: state-level systems ensure local electricity availability, regional grids optimize efficiency through cooperation, national power systems promote comprehensive energy policies, and global power systems aspire to achieve sustainable and integrated energy futures.
- Advancing power systems requires a harmonious blend of technical innovation, policy coherence, and commitment to environmental conservation, reflecting a collaborative effort to meet growing global energy demands while safeguarding the planet for future generations.

3.3 Losses in Transmission and Distribution System

Transmission and distribution losses pertain to the inefficiencies that arise during the transmission of energy from the power generation sources to the distribution locations. The losses are a result of the inherent resistance and inefficiency in the electrical conductors (such as conducting wires) and distribution transformers. The prevalence exceeds 20% in most states in our nation. To mitigate these losses, it is advisable to choose high-grade cables with suitable resistance and ensure the transformers are positioned correctly. Figure 3.4, showing the classification of power losses.

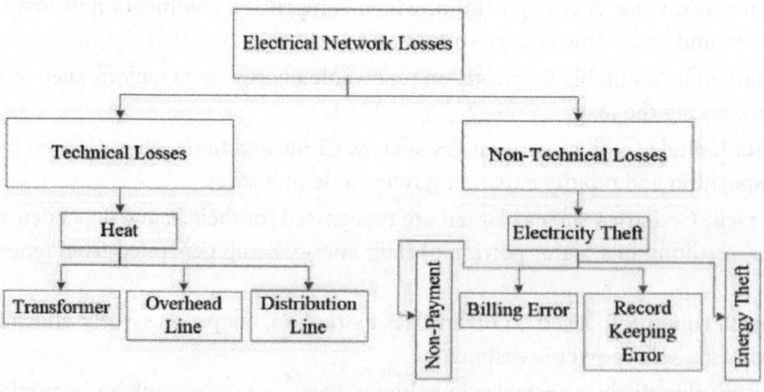

Figure 3.4 Classification of Power Losses

3.3.1 Technical Losses

- Technical losses in an electrical power system occur during generation, transmission, and distribution phases due to physical features and characteristics of power infrastructure components.

- These losses result from factors like electrical conductivity, material qualities, and device operation, rather than energy theft or unauthorized consumption.
- Energy wastage begins during the conversion processes in power plants generating electricity from fossil fuels, nuclear reactors, or renewable sources.
- Transmission lines, connecting power plants to load centers, incur losses due to resistance when transmitting electricity via conductive materials like copper or aluminum.
- Transformers optimize energy transmission but contribute to technical losses through core losses (e.g., hysteresis and eddy current losses) and copper losses.
- Switching and transmission equipment, such as circuit breakers and switches, further add to technical losses by converting electrical energy into heat during operation.
- Reactive power, essential for maintaining magnetic fields in AC systems, leads to technical losses during its conveyance and dispersion.
- Addressing technical losses involves strategies like using high-conductivity materials, improving transformer designs, and implementing advanced switchgear technologies and smart grid solutions.
- Harmonizing energy efficiency pursuits with practical aspects of power system design remains a complex and ongoing task in electrical engineering.

3.3.2 Components of Distribution Loss

Aggregated Technical and Commercial losses (AT&C) and Transmission and Distribution losses (T&D) loss are used in the electricity industry as benchmarks to assess the performance of distribution utilities. AT&C loss refers to the discrepancy between the energy input and the energy income obtained from consumers, whereas T&D Loss is the discrepancy between the energy supplied and the energy charged to the customer. The AT&C losses, also known as T&D losses, may be categorised into technical and non-technical losses.

3.3.3 Technical Loss

Technical losses occur because of electrical current passing across the network. While losses in energy distribution are unavoidable, they may be calculated and managed if the power system contains known loads. Technical losses are caused by harmonics distortion, long single-phase lines, unbalanced loading, overloading, low voltage, inadequate insulation, and lack of regular maintenance of equipment and machinery.

a) Controlling I^2R Losses

"The loss (converted into heat) due to the passage of a current through the resistance of a conductor."

The fundamental power equation in electrical systems is expressed as:

$$P = VI \tag{3.3}$$

Here, P=Power, V=Voltage and I=Current

Ohm's Law may also be used to represent the power for resistive components.

$$P = I^2R \tag{3.4}$$

Or

$$P = \frac{V^2}{R} \tag{3.5}$$

The symbol R represents the resistance, measured in ohms (Ω).

Effective control of I^2R or copper losses in transmission and distribution systems is crucial for maximising the overall efficiency of an electrical power network.

One successful technique is to transport power at high voltage, which decreases current values and so minimises I^2 R losses. Increasing the conductor size is a feasible way to lower resistance (R) and minimise I^2 R losses while the current value remains the same, according to the inverse proportionality (1/a).

Inductance and capacitance in line conductors in alternating current transmission systems result in the production of reactive power, leading to additional losses and a decrease in power factor.

To tackle this problem, several components including capacitor banks, phase shifting transformers, static VAR compensators, and Flexible A.C. Transmission Systems (FACTS) are strategically used.

These components regulate reactive power flow, leading to a decrease in I^2R losses and the maintenance of system voltage stability.

Replacing traditional Aluminium Cored Steel Reinforced (ASCR) conductors with low-resistance conductors such as All Aluminium Alloy Conductor (AAAC) is a beneficial strategy. This substitution reduces I^2R losses and improves overall transmission efficiency. Providing reactive power management and improving power factor are essential for lowering current flow and minimising I^2R losses.

Voltage controllers are a crucial tool in reducing I^2R losses. These controllers regulate current by keeping voltage levels steady and avoiding voltage drops, which helps reduce I^2R losses. Finally, it is important to reduce the distance between customer premises and distribution substation transformers. This method enhances energy distribution, minimises I^2R losses, and eventually enhances the efficiency of the overall power delivery system. Together, these solutions provide a thorough and integrated method to save energy and reduce I^2R losses in transmission and distribution networks.

Disadvantages of I^2R Losses

- **Energy Inefficiency**: The I^2R losses, also known as ohmic losses, lead to a substantial conversion of electrical energy into heat, resulting in the dissipation of energy. This diminishes the overall effectiveness of electricity generating, transmission, and distribution systems.
- **Heat Generation**: The dissipation of heat resulting from I^2R losses has the potential to induce excessive temperatures in electrical system components, which may lead to equipment damage and a decrease in its operational longevity. Excessive heat may also cause insulating materials to break down, which can further reduce the dependability of the system.
- **Capacity Constraints**: Transmission and distribution lines have maximum temperature thresholds. Excessive losses due to I^2R might compel utilities to run these lines at a capacity lower than their maximum to prevent overheating, so restricting the amount of power that can be delivered.

- **Power Quality Issues**: Excessive losses may result in diminished power quality, leading to issues like flickering lights and decreased functionality of delicate electrical devices, impacting both residential and industrial users.
- **System Reliability**: Excessive I^2R losses may decrease the dependability of the power system by inducing thermal overloads, which might result in possible failures and blackouts.

b) Optimizing Distribution Voltage

Distributors must consider voltage loss while designing, and the feeder size is dictated by the conductor's current carrying capability.

It is crucial to achieve an ideal balance between voltage control and economic efficiency in gearbox systems.

Increasing the voltage by a factor of 'n' allows the conductor size to be decreased to $1/n^2$ of the original size, assuming a consistent transmission efficiency.

It is important to recognise that greater voltage levels result in higher system costs owing to increasing expenditures associated with insulation, switchgear, and termination equipment.

Thus, selecting the ideal transmission voltage for a particular system requires a thorough evaluation of these aspects, weighing the benefits of smaller conductors against the increased expenses linked to higher voltage infrastructure.

This sophisticated method guarantees that the selected voltage level is in line with the system's economic efficiency and meets the required performance parameters.

c) Balancing Phase Currents

Balanced Load

A balanced load refers to a situation in a three-phase system where the currents in each phase are equal and the power factor is almost one.

Unbalanced Load

An Unbalanced load occurs when the three phases carry unequal currents. India's primary electrical energy distribution system consists of a three-phase, 4-wire configuration that serves both three-phase and single-phase loads. Three-phase loads are usually balanced, which means there is no current imbalance in the feeders. However, when it comes to household power supply via a three-phase 4-wire connection, an inherent imbalance may occur, depending on the various loads of consumers.

Single-phase supply is popular in residential settings, posing a particular issue at the three-phase connection point because of the presence of two loads typically associated with single-phase supplies.

Studying the three-phase feeder segment in Figure 3.5 uncovers the complexities of load distribution. Although a balanced load of 50 is uniformly distributed on each phase at the feeder's beginning end, imbalances occur at various places along the feeder. Phase A provides 230 A, Phase Y supplies 125 A, and Phase B supplies 165 A, leading to an imbalanced distribution causing circulating currents and higher losses. To address this problem, careful planning is needed to evenly spread various loads throughout each phase, aiming for about equal load currents, preferably around 175 A per phase.

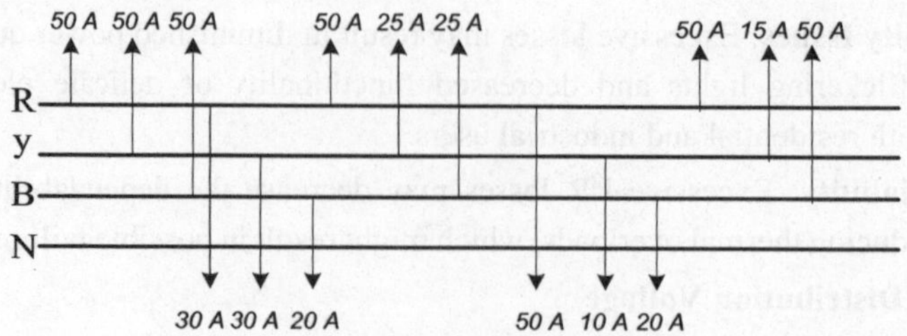

Figure 3.5 Unbalanced Feeder

Attaining this equilibrium by manual means presents difficulties, leading to the use of suitable optimisation methods. Implementing an optimised load balancing technique is crucial for achieving the optimal balance at both the feeder supply point and over the full feeder length. This strategic approach reduces losses owing to imbalanced currents, boosting the overall efficiency and stability of the electrical distribution system.

Single Phase System:

Phase Voltage (V)

In a single-phase system, the phase voltage *V* refers to the voltage directly sent to the load. The line-to-neutral voltage, sometimes denoted as $V_{L\text{-}N}$, is often expressed as

$$V = V_{L-N} \quad 3.6$$

Phase Current (I)

In a single-phase system, the phase current I, I refers to the current that passes through the load. The calculation may be performed using Ohm's Law when the load impedance Z is known.

$$I = \frac{V}{Z} \quad 3.7$$

Where,

V=Phase voltage and Z= Load Impedance

Three Phase System:

Within a three-phase system, it is necessary to differentiate between two distinct configurations: the Star (Wye) Configuration and the Delta Configuration.

- **Star (Wye) Configuration**

  Phase Voltage (*I_{ph}*), V_{ph} is the voltage across the each phase

  $$V_{ph} = \frac{V_{L-L}}{\sqrt{3}} \quad 3.8$$

  Where, $V_{L\text{-}L}$ line to line voltage

  Phase Current (I_{ph}), in star connection, the phase current (I_{ph}) is the same as the line current I_L

  $$I_{ph}=I_L \quad 3.9$$

- **Delta Configuration**

  Phase Voltage (V_{ph}), the phase voltage V_{ph} *is equal to the line-to-line voltage* $V_{L\text{-}L}$.

  $$V_{ph}=V_{L\text{-}L} \quad 3.10$$

  Phase current (I_{ph}), is related to the line current I_L by

$$I_{ph} = \frac{I_L}{\sqrt{3}} \quad 3.11$$

d) Compensating reactive power flow

Power in electrical systems refers to the rate at which electrical energy is transmitted via an electric circuit. The watt (W) is the standard unit of power. The classification of power is provided in Figure 3.6.

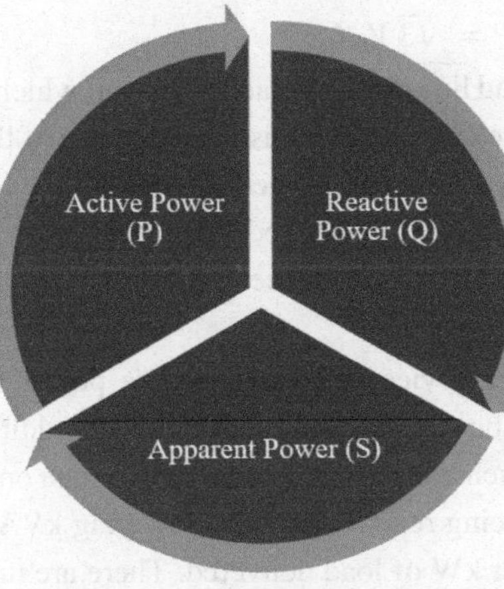

Figure 3.6 Types of Power

Active Power, sometimes referred to as genuine power or true power, is the power that is effectively used to produce work in an electrical circuit. Power is quantified in units of watts (W).

Formula for Single Phase

$$P = V.I\,Cos(\emptyset) \quad 3.12$$

Formula for three Phase

$$P = \sqrt{3}V_L\, I_L\, Cos(\emptyset) \quad 3.13$$

Where,

V/V_L is the line voltage,

$I/I_L$is the line current,

ϕ is the phase angle between the voltage and current,

Cos ϕ is the power factor.

Reactive power refers to the power that alternates between the source and the reactive components, such as inductors and capacitors, inside a circuit. The unit of measurement is volt-amperes reactive (VAR).

Formula for Single Phase

$$P = V.I\,Sin\,(\emptyset) \quad 3.14$$

Formula for three Phase

$$P = \sqrt{3}\;V_L\, I_L\, Sin(\emptyset) \quad 3.15$$

Apparent power is the result of multiplying the current and voltage in the circuit, without considering the phase angle. The term "apparent power" refers to the overall power that is being transferred in an electrical circuit, and it is quantified in units of volt-amperes (VA).

Formula for Single Phase

$$P = V.I \qquad 3.16$$

Formula for three Phase

$$P = \sqrt{3}\, V_L\, I_L \qquad 3.17$$

When fully loaded, an overhead line absorbs reactive power, which is calculated by the formula I^2X, where I represents the line current, and X is the reactance of the line per phase. Under low loads or no load, the shunt capacitance dispersed throughout the line is the main factor for the line to produce charging VAR ($V^2\omega C$), where V represents the line voltage, ω is the system frequency, and C is the line-to-earth capacitance. Cables, with their different capacitances, also have a role in producing reactive power.

Reactive power compensating devices provide reactive power at the receiving end bus in transmission systems or load bus in distribution systems. In addition to voltage control, these devices provide advantages such alleviating the reactive burden on the supply side, minimising system copper losses by reducing reactive current, lowering kVA loading on alternators, and minimising the investment per kW of load delivered. There are many kinds of reactive power compensators.

Shunt Capacitors are groups of static capacitors linked in star/delta formation at substations to provide reactive power to the system, enhancing the power factor of the load and sustaining the voltage profile.

Shunt-connected inductors are used at the load end of the gearbox line to regulate over-voltage under light load circumstances. The inductors exhibit linear characteristics, and their reactive power absorption is defined by,

$$QL = - V^2/\omega L. \qquad 3.18$$

Synchronous Compensators are basically synchronous motors operating without a load, capable of producing or consuming reactive power, providing operational flexibility. Nevertheless, they have disadvantages such as high expenses, elevated short-circuit current, increased losses, and more maintenance requirements.

Sequence Connecting capacitors in series with line conductors decreases the overall inductive reactance, which enhances voltage stability, maintains the voltage profile, and improves steady-state stability. Yet, their use is restricted by challenges like as excessive over-voltage during line failures and sub-synchronous resonance. Static VAR Compensators use inductors and capacitors that may be switched to the line to address lagging or leading reactive VA needs, offering a flexible option for reactive power compensation.

Disadvantage of Reactive Power

- Reactive power does not contribute to any productive labour, but it does induce the flow of electric current in the system, resulting in increased resistive losses (I^2R) in transmission and distribution lines. Therefore, the overall efficiency of the system is diminished.

- Excessive reactive power may result in substantial voltage reductions along transmission lines, which can impact the voltage levels at the receiving end. This may result in instability and inadequate voltage control, posing difficulties in maintaining constant and stable voltage levels for users.
- Reactive power takes up space in transmission lines and transformers, which decreases the amount of active power that can be transported. This constrains the operational capability of the power system to transmit useful electrical energy to loads.
- In order to regulate reactive power and maintain power quality, supplementary apparatus such as capacitors, reactors, and synchronous condensers are necessary. This contributes to the financial expenses for both capital and operating charges, hence augmenting the intricacy of the power system architecture.

Needs and Necessities of Reactive Power

- Reactive power is crucial for maintaining voltage stability within tolerable thresholds. It aids in offsetting voltage reductions caused by inductive loads and impedance in transmission lines. This regulation guarantees that electrical equipment functions within its designated voltage range, so avoiding any harm and assuring consistent and dependable functioning.
- Power factor adjustment is necessary in several industrial and commercial buildings to enhance the efficiency of electrical systems. Power factor adjustment entails the modification of the proportion between active power (work that is really used) and perceived power (total power). Power factor correction optimises energy use and saves electricity costs by injecting or absorbing reactive power when required, hence minimising the amount of reactive power pulled from the grid.
- Inductive loads, such as motors, transformers, and fluorescent lights, need reactive power for optimal operation. Reactive power is used to offset the delay in the phase angle between voltage and current in these devices, guaranteeing their proper operation and reducing power wastage.

3.3.4 Non-Technical loss

Non-technical losses refer to the energy spent in the distribution system that is not accounted for. These losses may be further categorised as follows.

- **Internal Non-Technical Losses**

Internal non-technical losses can occur due to various reasons such as mismanagement of connections (e.g., releasing connections without metres, under-recording of load, illegitimate consumers), theft (metre tampering or bypassing), inaccurate metre reading, incorrect billing (e.g., generating average bills due to delayed readings, faulty billing software), and lack of field supervision.

- **External Non-Technical Losses**

External non-technical losses result from failures in collecting dues, mismanagement of collections and credits, such as limited collection options, lack of follow-up on defaulters, incorrect revenue postings, delayed disconnections, and unpaid bills.

Commercial Losses

Commercial losses in electrical power systems refer to non-technical causes that result in revenue loss for utilities. The main causes of these losses are theft, flaws in metering, problems in invoicing, and inefficiencies in administration, rather than the actual waste of energy during transmission and distribution.

Commercial losses have many consequences, such as diminished profitability, elevated operating expenses, and heightened consumer tariffs. Detection and prevention tactics include the deployment of sophisticated metering technologies, the implementation of resilient billing systems, the enhancement of data analytics for the identification of anomalies, and the execution of consumer awareness campaigns. Regulatory frameworks are essential for supervising and enforcing initiatives to reduce losses and guaranteeing adherence to standards.

Real-life instances showcase effective implementations of smart metering and anti-theft techniques.

Future developments prioritise the incorporation of cutting-edge technology and sustainable energy sources to reduce losses and improve the overall efficiency of the system.

It is crucial to address commercial losses to provide financial stability, enhance service dependability, and preserve the long-term economic sustainability of electrical utilities. Commercial losses occur in three way, shown in Figure 3.7.

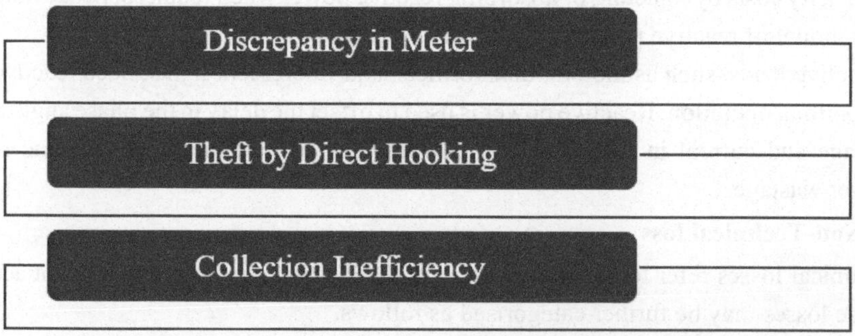

Figure 3.7 Commercial Losses Occurs in System

There are some methods for minimization of commercial losses and shown in Figure 3.8.

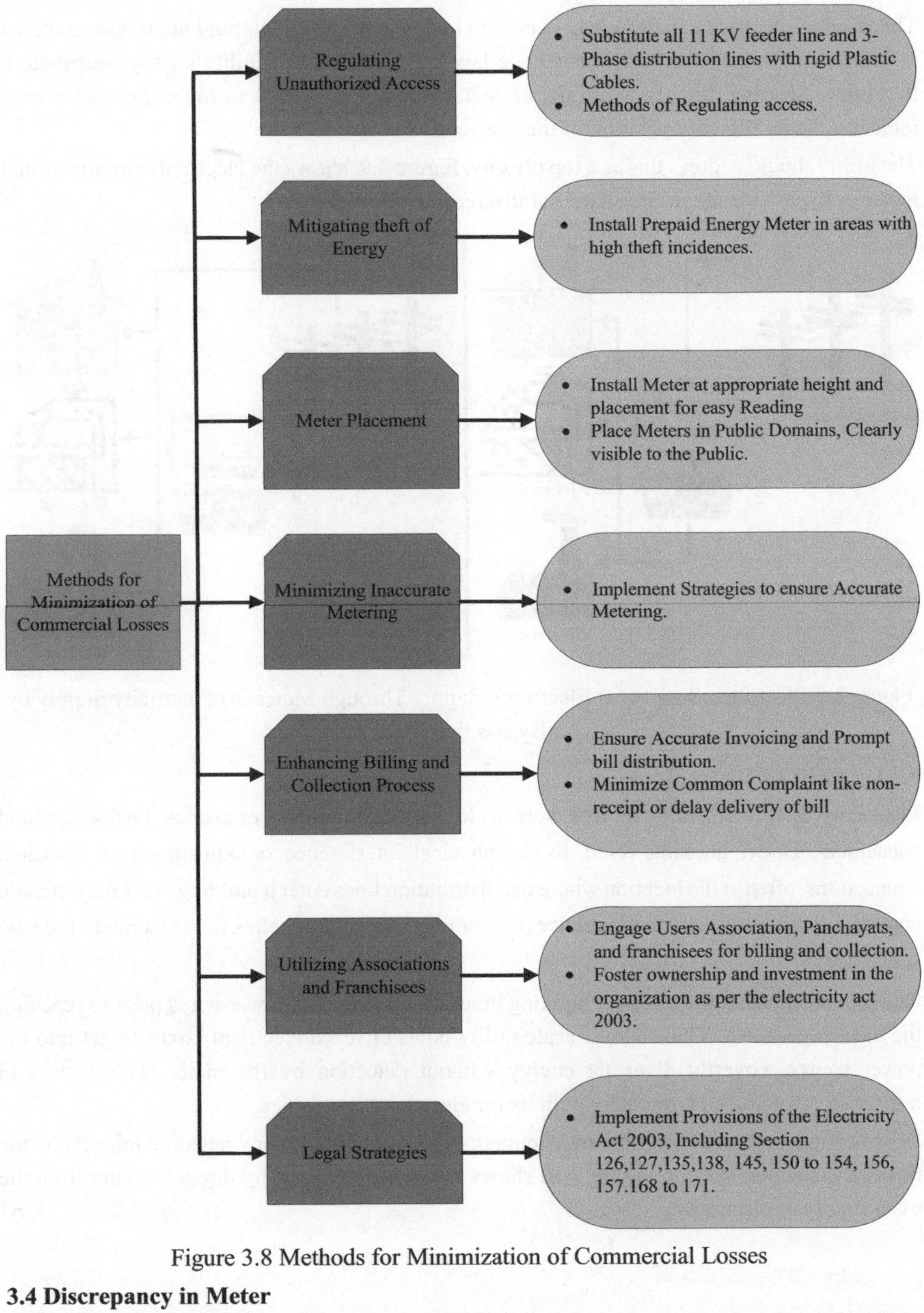

Figure 3.8 Methods for Minimization of Commercial Losses

3.4 Discrepancy in Meter

Dishonest users illicitly get energy by circumventing the energy metre or by directly connecting leads to the distribution lines. In certain regions, unauthorised power use by non-subscribers is common.

This kind of electricity theft mostly occurs in residential and agricultural areas. Geographical isolation, widespread thievery, inadequate law enforcement, and utility apathy contribute to this issue. Stealing directly is an affront and, thus, a provocation to the utility engineer. It indicates the inefficient operation of the distribution utility.

The utility should address this as a top priority. Figure 3.9, shows the electricity supply through meter or bypass the meter, it is a part of discrepancy in meter.

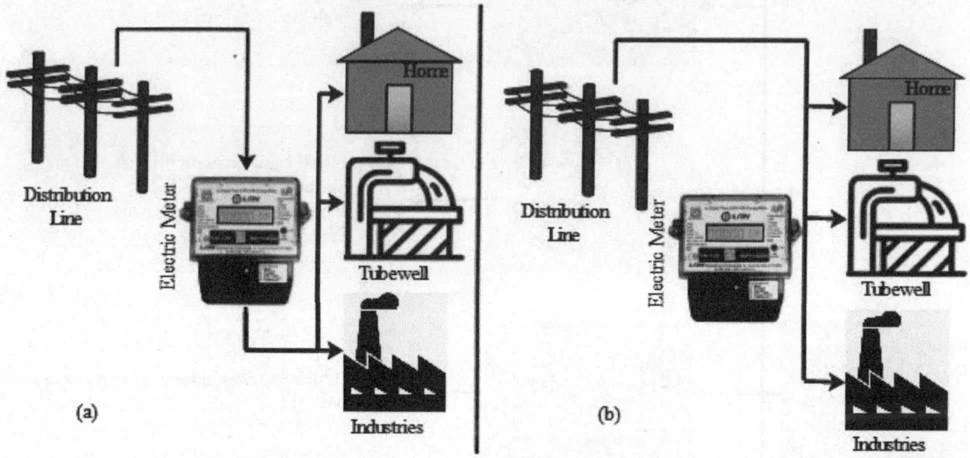

Figure 3.9 Electricity Supply (a) Electricity Supply Through Meter (b) Electricity Supply by Bypass the Meter

3.4.1 Theft by Direct Hooking

Electricity theft is a major problem worldwide, impacting utility companies, businesses, and consumers. Direct hooking refers to the physical interference or adjustment of electrical connections, often at the location where the distribution lines enter a building. This may include connecting cables directly to electricity lines or tampering with metres to inaccurately indicate actual use.

One prevalent technique of direct hooking involves intercepting power wires prior to reaching the metering system. Thieves may scale utility poles or reach electrical boxes to get into the power source, covertly diverting energy without detection by the meter. This results in imprecise invoicing and monetary deficits for electricity companies.

Direct connecting causes significant commercial losses and has many negative impacts on the power distribution system. Figure 3.10 shows the electricity theft by direct hooking from the main supply of electricity.

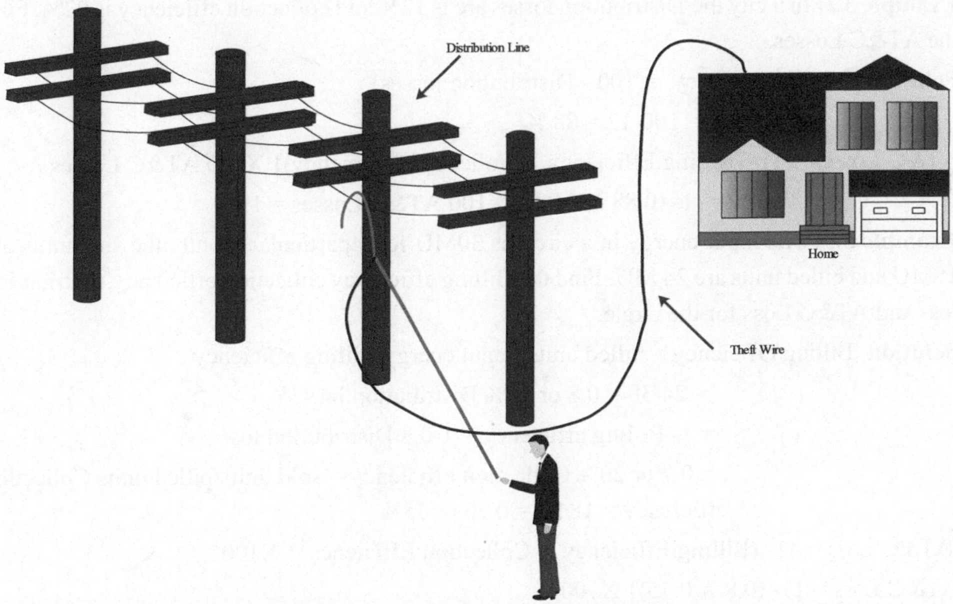

Figure 3.10 Electricity Theft by Direct Hooking

3.4.2 Collection Inefficiency

Collection inefficiency in energy commercial losses pertains to the difficulties and deficiencies utility companies have in recovering money from customers for the power they provide.

This problem may arise due to a variety of circumstances, such as non-payment, invoicing inaccuracies, and challenges in collecting payment from clients who are behind on payments. Consumers not making payments is a main reason for collection inefficiencies. Some clients may deliberately avoid paying their power bills, resulting in unpaid amounts.

Improving collection efficiency is essential for the financial viability of utility companies and the overall reliability of the power distribution system.

Utility companies utilise numerous ways to improve collection efficiency. One popular strategy involves using advanced metering infrastructure (AMI) and smart grid technology.

The solutions allow for real-time monitoring of use, precise invoicing, and the identification of anomalies that might suggest theft or tampering with the metre. AMI also enables the deployment of prepaid metering systems, enabling users to make advance payments for power, minimising the likelihood of non-payment.

Example 3.1

In a certain area the energy input is 90 MU and sold units are 74 MU with the collection efficiency of 95 %. Find the AT&C Losses.

Solution:

Energy realized = sold units X Collection Efficiency Energy realized

= 74 X 0.95 = 70.3 MU

AT&C Losses = {(Total Energy Input LESS Energy Realized)/ Total Energy Input} X 100

AT&C Losses = {(90- 70.3)/90 } X 100 = 21.88 %

Example 3.2: In a city the Distribution losses are is 12% and collection efficiency is 92%. Find the AT&C Losses.

Solution: Billing efficiency = (100 - Distribution losses}

= 100-12 = 88 %

AT&C Losses = {1- (Billing Efficiency X Collection Efficiency)} X100 AT&C Losses

= {1- (0.88 X 0.92)} X100 AT&C Losses = 19%

Example 3.3: The input energy in a circle is 30MU for a particular month, the sold units are 18MU and billed units are 24 MU. Find the Billing efficiency collection efficiency, distribution loss and AT&C Loss for the circle.

Solution: Billing efficiency = billed units/ input energy Billing efficiency

= 24/30 = 0.8 or 80% Distribution loss

= 1- Billing efficiency = 1-0.8 Distribution loss

= 0.2 or 20% Collection efficiency = sold units/billed units Collection efficiency = 18/24 = 0.75 or 75%

AT&C Loss = {1- (Billing Efficiency X Collection Efficiency)} X100

AT&C Loss = {1- (0.8 X 0.75)} X100

AT&C Loss = 0.4 or 40%

Example 3.4: Calculate the electricity bill amount for a month of 31 days, if the following devices are used as specified:

- 3 bulbs of 30 watts for 5 hours
- 4 tube lights of 50 watts for 8 hours
- 1 fridge of 300 watts for 24 hours

Given the rate of electricity is Rs. 2 per unit.

Solution:

The energy consumed by the bulbs,

As we know Energy = Power × Time

3 bulbs × 30 watts × 5 hours × 31 days = 13950 Wh

The energy consumed by the tubes,

4 tubes × 50 watts × 8 hours × 31 days = 49600 Wh

The energy consumed by the fridge,

1 fridge × 300 watts × 24 hours × 31 days = 223200 Wh

Therefore, the total energy consumption is given by,

13950+49600+223200 = 286750 Wh = 286.75 KWh

We need to convert it into units, where 1 unit = 1 kWh

So, electricity bill = 286.75 units × 2 = Rs. **573.5**

3.5 Collection efficiency

Collection efficiency is a metric that measures the percentage of money received from customers compared to the amount invoiced to them. There is a significant number of customers that have a proclivity to fail on their payments due to numerous factors. Therefore, the utility is unable to fully collect the amount it has invoiced, leading to financial losses.

$$\text{Collection Efficiency} = \frac{\text{Revenue Collected}}{\text{Billed Amount}} \quad 3.19$$

3.6 Energy Conservation Equipment

Energy-saving devices are crucial in tackling the worldwide issue of dwindling resources and environmental sustainability. The revolutionary technologies are designed to enhance energy efficiency, decrease waste, and lower the environmental impact of different businesses and homes. Figure 3.11 showing the effective tools for energy conservation and management.

- Smart thermostats provide precise management of heating and cooling systems, optimising energy use.
- LED lighting systems provide a more efficient option than conventional bulbs, reducing power consumption while yet providing sufficient illumination.
- Energy-efficient products like refrigerators and washing machines use modern technology to reduce power usage while maintaining functioning.
- Renewable energy systems such as solar panels and wind turbines use natural resources to produce clean energy, aiding in the transition from fossil fuels.
- Building management systems use sensors and automation to control energy consumption in commercial buildings, improving efficiency.

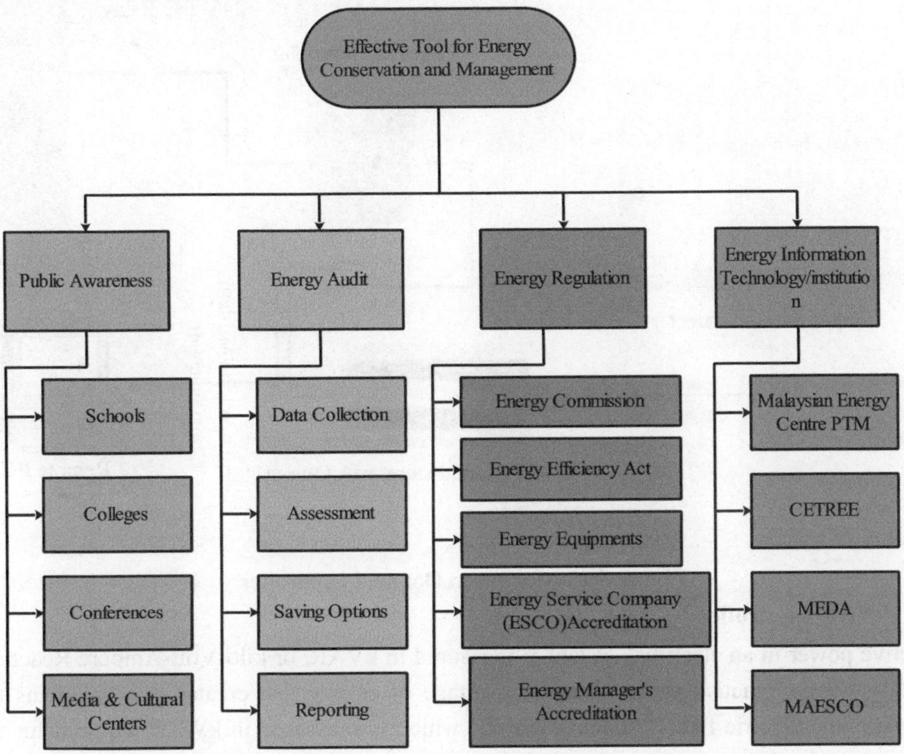

Figure:3.11 Effective Tools for Energy Conservation and Management

Energy conservation equipment comprises a broad variety of instruments, technologies, and systems that are aimed to decrease energy use, boost efficiency, and minimise waste in a variety of industries. These include the following:

- Maximum Demand Controller
- kVAR Controller
- Automatic Power Factor Controller (APFC)

3.6.1 Maximum Demand Controller

A Maximum Demand Controller (MDC) is an electrical device used for the purpose of monitoring and regulating the highest power need of a system, in order to prevent beyond a pre-established threshold. It aids in optimising energy use, minimising peak demand, and avoiding fines from utility suppliers for exceeding the agreed-upon limit of energy consumption. The MDC does this by shedding or deferring non-essential loads during times of high demand, thereby ensuring that the aggregate demand remains within the prescribed limit. It is often used in industrial and commercial environments to optimise energy efficiency and efficiently control operating expenses. Circuit diagram of maximum demand controller is shown in Figure 3.12.

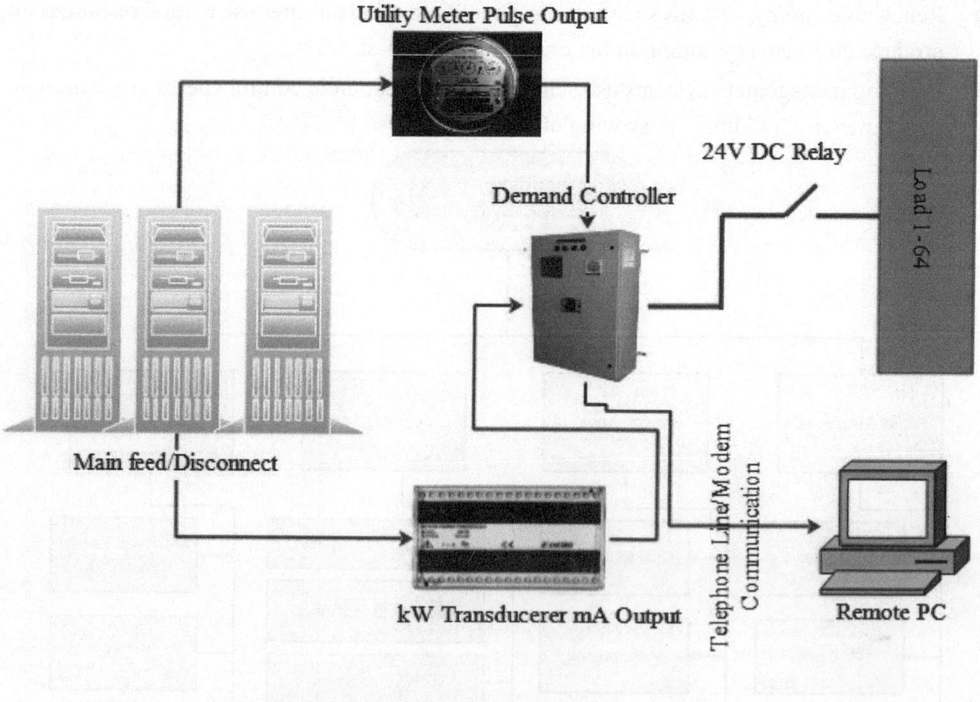

Figure 3.12 Maximum Demand Controller

3.6.2 kVAR Controller

Reactive power in an electrical system is measured in kVAR, or kilo-Volt-Ampere Reactive. In AC systems, reactive power is the percentage of energy that creates and maintains the magnetic and electric fields. Reactive power, which is measured in kW, is required for the operation of inductive loads such as motors and transformers but does not carry out any beneficial work. Figure 3.13 shows the circuit diagram of kVAR controller.

Reactive power (Q) maybe expresses as,

$$Q = V \times I \times Sign\ \varphi \qquad 3.20$$

where:

Q is the Reactive Power

active power in VAR (Volt-Ampere Reactive),

V is the RMS voltage,

I is the RMS current,

ϕ is the phase angle between the voltage and current.

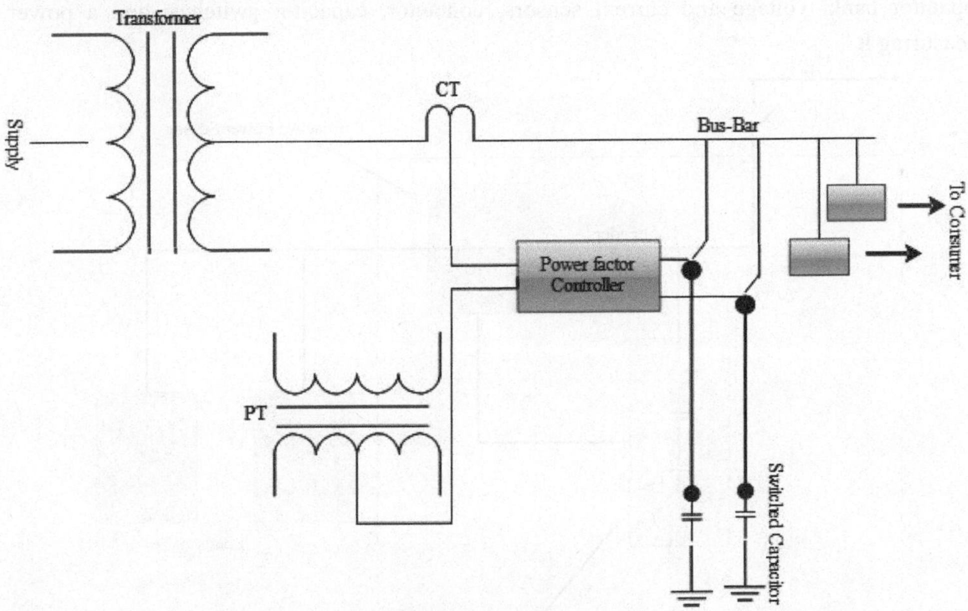

Figure 3.13 kVAR Controller

3.6.3 Automatic Power Factor Controller (APFC)

The capacitor bank in APFC setup is connected across the line to regulate power factor, and it is controlled by a micro controller and contactor system.

- The control system detects the power factor of the load using kVAR demand to manage the connection and removal of capacitors as needed.
- Maintaining a power factor of unity reduces the current flowing through the lines, as per the formula Real Power = Apparent Power × Power Factor.
- Maximum demand for billing is calculated based on the apparent power in kilovolt-amperes (kVA).
- The APFC system functions by connecting the A.C. supply mains to the APFC panel, where current transformers (CT) and potential transformers (PT) on the line side detect the power factor.

- The capacitor banks are turned on or off as required to meet the estimated power factor.
- A microprocessor-controlled Automatic Power Factor Correction (APFC) relay is essential in this procedure.
- The APFC relay guarantees that the capacitor bank works at the necessary kVAR to achieve the specified power factor defined by the APFC panel.
- The CT and PT confirm the feedback from the switching capacitors, aiding in reaching the required set power factor.
- The APFC system's coordinated action enables efficient power factor adjustment in accordance with the system's changing requirements.

The block diagram in figure 3.14 shows the main elements of the controller: AC power supply, capacitor bank, voltage and current sensors, contactor, capacitor switches, and a power measuring IC.

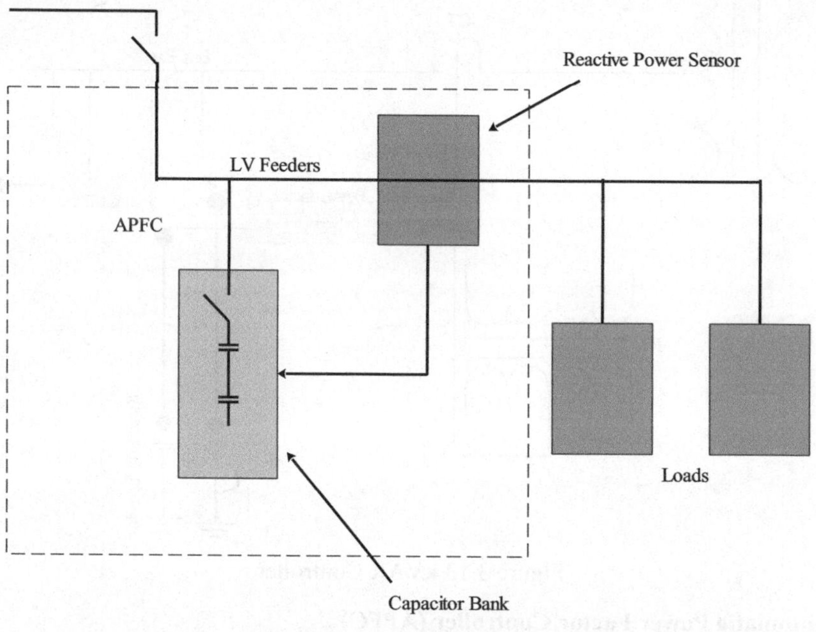

Figure 3.14 Block Diagram of Automatic Power Factor Correction

3.7 Energy Conservation in Lighting System

Conserving energy in lighting systems is crucial for sustainable and effective resource management. Lighting accounts for a substantial amount of worldwide energy use, highlighting the need to implement tactics that lower power usage and lessen environmental harm. The advancement of lighting technology, such Light Emitting Diodes (LEDs) and Compact Fluorescent Lamps (CFLs), has transformed energy-efficient lighting. LEDs have longer lifespans and better energy efficiency than typical incandescent lights, leading to significant energy savings.

Smart control systems are crucial for conserving energy. Occupancy sensors, daylight harvesting devices, and smart lighting controls allow lights to adjust based on ambient conditions and human presence, ensuring they are only on when needed. Timers and task lighting techniques improve efficiency by optimising lighting schedules and directing illumination to specific areas.

3.7.1 Lighting Technologies

Lighting technologies are crucial in determining how we light up our environment, affecting energy efficiency, visual comfort, and adherence to lighting standards. This section provides a detailed summary of several lighting systems, each offering distinct characteristics to the wide range of illumination choices now accessible. Comprehending these technologies is essential for making well-informed decisions on lighting laws.

The group includes conventional alternatives such as incandescent lighting, valued for its warm and familiar glow, and fluorescent lighting, recognised for its energy efficiency. High-intensity discharge lighting, known for its intense and efficient illumination, is compared with the innovative LED lighting, which has become a diverse and revolutionary solution in recent years. Our goal is to provide a basis for evaluating the characteristics of each technology in the regulatory environment as we explore them.

3.7.2 Incandescent Lighting

Incandescent lamps produce light by running electricity through a coiled tungsten wire filament, heating it till it emits light. The lamps the bulbs are typically filled with an inert gas mixture mostly composed of argon. Only 10 to 15 percent of the energy inputted into the incandescent filament is released as light, while the remaining percentage is emitted as heat. Incandescent lights are available in many forms and sizes.

The letter designation signifies the lamp's form, while the number denotes the maximum diameter in eighths of an inch. The glass bulb might be transparent, opaque, or coloured, or it can have a reflecting coating on the interior. Both directional and nondirectional incandescent bulbs are offered. Different parts of incandescent lamp are shown in Figure 3.15.

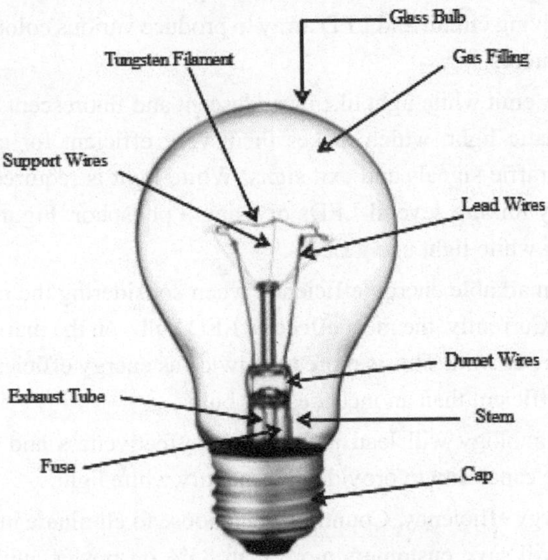

Figure 3.15 Typical Incandescent Lamp

3.7.3 Fluorescent Lighting

CFLs are easily replaceable for incandescent lamps since they have an electronic ballast and a glass tube coated with phosphor. When an electrical arc is created at the electrodes of the tube, mercury atoms release ultraviolet (UV) light, which excites the phosphor coating and produces visible light. The picture of fluorescent lamp is shown in Figure 3.16.

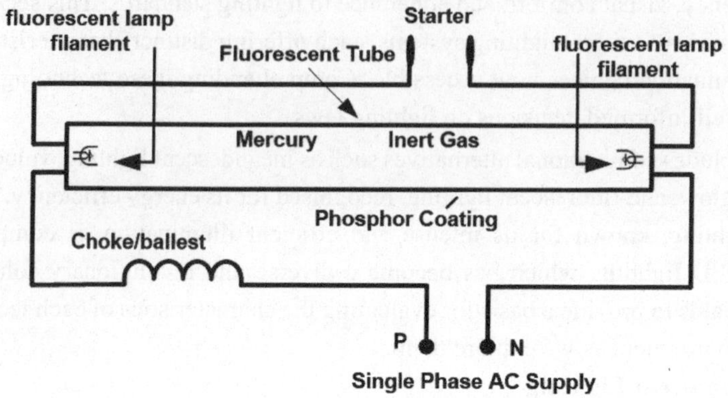

Figure 3.16 Typical Fluorescent Lamp

3.7.4 LED Lighting

LED lights and luminaires are quickly becoming more prevalent in general lighting applications worldwide. As LED technology advances and becomes more affordable, the market growth will speed up, replacing conventional light sources with more efficient and superior LED technology.

LEDs possess certain qualities that make them a captivating light source. The lights are durable, long-lasting, resistant to damage and vibration, function well in cold conditions, turn on instantly, and certain variants can be dimmed. Contingent LEDs in a specific light source may be modified on the driving circuit and LED array to produce various colours or white light with varied colour temperatures.

LEDs do not naturally emit white light like incandescent and fluorescent bulbs. LEDs generate virtually monochromatic light, which makes them very efficient for applications requiring coloured light, such traffic signals and exit signs. White light is required for general lighting purposes, achieved by mixing several LEDs or using a phosphor. Figure 19 illustrates many methods of producing white light using LEDs.

LEDs demonstrate remarkable energy efficiency when considering the ratio of light output to power input in watts. Currently, the most effective LED bulbs on the market have an efficiency of around 130 lumens per watt. This is more than twice as energy efficient as a CFL and more than ten times more efficient than an incandescent bulb.

Advancements in technology will lead to increased effectiveness and reduced costs in the future. LEDs have the capability to provide high-quality white light.

with unparalleled energy efficiency. Countries that choose to eliminate incandescent bulbs and go directly to LED will save customers more than 85% on power, without sacrificing light quality, and benefit from a much longer service life.

Example 3.5: A 100 W lamp is connected to a 230 V supply. Determine (a) the current flowing in the bulb, and (b) the resistance of the lamp.

Solution: *Power* $P = V \times I$

Current, I= 100/230=0.435 A

Resistance, R = V/I; 230/0.435= **528.74 Ω**

Example 3.6: An energy audit was conducted in a factory and the following observations were made. The output of three phase induction motor: 20 kW at 0.9 p.f. The industry operates for 5000 hours is a year with the electrifying cost of Rs.8 per unit. If the existing motor is replaced with 15 kW energy efficient motor with 90% efficiency and 0.95 p.f. The cost of energy efficient motor is Rs. 90,000 and the salvage value of existing motor is Rs. 10,000.

Solution:

Power consumption by existing motor = 20×0.9 = 18 kW

Energy consumption in one year= 18 kW×5000

=90,000 kWh

Bill per Annum= 90,000×8.0

=Rs. 7,20,000

Power consumption by energy efficient motor= $\frac{15}{0.9} \times 0.95$

= 15.83 kW

Energy Consumption in a year= 79167 kW

Bill Per Annum= Rs. 6,33,333

Annul Saving= Rs. 720000 – Rs. 6,33,333

= Rs. 86,667

Payback period = $\frac{90{,}000-10{,}000}{86{,}667}$ =0.92 years

=1 year (Approx)

a) Bharat Lamp Yojana

The Bharat Lamp Yojana is an Indian government effort that seeks to promote energy efficiency by incentivizing the use of energy-efficient lighting alternatives, particularly LED lights. This initiative is a component of a more comprehensive approach aimed at diminishing energy use and mitigating greenhouse gas emissions across the whole nation. The Bharat Lamp Yojana provides customers with LED lights at reduced prices, making them more inexpensive and easily obtainable. The program's main objective is to replace conventional incandescent and compact fluorescent lights (CFLs) with LEDs, which are characterised by higher energy efficiency and a longer lifetime. This substitution aims to decrease both total energy expenses and environmental consequences.

The Bharat Lamp Yojana, commonly referred to as the Unnat Jyoti by Affordable LEDs for All (UJALA) project, is a prominent endeavour of the Indian government with the objective of fostering energy efficiency across the country.

Key Features:

- **Cost-Effective Pricing:** LED bulbs are offered to customers at reduced rates, resulting in a substantial reduction in price compared to market pricing.
- **Nationwide Implementation:** The programme is being implemented across India, with the aim of promoting the extensive use of LED lighting in both urban and rural regions.
- **Distribution Network:** LEDs are delivered via specific distribution centres, such as government offices, utility companies, and unique kiosks located in different areas.
- **Quality Assurance:** The LED bulbs given under this plan are of superior quality, guaranteeing both longevity and performance.

Benefits:

- **Energy Savings:** LEDs have a far lower power consumption compared to incandescent lights, resulting in considerable energy savings.
- **Cost Reduction:** Decreased energy use results in decreased power costs for customers.
- **Environmental Impact:** Decreased energy use results in decreased carbon emissions, so helping to the preservation of the environment.
- **Economic Impact:** The initiative contributes to improved energy management by decreasing electricity usage and alleviating the burden on the national power infrastructure.

3.8 Energy Conservation in Fans

When purchasing and installing fans, it is crucial to prioritize energy efficiency. Selecting the appropriate fan size for a room is essential, ensuring optimal energy utilization.

For instance, a 48 cm fan is suitable for a 10 feet x 10 feet room, and exceeding this size may result in unnecessary energy wastage. During installation, careful attention should be paid to blade balance, minimizing noise and vibration that can otherwise increase power input. Ensuring the quality of bearings is vital to prevent unnecessary friction, overheating, and the loss of additional energy. The choice of regulators for the fan is equally important. Electrical-type regulators employing barrette-type resistance or chokes can lead to higher power losses. Therefore, opting for electronic regulators, which consume minimal electrical energy, is advisable.

Electronic controlled regulators offer the convenience of adjusting fan speed effortlessly from any location within the room, allowing for efficient energy management. Figure 3.17 shows the connection diagram of ceiling fan and capacitor used in ceiling fan.

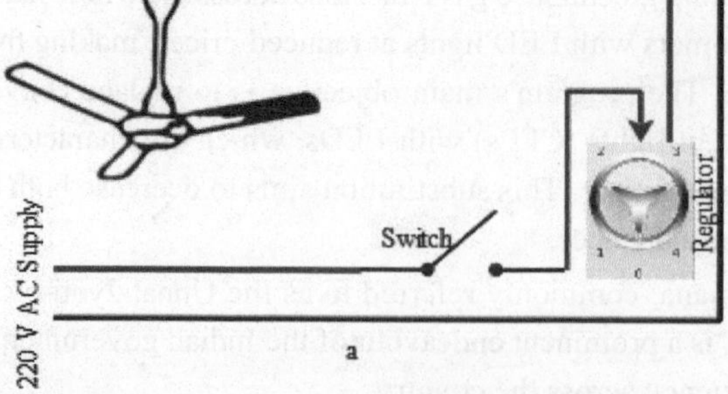

a

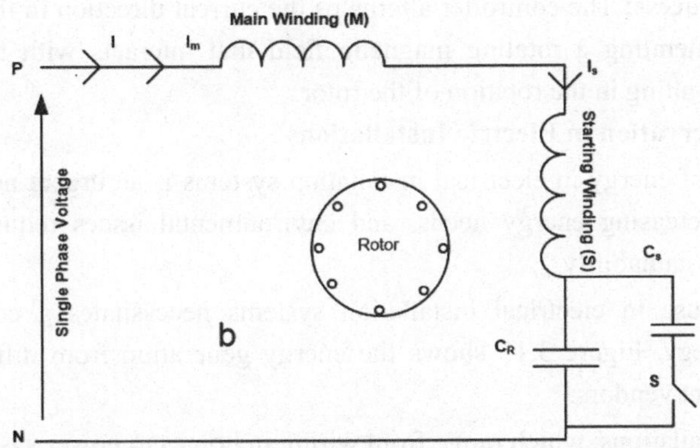

Figure:3.17 Ceiling Fan, (a) Connection Diagram of Ceiling Fan, (b) Ceiling Fan Capacitor Connection Diagram

Moreover, utilizing electronic regulators provides the flexibility to turn off the fan conveniently, contributing to energy savings. It is essential to consider the proper height of fan placement relative to the working plane, as this also impacts energy consumption. Overall, these precautions and considerations contribute to an energy-efficient and optimized fan usage experience.

- Electronic regulators replace conventional ones, saving more than 25% energy.
- Energy-efficient fan motors reduce consumption.
- Utilize windows for natural air circulation, reducing fan usage and energy bills.
- Turn off fans when leaving home, office, or any unoccupied space.
- Optimize fan efficiency with properly designed blades, especially in whole-house fans.
- Regular maintenance ensures fans operate efficiently and last longer.

i. BLDC fan and its working

A Brushless DC (BLDC) fan is a highly efficient fan that uses a brushless DC motor to transfer electrical energy into mechanical energy, resulting in rotational movement.

BLDC fans, in contrast to traditional AC fans, provide superior efficiency, extended lifespan, and quieter performance.

Working Principle:

- **Brushless DC Motor**
  - **Structure:** The BLDC motor comprises a rotor equipped with permanent magnets and a stator containing windings. Unlike conventional motors, it lacks brushes or a commutator.
  - **Electronic Commutation:** An electronic controller governs the functioning of the motor, eliminating the need for mechanical commutation performed by brushes in conventional motors.
- **Electronic Controller**
  - **Function:** The electronic controller regulates the power sent to the stator windings. The system employs sensors to ascertain the precise location of the rotor and then modulates the electric current in the windings appropriately.

- **Process:** The controller alternates the current direction in the stator windings, generating a rotating magnetic field that interacts with the rotor magnets, resulting in the rotation of the rotor.

ii. Energy Conservation in Electric Installations

The preservation of energy in electrical installation systems is an urgent need in our modern society, where increasing energy needs, and environmental issues require a fundamental change towards sustainability.

Efficient energy use in electrical installation systems necessitates a comprehensive and multifaceted strategy. Figure 3.18 shows the energy generation from different aspects and transmit to different vendors.

- Electrical installations, which range from wiring in homes to power systems in industries, are essential for the foundation of contemporary infrastructure.
- The need for energy conservation in electrical infrastructure is emphasized by the limited availability of traditional energy sources and the environmental consequences linked to their use.
- Electricity production that relies on fossil fuels supply a substantial contribution to the release of greenhouse gases, air pollution, and the occurrence of climate change.
- An essential approach to conserving energy in electrical installations is implementing energy-efficient lighting systems.

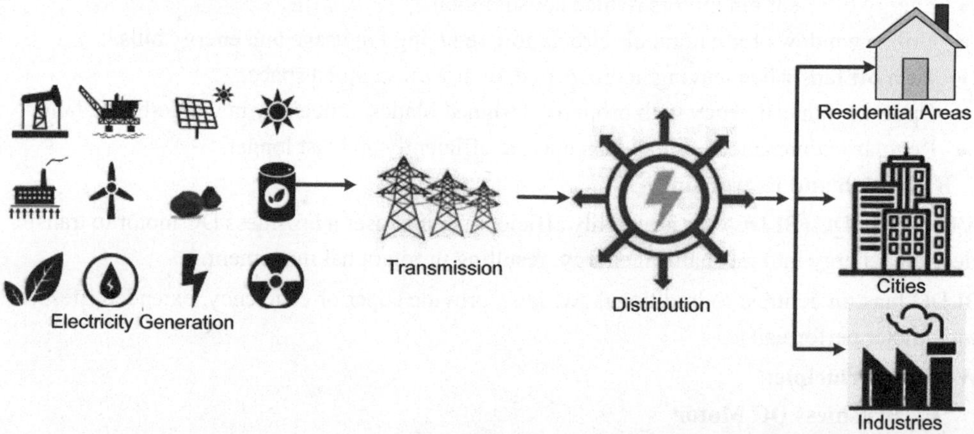

Figure 3.18: A Schematic of the Conventional Electrical Grid

- Conventional incandescent bulbs, known for their lack of energy efficiency, are slowly being replaced with more energy-efficient options like Light Emitting Diodes (LEDs) and Compact Fluorescent Lamps (CFLs). These technologies have both lower power consumption and longer lifespans, resulting in decreased maintenance expenses. In addition, the incorporation of intelligent lighting systems that are equipped with occupancy sensors and daylight harvesting capabilities guarantees that lights are only operational when needed, thereby reducing excessive energy use. Figure:3.19 showing the five important part of Smart Building Management System (BMS).

- The integration of Smart Building Management Systems (BMS) as shown in figure 3 is becoming a disruptive approach as buildings remain significant consumers of electrical energy.
- BMS technology enables the centralised management and supervision of diverse electrical systems, such as HVAC, lighting, and security.
- BMS systems optimise the performance of systems by analysing occupancy patterns, weather conditions, and time-of-day parameters.

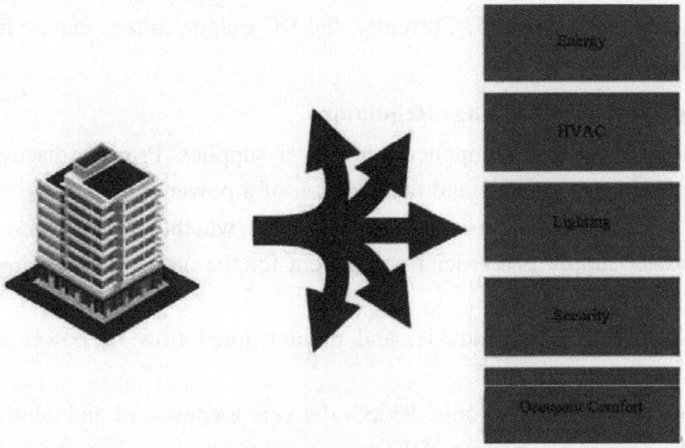

Figure: 3.19 Important Part of Smart Building Management System (BMS)

3.9 Electronic Regulator

A voltage regulator is an automated device meant to consistently maintain a stable voltage.

- It might be used a basic feed-forward structure or include negative feedback.
- It may use either an electromechanical mechanism or electrical components.
- Depending on the configuration, it may be used to control one or several alternating current (AC) or direct current (DC) voltages.
- A voltage regulator is also used to control and stabilise voltage levels.
- A voltage regulator produces a stable output voltage that stays consistent despite any changes in an input voltage or load circumstances.
- It serves as a protective barrier to prevent damage to components.
- A voltage regulator is a device that has a straightforward feed-forward architecture that utilises negative feedback control loops.

There are primarily two categories of voltage regulators:

- Linear voltage regulators are electronic devices that are used to maintain a constant voltage output regardless of changes in the input voltage or load conditions. The linear voltage regulator is the simplest kind of voltage regulator. There are two variants available: small and suitable for use in low power, low voltage systems.
- Switching voltage regulators find use in a broader range of applications.

These are the primary components that are used in the voltage regulator:

- Feedback Circuit

- Stable Reference Voltage
- Pass Element Control Circuit

The method of voltage control may be easily accomplished by using the three components. The first element of the voltage regulator, such as a feedback circuit, is used to detect variations in the DC voltage output. Derived from the reference voltage, as well as Feedback is used to provide a control signal that directs the Pass Element to compensate for the changes. A pass element is a kind of solid-state semiconductor device that is comparable to a BJT transistor, PN-Junction Diode, or a MOSFET. Currently, the DC output voltage can be maintained at a somewhat steady level.

3.9.1 Working Principle of Voltage Regulators

Voltage regulators are crucial components in power supplies. Prior to discussing a voltage regulator, it is important to understand the function of a power supply in system design. For example, in any operational system such as a smartphone, whether it is a wristwatch, computer, or laptop, the power supply is a crucial component for the proper functioning of the whole system.

- It ensures a steady, dependable, and uninterrupted flow of power to the internal components of the system.
- The power supply in electronic devices delivers a consistent and controlled power to ensure the correct functioning of the circuits.
- There are two sorts of power supply sources: AC power supply, which is obtained from mains outlets, and DC power supply, which is obtained from batteries.

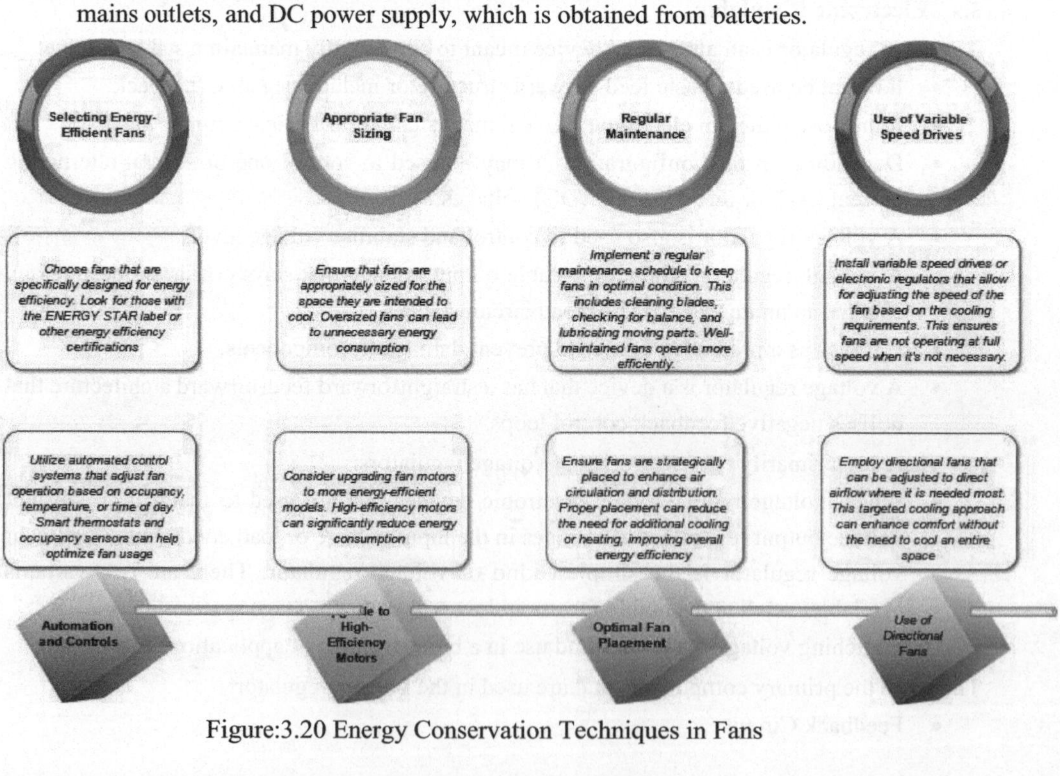

Figure:3.20 Energy Conservation Techniques in Fans

SUMMARY

The pursuit of sustainability in the electrical industry involves implementing innovative practices and responsibly using resources, such as optimising lighting and electrical systems, adopting smart technology, and incorporating renewable energy sources with responsible environmental management. This results in reduced energy usage and operating expenses, while also improving occupant comfort. Integrating solar panels, wind turbines, and other renewable sources into the electrical grid enhances the energy portfolio, reducing dependence on traditional, often carbon-intensive, power production. This not only reduces the negative effects on the environment but also helps to achieve energy self-sufficiency and the ability to recover quickly from disruptions. Here in this unit, energy conservation in electrical installations and energy conservation in lighting systems and different equipment required to achieve energy conservation are presented.

EXERCISE

Short Answer Type Questions

1. Why energy conservation is important in electrical installations?
2. Define aggregate technical and commercial losses, ATC?
3. Present a case study of aggregate technical and commercial losses, ATC of an Indian power systems.
4. Write a short note of energy conservation on lighting system.
5. Discuss the followings

   I) Maximum demand controller

   II) kVAR controller

   III) Automatic power factor controller, APFC
6. Discuss energy conservation techniques used for fans.
7. Define power systems. Draw a single line diagram of power system.
8. What are the main causes of commercial losses in power systems, and how can pilferage be prevented?
9. What role do Maximum Demand Controllers and kVAR Controllers play in energy conservation?
10. List some energy conservation techniques for lighting systems.

Long Answer Type Questions

1. Explain the significance of energy conservation in electrical installations.
2. Define Aggregate Technical and Commercial (ATC) losses in the context of electrical power systems.
3. Compare and contrast the energy conservation techniques used in traditional lighting systems with modern LED lighting systems. Discuss the advantages and challenges associated with transitioning to LED lighting in terms of energy efficiency and environmental impact.

4. Using a specific case study from an Indian power system, analyze the factors influencing Aggregate Technical and Commercial (ATC) losses. Evaluate the effectiveness of measures implemented to reduce these losses and their impact on overall system efficiency.
5. Describe voltage optimisation techniques to reduce technical loss.
6. Discuss the impact of ATC losses on power systems at the state, regional, national, and global levels.
7. Explain the causes of technical losses in power systems and describe methods to control I2R losses, optimize distribution voltage, balance phase currents, and compensate reactive power flow.
8. Analyze the various commercial losses in power systems, including pilferage, and suggest remedies to address these issues.
9. Evaluate the effectiveness of energy conservation equipment such as Maximum Demand Controllers, kVAR Controllers, and Automatic Power Factor Controllers (APFC) in reducing energy consumption.
10. Describe energy conservation techniques in lighting systems, including replacing lamp sources, using energy-efficient luminaires, employing light-controlled gears, installing separate transformers or servo stabilizers for lighting, and implementing periodic surveys and maintenance programs.

Multiple Choice Questions

1. What are Aggregated Technical and Commercial (ATC) losses?
   A. Losses due to natural disasters
   B. Losses in the transmission and distribution of electricity
   C. Losses due to administrative errors
   D. Losses due to equipment failures
2. Which of the following is a cause of technical losses in a power system?
   A. Unauthorized connections
   B. Energy pilferage
   C. I^2R losses in conductors
   D. Incorrect meter reading
3. Which measure can reduce I^2R losses?
   A. Increasing current
   B. Using conductors with higher resistance
   C. Using conductors with lower resistance
   D. Reducing voltage
4. How can optimizing distribution voltage help in reducing technical losses?
   A. By minimizing voltage drops
   B. By increasing the current flow

C. By decreasing the load demand

D. By increasing power factor

5. What is the effect of balancing phase currents in a power system?

A. Increases I^2R losses

B. Decreases I^2R losses

C. Decreases system reliability

D. Increases system instability

6. What does compensating reactive power flow help with?

A. Reducing voltage levels

B. Increasing system losses

C. Improving voltage stability and reducing losses

D. Decreasing power factor

7. What is a common cause of commercial losses in power systems?

A. High conductor resistance

B. Unauthorized electricity usage (pilferage)

C. Poor power factor

D. Overloading transformers

8. Which device helps in controlling maximum demand?

A. Lux meter

B. Ammeter

C. Voltmeter

D. Maximum Demand Controller

9. What is the primary function of a kVAR controller?

A. Measure current

B. Measure voltage

C. Control reactive power flow

D. Control active power flow

10. What does an Automatic Power Factor Controller (APFC) do?

A. Automatically adjusts the power factor

B. Measures the power factor

C. Manually adjusts the power factor

D. Increases energy consumption

11. How can energy conservation be achieved in lighting systems?

A. Using incandescent lamps

B. Replacing lamp sources with energy-efficient ones

C. Using high resistance wiring

D. Increasing lighting duration

12. Which type of luminaries is considered energy efficient?
   A. Incandescent bulbs
   B. Halogen lamps
   C. LED lights
   D. Neon lights
13. What is the benefit of using light control gears?
   A. Increased power consumption
   B. Reduced energy usage
   C. Increased maintenance costs
   D. Decreased light quality
14. Why is it beneficial to install a separate transformer or servo stabilizer for lighting?
   A. To increase energy losses
   B. To decrease initial costs
   C. To increase overall power consumption
   D. To ensure stable voltage and reduce losses
15. How often should periodic surveys and maintenance programs be conducted for lighting systems?
   A. Annually
   B. Monthly
   C. Periodically as per manufacturer's recommendation
   D. Never
16. What is an energy conservation technique for fans?
   A. Using mechanical regulators
   B. Using electronic regulators
   C. Increasing fan speed
   D. Using older fan models
17. What is the primary advantage of electronic regulators for fans?
   A. Higher energy consumption
   B. Lower energy consumption
   C. Higher initial cost
   D. Lower speed control
18. How can pilferage of electricity be reduced?
   A. Increasing voltage levels
   B. Decreasing surveillance
   C. Ignoring unauthorized connections
   D. Installing tamper-proof meters
19. What role does a Maximum Demand Controller play in energy conservation?
   A. Reduces reactive power flow

B. Manages and limits peak demand

C. Increases active power consumption

D. Decreases power factor

20. Why is compensating reactive power flow important in a power system?

A. It improves voltage regulation and reduces system losses

B. It increases system losses

C. It decreases the overall system efficiency

D. It increases voltage drops

21. A 400W lamp was switched on for 10 hours per day. The supply volt is 230V (current= 2 amps & PF= 0.8). What is the energy consumption per day

A. 3.68 kWh

B. 6.37 kWh

C. 0.37 kWh

D. 4.0 kWh

22. Matching energy usage to requirement means providing

A. just theoretical energy needed

B. just the design needs

C. energy with minimum losses

D. less than what is needed

Answer of Multiple Choice Questions

1	**B**	**2**	**C**	**3**	**C**	**4**	**A**	**5**	**B**
6	**C**	**7**	**B**	**8**	**D**	**9**	**C**	**10**	**A**
11	**B**	**12**	**C**	**13**	**B**	**14**	**D**	**15**	**C**
16	**B**	**17**	**B**	**18**	**D**	**19**	**B**	**20**	**A**
21	**A**	**22**	**C**						

REFERENCES

1. BEE. “Energy Efficiency in Electrical Utilities” New Delhi, India: BEE; 2015.

2. BEE. “General Aspects of Energy Management and Energy Audit” New Delhi, India: BEE; 2015.

3. BEE. “Energy Efficiency in Thermal Utilities” New Delhi, India: BEE; 2015.

4. BEE. “Energy Performance Assessment For Equipment and Utility Systems” New Delhi, India: BEE; 2015.

5. K. M. Mahbub and M. E. Haque, "Reduction of technical and non-technical losses in distribution system," IEEE International Conference on Electrical and Computer Engineering, 2008, pp. 326-329.

6. S. P. Chowdhury, S. Chowdhury, and P. Crossley, Microgrids and Active Distribution Networks, The Institution of Engineering and Technology, 2009.

7. T. J. Hammons, "Reducing technical losses in electric power systems: Aspects and prospects," *IEEE Power Engineering Society General Meeting*, 2006.
8. H. H. Happ, "Improving power system efficiency and reliability through technical loss reduction," *IEEE Transactions on Power Systems*, vol. 6, no. 2, pp. 424-430, 1991.
9. M. G. Da Silva, M. S. Castro, and J. L. R. Pereira, "Voltage optimization and its impact on energy loss reduction," *IEEE Transactions on Power Delivery*, vol. 23, no. 4, pp. 2065-2071, 2008.
10. R. C. Dugan, M. F. McGranaghan, and H. W. Beaty, *Electrical Power Systems Quality*, 3rd ed., McGraw-Hill, 2012.
11. M. H. Haque, "Compensation of distribution systems using custom power devices," *IEEE Power and Energy Society General Meeting*, 2010.
12. S. K. Khaitan and J. D. McCalley, "Design techniques and analysis of electricity theft detectors," *IEEE Transactions on Power Delivery*, vol. 22, no. 4, pp. 1981-1989, 2007.
13. A. S. A. Aqel, "Electricity theft and illegal connection as a problem of energy poverty: A perspective on energy justice," *Energy Policy*, vol. 123, pp. 636-645, 2018.
14. N. Kumar, A. Swarnkar, and A. Kumar, "Energy conservation in industry using maximum demand controller," *International Journal of Advanced Research in Electrical, Electronics and Instrumentation Engineering*, vol. 2, no. 12, pp. 5866-5872, 2013.
15. P. Kundur, *Power System Stability and Control*, McGraw-Hill, 1994.
16. A. W. Galli, G. L. Vecchio, and F. Tinè, "Design of an automatic power factor controller for induction motor loads," *IEEE Transactions on Power Electronics*, vol. 12, no. 3, pp. 452-459, 1997.
17. I. Mills, "Energy-efficient lighting: The role of government and private sector," *Energy Policy*, vol. 34, no. 2, pp. 158-166, 2006.
18. J. D. Bullough, "Lighting quality and energy efficiency," *IEEE Industry Applications Magazine*, vol. 15, no. 5, pp. 36-43, 2009.
19. J. J. Chalmers, "The application of daylight-responsive dimming systems," *IEEE Transactions on Industry Applications*, vol. 34, no. 4, pp. 675-681, 1998.
20. S. K. Ganguli and A. M. Bhat, "Design and implementation of a servo stabilizer for load voltage regulation," *IEEE Transactions on Power Electronics*, vol. 9, no. 3, pp. 282-287, 1994.

4 Energy Conservation Through Co-generation and Tariff

UNIT SPECIFICS

In this unit, energy conservation through co-generations and its advantages are explained covering the following related topics.

- Concept and significance of energy conservation through co-generation.
- Importance and types of co-generation.
- Factors governing the selection of co-generation system.
- Types of power tariff and methods of reducing energy bills.

RATIONALE

Co-generation promotes energy sustainability by making efficient use of heat or fuel that would otherwise be wasted.

PRE-REQUISITES

Basic knowledge about electricity generations from different fuels.

UNIT OUTCOMES

The outcomes of this unit are as follows

U4-O1: To understand the concepts of energy conservation through energy co-generation.

U4-O2: To describe the benefits of co-generation.

U4-O3: To assess the factors governing the selection of co-generation system.

U4-O4: To study the technologies used for co-generation.

U4-O5: To understand the types of power tariff and application of tariff system to reduce energy bill.

Unit outcomes	EXPECTED MAPPING WITH COURSE OUTCOMES (1- Weak Correlation; 2- Medium correlation; 3- Strong Correlation)				
	CO-1	CO-2	CO-3	CO-4	CO-5
U4-O1	2	2	1	3	3
U4-O2	1	1	3	3	2
U4-O3	1	1	2	3	3
U4-O4	1	2	2	3	3
U4-O5	1	-	-	3	3

4.1 Introduction

Cogeneration refers to the process of generating and using energy on-site in various forms concurrently, while maximising the efficiency of fuel energy and ensuring cost-effectiveness and environmental responsibility. Energy conservation in co-generation, or combined heat and power (CHP), is essential since it greatly improves energy efficiency and minimises environmental harm. In this unit significance of co-generation in fulfilling the objectives of energy conservation, types of cogeneration on basis of sequence of energy use, Topping cycle, Bottoming cycle, factors governing the selection of cogeneration system and advantages of cogeneration are discussed. Since co-generation helps in energy conservation means reduction in energy consumption, therefore tariffs and types of tariffs are also included here in this unit.

4.2 Need of Co-Generation

Co-generation, also known as Combined Heat and Power (CHP), refers to the simultaneous generation of electricity and useful heat from the same energy source. India gets a lot of its power from thermal power plants. Conventional power plants lose 65% of the energy they generate, resulting in an efficiency of just 35%. Heat rejected to the surrounding water or air is the primary source of conversion loss because of the inherent restrictions of the many thermodynamic cycles used to generate electricity.

Here are some key reasons for the need of co-generation:

- Reduces energy demand.
- Reduces rise in energy cost.
- Provides economical solution to energy shortages.
- Increase financial capital.
- Increases environmental value.

4.2.1 Significance of Energy Conservation for Co-Generation

- **Increased Energy Efficiency:** Co-generation systems may attain efficiency levels of up to 80-90%, in contrast to conventional power plants that generally run at about 30-50% efficiency. This significant improvement is a result of the efficient use of waste heat that would otherwise be wasted in traditional energy producing techniques.
- **Cost Savings:** Co-generation decreases fuel use and decreases energy costs for industrial, commercial, and residential customers by enhancing energy efficiency. This is especially advantageous for extensive activities, such as industrial facilities and hospitals, where there is a significant need for energy.
- **Environmental Benefits:** Increased efficiency in co-generation results in a decrease in greenhouse gas emissions and other pollutants. Co-generation reduces the environmental consequences of fossil fuel use by minimising fuel consumption while maintaining the same energy output.
- **Energy Security and Reliability:** Co-generation systems often function on the premises and may be customised to fulfil precise energy requirements, offering enhanced energy security and dependability. This is particularly crucial in regions with unstable power infrastructure or where the availability of electricity is of utmost importance.
- **Reduced Transmission Losses:** Co-generation systems, being usually situated near the point of use, reduce energy losses related to long-distance transmission and distribution, hence improving total energy efficiency.
- **Flexibility and Fuel Diversity:** Co-generation may use a range of fuel sources, including renewable ones, to improve energy resilience and flexibility. This flexibility

enables the integration of various energy systems and supports the shift towards more environmentally friendly energy sources.

4.3 Component of Co-generation Process

The essential components of a combined heat and power system shown in figure 4.1 consist of the followings.

- Fuel System
- A Prime Mover is a kind of engine that is specifically designed to power and operate a generator.
- The generator is used to convert electrical energy from the power distribution system into the building's internal power supply.
- A Heat Recovery System is used to capture and utilize heat from the locomotive's engine.
- The cooling system is designed to efficiently dissipate the heat that is expelled by the locomotive and cannot be enhanced further.
- Combustion and ventilation air systems are used to provide fresh air and remove exhaust gases generated by the engine.
- A control system is used to ensure the secure and efficient functioning of a system.
- *The enclosure serves the purpose* of safeguarding the engine and machines, while also minimizing noise.

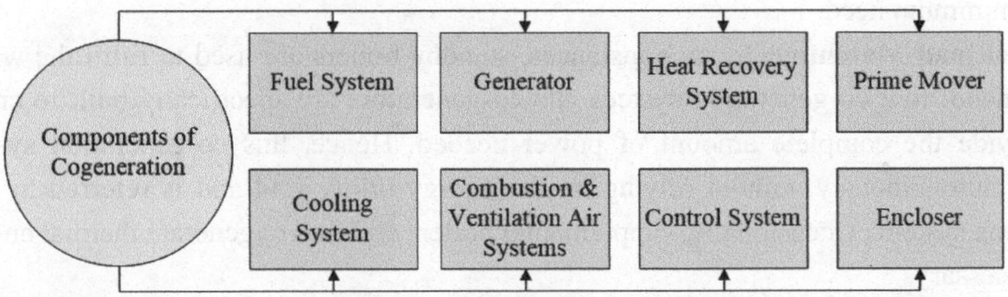

Figure 4.1: Components of Co-generation

4.4 Factors Governing the Selection of Cogeneration System

- **Heat to Power Ratio:** The heat-to-power ratio of the consuming system should align with the parameters of the co-generation system. It is quantified using the energy unit kilowatt (kW). The heat power ratio is calculated by dividing the heat energy by the amount of electricity needed.
- **Load Pattern:** When choosing a co-generation system, it is important to consider the load pattern for both heat and electricity needs.
- **Type of Fuel Available:** The choice of co-generation system is contingent upon the availability of fuel for the system. If the cost of available fuel for the system is minimal, then selecting the co-generation system will provide optimal results.
- **Quality of Thermal Energy Required:** The needed quality of thermal energy is dependent on the temperature and pressure, and thus plays a significant influence in determining the kind of co-generation system.

- **System Reliability:** Reliability is a crucial issue when it comes to a certain power source utilising the co-generation system. If there is a crucial phase in the power-consuming system that cannot tolerate the absence of a co-generation system, it is necessary for the co-generation system to be modular in such situations.
- **Electricity Buy-back:** When constructing a co-generation system, it is necessary to consider and understand the local legislation regarding the purchase of power from the co-generating system and the sale of electricity to the co-generation system.
- **Grid Dependent System And Independent System :** The technical setup of a grid-dependent co-generation system is contingent upon this element.
- **Local Environmental Regulations:** The kind of fuel utilized has varying environmental impacts. To achieve a greater decrease in a certain kind of fuel, it is necessary to consider the environmental regulations in that area. The environmental regulations in metropolitan regions may vary from those in suburban areas and villages.

Base Electrical Load Matching

The co-generation system is specifically built to provide the essential amount of power required to meet the minimal demand of the system. The remaining power requirement is procured from the utility grid. This kind of co-generation is used to generate the necessary thermal energy.

- **Base Thermal Load Matching:** The co-generation system is specifically intended to provide the lowest amount of thermal energy needed when the demand for heat exceeds the base or minimum need.
- **Electrical load Matching:** In such instances, standby boilers are used to fulfil the whole load demand. In a co-generation system, the co-generators are specifically built to create and provide the complete amount of power needed. Hence, this co-generation system operates autonomously without relying on the energy utility grid and is referred to as a 'standalone system'. Occasionally, supplemental boilers are used to generate thermal energy when necessary.
- **Thermal Load Matching:** The co-generation system is intended to provide the necessary thermal energy, and if needed, electricity may be obtained from the utility grid.

4.5 The Different Categories of Co-generation Power Plants

The classification of cogeneration power plants is mostly based on the operational process and energy utilisation series. Hence, the two categories, showing in figure 4.2, of cogeneration systems are the topping cycle and the bottoming cycle.

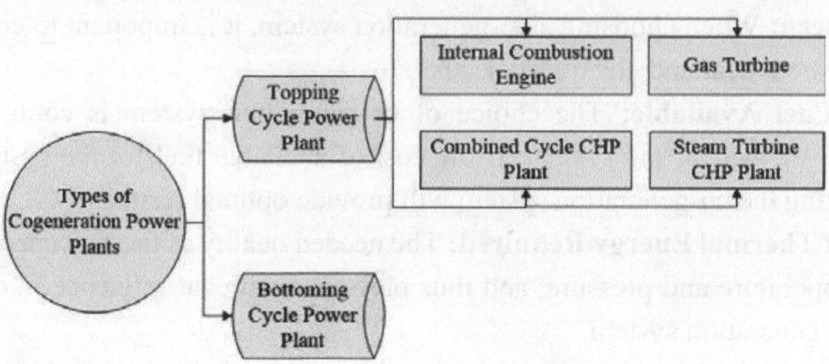

Figure: 4.2 Types of Cogeneration Power Plants

4.6 Co-Generation systems by Energy Consumption Sequences

Co-generation systems, also known as combined heat and power (CHP) systems are specifically engineered to produce electricity and valuable thermal energy concurrently from a single energy source as shown in figure 4.3. The efficiency and applicability of these systems may be classified according to the order in which energy is used and utilised within the system. Typically, this classification may be divided into two primary categories.

a) Topping cycle
b) Bottoming cycle

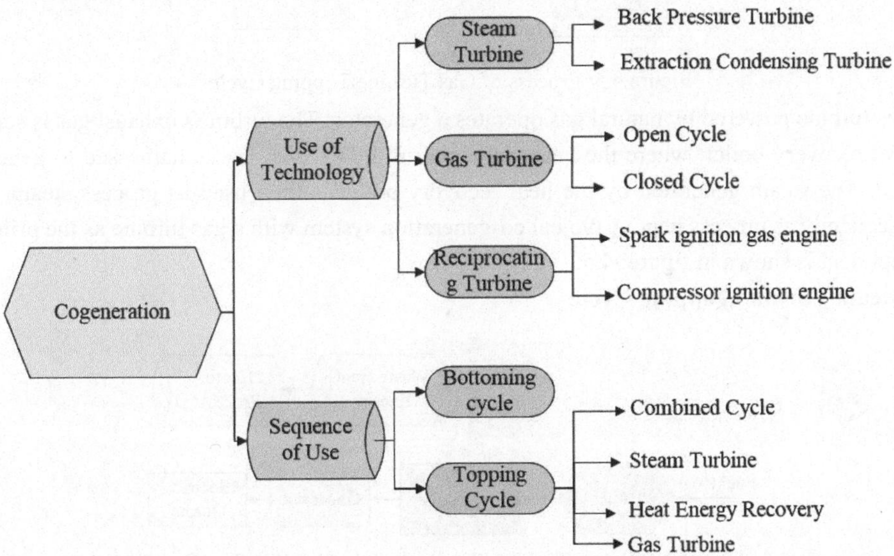

Figure 4.3: Classification of Co-generation System Based on Sequence of Energy Use

a. Topping Cycle

A topping cycle is a thermodynamic cycle in which the primary purpose is to generate electricity. The thermal energy generated is used for the purpose of heating different processes or it is employed for other applications. Co-generation is extensively used in most topping cycle systems, making it the fundamental technique of co-generation. The figure 4.4 is a basic and typical example of a topping cycle co-generation system used in thermal power production plants.

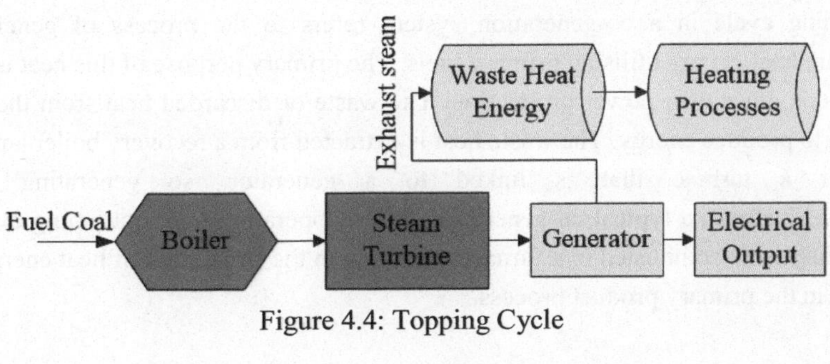

Figure 4.4: Topping Cycle

i. Gas Turbine Topping Cycle

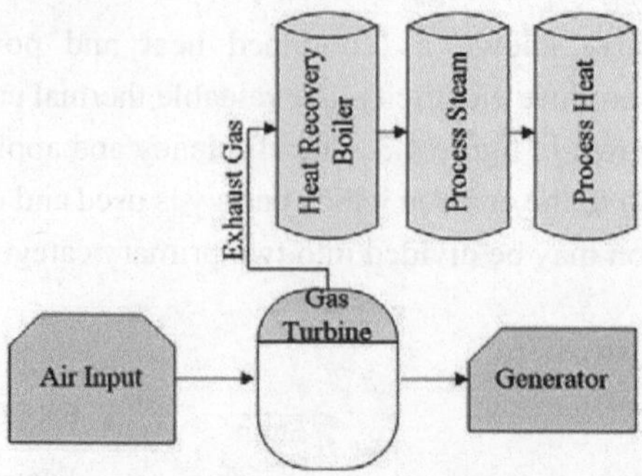

Figure 4.5: Process of Gas Turbine Topping Cycle

A gas turbine powered by natural gas operates a generator. The turbine's exhaust gas is sent to a heat recovery boiler, where the heat contained in the exhaust gas is harnessed to generate steam. The steam generated by the heat recovery boiler is then used as process steam, and subsequently as process heat. A typical co-generation system with a gas turbine as the primary component is shown in figure: 4.5.

ii. Steam Turbine Topping Cycle

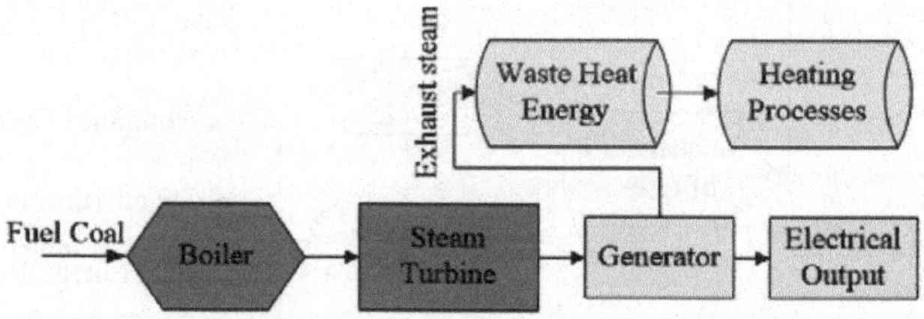

Figure 4.6: Steam Turbine Topping Cycle (Same as Topping Cycle)

In this topping co-generation system, several types of fuel such as coal, oil, and wood are combusted to generate high-pressure steam, which is then directed via a steam turbine. The low-pressure steam extracted from the turbine's exhaust may be used for several applications, including heating industrial items, homes, or as a heat source for the feed water in a power plant.

Additionally, the flue gases that are directed towards the chimney from the boiler may be used in the economizer to warm the feed water that is supplied to the boiler as shown in figure 4.6.

b. Bottoming Cycle

A bottoming cycle in a co-generation system refers to the process of generating high temperature heat energy utilising primary fuels. The primary purpose of this heat is to be used in operations other than power production. The waste or discarded heat from the process is harnessed to produce energy. The waste heat is extracted from a recovery boiler and then used to power a turbine that is linked to a generator, so generating electricity. Figure 4.7 illustrates a typical co-generation facility operating on a bottoming cycle. In this process, the fuel is combusted in a furnace, resulting in the generation of heat energy which is then used in the primary product process.

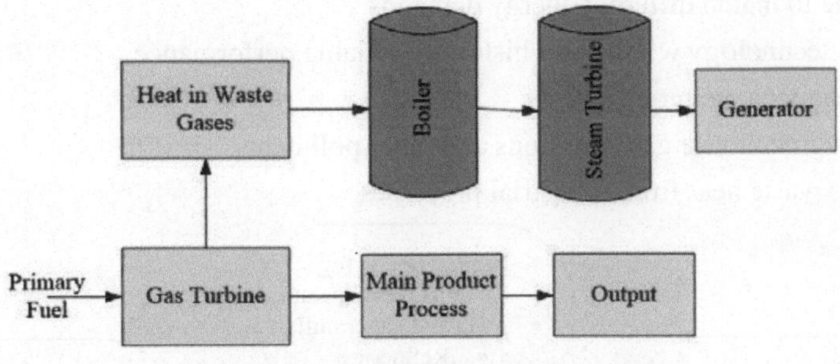

Figure 4.7: Process of Bottoming Cycle

4.7 Types of co-generation Basis of Technology

Commonly used co-generation methods include extraction/back pressure steam turbines, gas turbines with heat recovery boilers and reciprocating engines with heat recovery boilers.

a. Steam Turbine Co-generation Systems

The two main kinds of steam turbines are the back pressure and extraction turbines. A modified version of the co-generation system, known as the extraction-back pressure turbine, may be used when the end-user requires thermal energy at two distinct temperature levels. Full-condensing steam turbines are often installed at locations where the waste heat from the process is used to produce electricity. Steam Turbine Co-generation System Schematic Diagrams shown in figure 4.8.

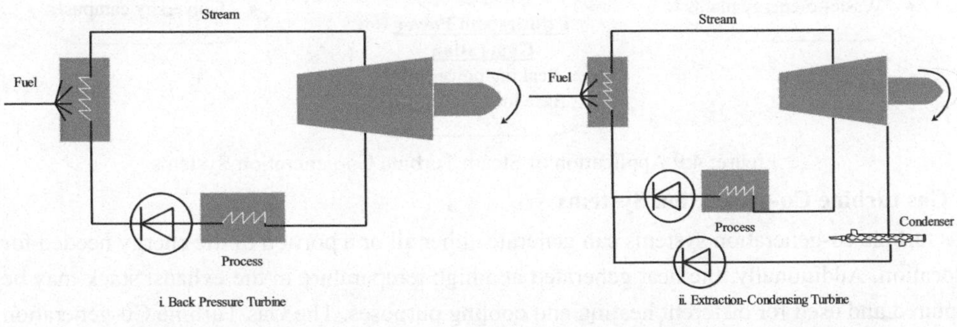

Figure 4.8: Steam Turbine Co-generation System Schematic Diagrams

i. Advantage of Steam Turbine Co-generation Systems

Steam turbine co-generation systems have several benefits, which contribute to their widespread use in various industrial and commercial settings.

- Achieves overall efficiencies of up to 80-90%.
- Significant cost savings due to high efficiency and reduced fuel consumption.
- Provides greater energy security and reliability.
- Reduces fuel consumption for the same energy output.
- Suitable for industrial processes, commercial buildings, hospitals, and district heating systems.
- Can be used for peak load management.
- Operates on various fuels (natural gas, coal, biomass, waste heat).

- Scalable to match different energy demands.
- Proven technology with a long history of reliable performance.
- Low maintenance requirements.
- Lowers greenhouse gas emissions and other pollutants.
- Utilizes waste heat from industrial processes.

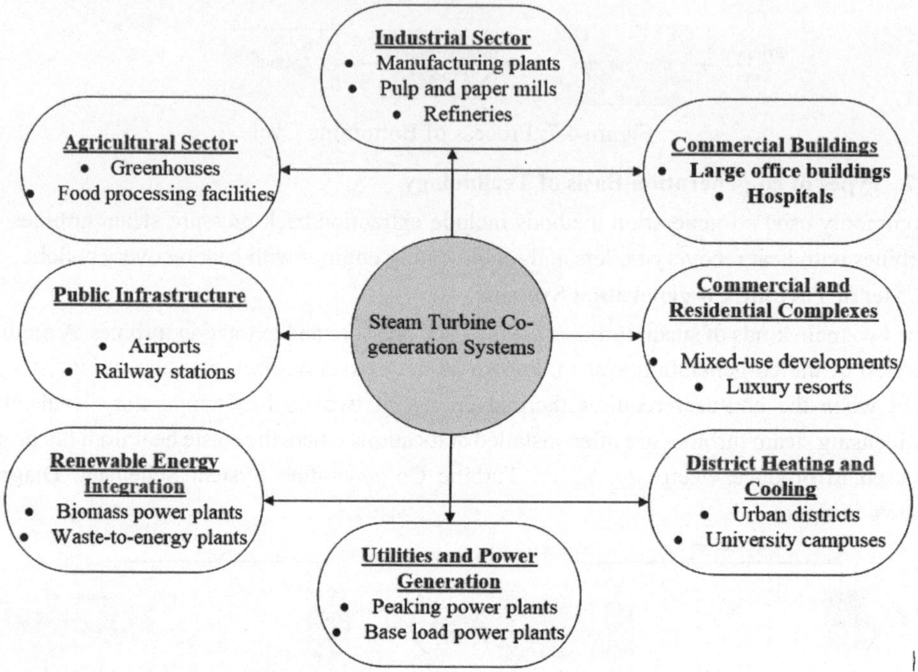

Figure: 4.9 Application of Steam Turbine Co-generation Systems

b. Gas turbine Co-generation Systems

Gas turbine co-generation systems can generate either all or a portion of the energy needed for a location. Additionally, the heat generated at a high temperature in the exhaust stack may be captured and used for different heating and cooling purposes. The Gas Turbine Co-generation Schematic Diagram shown in figure 4.10.

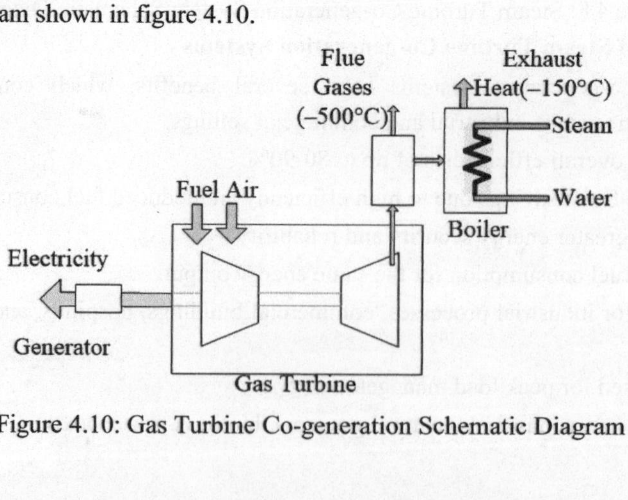

Figure 4.10: Gas Turbine Co-generation Schematic Diagram

i. Advantages of Gas Turbine Co-generation Systems

Gas turbine co-generation systems, or combined heat and power (CHP) systems, provide several notable benefits. These systems can produce both electrical and heat energy at the same time using just one fuel source.

- Achieves overall efficiencies of up to 75-85%.
- Effective utilization of both electricity and thermal energy.
- Can operate on natural gas, biogas, and other gaseous fuels.
- Capable of switching between different fuel sources.
- Lower greenhouse gas emissions compared to conventional power generation.
- Combustion process produces fewer pollutants like NOx and CO_2.
- Rapid start-up times enhance operational flexibility.
- Suitable for applications requiring variable load demands.
- Easier integration into existing facilities.
- Suitable for small to medium-scale applications.
- Provides reliable power supply in remote or isolated areas.

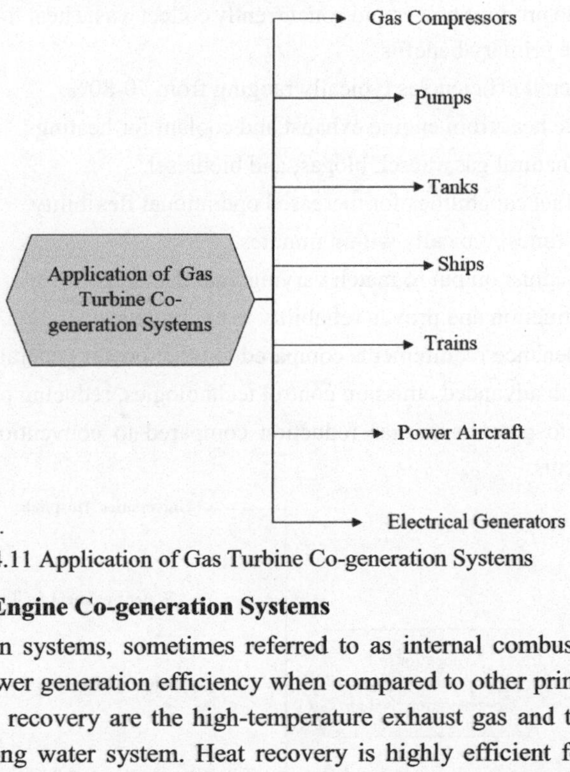

Figure: 4.11 Application of Gas Turbine Co-generation Systems

c. Reciprocating Engine Co-generation Systems

These co-generation systems, sometimes referred to as internal combustion (I.C.) engines, exhibit superior power generation efficiency when compared to other prime movers. The two sources of heat for recovery are the high-temperature exhaust gas and the low-temperature engine jacket cooling water system. Heat recovery is highly efficient for smaller systems, making them more popular among smaller energy-consuming facilities. These facilities typically have a greater demand for electricity than thermal energy and require lower quality heat, such as low-pressure steam or hot water. The Reciprocating Engine Co-generation Schematic Diagram shown in figure 4.12.

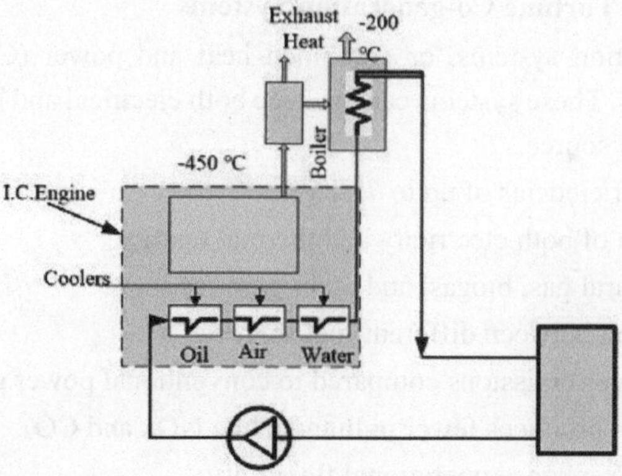

Figure 4.12: Reciprocating Engine Co-generation Schematic Diagram

i. Advantages of Reciprocating Engine Co-generation Systems

Reciprocating engine co-generation systems are favoured for combined heat and power (CHP) applications in many sectors due to their numerous benefits. These systems use internal combustion engines to produce power and concurrently collect waste heat for thermal purposes. The following are the primary benefits:

- Achieves overall efficiencies typically ranging from 70-80%.
- Utilizes waste heat from engine exhaust and coolant for heating.
- Operates on natural gas, diesel, biogas, and biodiesel.
- Offers dual-fuel capabilities for increased operational flexibility.
- Fast start-up times, typically within minutes.
- Can quickly adjust output to match varying load demands.
- Robust construction and proven reliability in continuous operation.
- Lower maintenance requirements compared to other power generation technologies.
- Equipped with advanced emission control technologies, reducing pollutants.
- Contributes to greenhouse gas reduction compared to conventional electricity and heating systems.

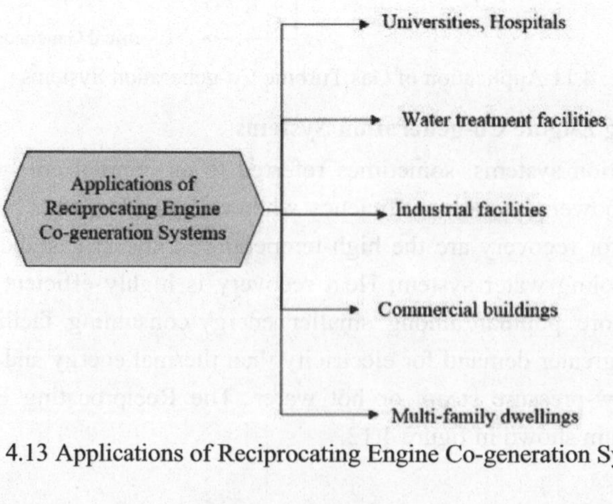

Figure: 4.13 Applications of Reciprocating Engine Co-generation Systems

Example 4.1: *Calculate the monthly electric bill, if the following load are connected.*

- *3 LEDs of 20 W each for 5 Hr.*
- *2 fan of 40 W each for 10 Hr.*
- *1 refrigerator of 300 W for 24 Hr.*

The billing is done at ₹-5.00 per Unit

Solution: *The energy consumed by LEDs*= 3 × 20 × 8 × 30

=14,400

=14.4 kWh

The energy consumed by fan= 2 × 40 × 10 × 30

=24 kWh

The energy consumed by refrigerator= 1 × 300 × 24 × 30

=216 kWh

Total Energy Consumption = 254.4 kWh

Electricity bill for one month =254.4 × ₹ 5.0

=₹ 1272

4.8 Co-generation Technologies

Co-generation, or Combined Heat and Power (CHP), is a technique that enables the simultaneous production of electricity and useable heat from a single energy source. This technique greatly enhances the total energy utilisation efficiency when compared to the traditional independent production of electricity and heat. Several regularly used co-generation technologies exist:

- **Piston Engine Facilities:** The most popular cogeneration approach. The radiator or exhaust of smaller piston engines, mainly diesel, absorbs heat. These systems are popular because they are cheap, simple to maintain, and adaptable to different sizes.
- **Gas Engine Facilities:** These plants use gas engines, which are simpler to maintain than 5 MW gas turbines. Most fuels are natural gas or propane. These plants arrive assembled and are kept in a big warehouse with heating, electricity, and gas connections.
- **Gas Turbine Facilities:** Waste heat is produced in turbine flue gas in these facilities. Most fuel is natural gas. Large gas turbine plants are housed outside in sound-attenuated containers with gas lines.
- **Steam Turbine Facilities:** The steam condenser powers the steam turbine in these basic heating systems.
- **Biofuel Facilities:** The biofuel configuration determines whether these plants employ a reciprocating petrol or diesel engine. The design resembles a gas engine plant. A biofuel plant reduces hydrocarbon fuel usage and carbon emissions, its main benefit. Biofuel cogeneration facilities need less permission than conventional cogeneration plants but produce less.

- **Heavy Fuel Oil Facilities:** HFO cogeneration facilities are rare in the US but prevalent in underdeveloped nations. Fuel oil, the heaviest commercial fuel derived from crude oil, is low-grade. Most cogeneration facilities employ HFO Number 5 and Number 6, which need 170–260 °F preheating. HFO is inexpensive yet emits a lot.
- **Combined Cycle Facilities:** Combining cycle plants use heat engine exhaust to generate electricity or power mechanical activities. Multiple thermodynamic cycles boost efficiency and decrease fuel costs. The problem is that most cogeneration plants must be modified for this technology.
- **Fuel Cell Facilities:** Fuel cell technology converts chemical energy to electricity by reacting with an oxidizer. Hydrogen is preferable, although cogeneration facilities employ molten-carbonate or solid oxide because to their high exhaust temperatures, which may exceed 1,200 °F.
- **Nuclear Power Facilities:** Refitting nuclear power stations with taps after the turbines may provide steam for central heating. Due to the 10 MW power loss required to create 95°C heat, these systems are rare.
- **Biomass Power Facilities:** Growing in popularity, biomass plants use hydrogen, carbon, or oxygen from industrial waste or rubbish. Recently, technology has been improved to collect more energy from wood, rubbish, waste, alcohol fuels, and landfill gases.

4.9 Reduces Energy Demand and Cost

Energy demand is the quantity of energy required by people, enterprises, industries, and communities to fulfil different activities and functions. It includes the use of energy for various reasons such as heating, cooling, transportation, industrial operations, lighting, electronic gadgets, and other activities.

Energy demand is subject to several variables, including population expansion, economic progress, technical breakthroughs, weather conditions, lifestyle changes, and government regulations. Comprehending energy demand is essential for energy planners, policymakers, and enterprises to guarantee a dependable and sustainable energy supply, optimise energy use, and alleviate environmental consequences such as greenhouse gas emissions and resource exhaustion. Some basic tips of reduce energy use in different areas shown in figure 4.14.

Example 4.2: The Illuminance from lamp at 1 meter distance is 20 lm/m². Determine the Illuminance at 0.5 m distance.

Solution:

$$E = \left(\frac{1.0}{0.5}\right)^2$$

$$= 80 \text{ lm/m}^2$$

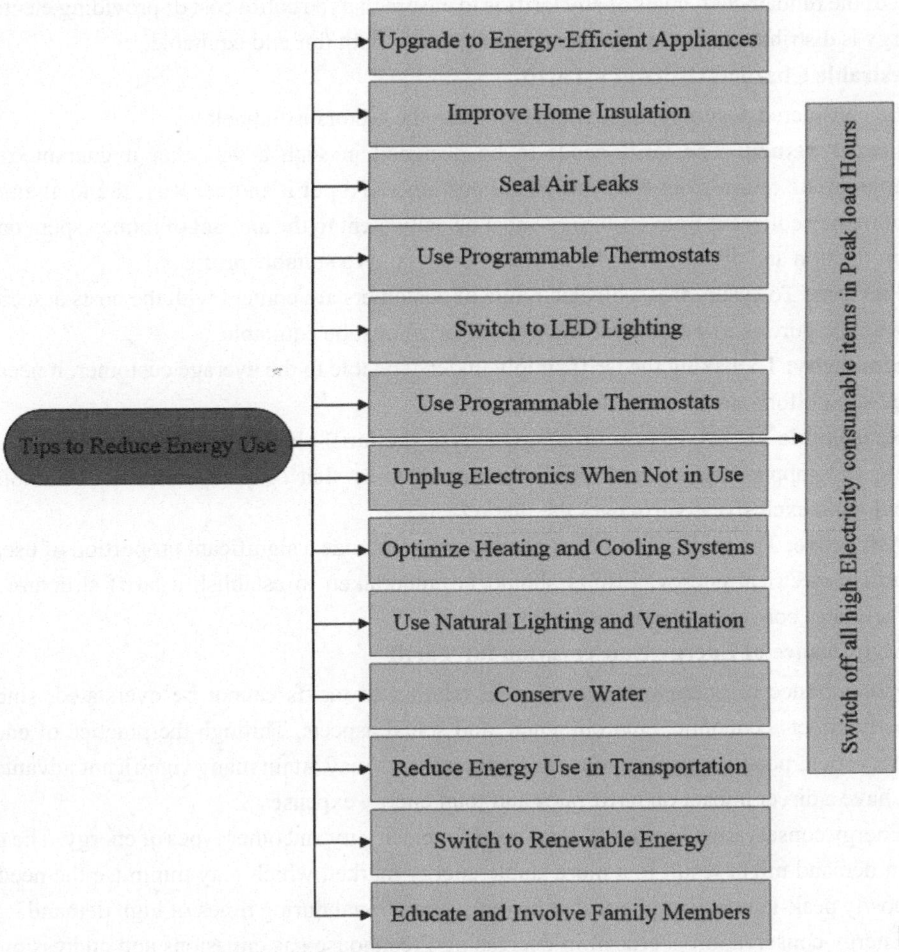

Figure 4.14: Methods of Reduce Energy Consumption

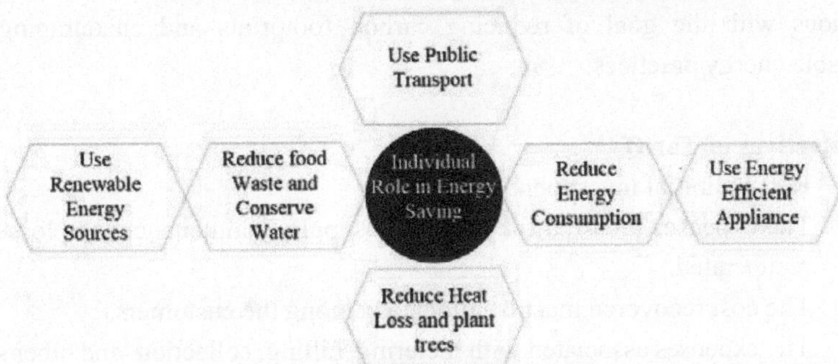

Figure 4.15 Individual Role in Energy Saving

4.10Tariff

Tariff is the rate or pricing structure set by an energy provider for the supply of electricity or other forms of energy to its customers.

One of the fundamental goals of any tariff is to ensure that the entire cost of providing electrical energy is distributed among its users in a way that is both fair and equitable.

i. Desirable Characteristics of a Tariff

To be considered desirable, a tariff must possess the factors listed below:

- **Proper return:** The tariff needs to be designed in such a way that it guarantees the appropriate return from each individual customer. To put it another way, the total amount of money collected from customers must be equivalent to the amount of money spent on the production and distribution of electrical energy, plus a suitable profit.
- **Fairness:** To ensure that a diverse range of customers are content with the costs associated with the purchase of electrical energy, the tariff must be equitable.
- **Simplicity:** To making the tariff simply understandable to the average customer, it needs to be straightforward.
- **Reasonable profit:** The profit component of the tariff should be fair and justifiable. An electric supply business is a publicly owned utility that often operates as a monopoly, enjoying exclusive control over the market.
- **Attractive:** The tariff should be appealing to incentivize a significant proportion of users to utilise electrical energy. Efforts should be undertaken to establish a tariff structure that facilitates convenient payment for customers.

ii. Significance of Energy Conservation for Tariff

The importance of energy conservation in relation to tariffs cannot be overstated, since it directly affects economic, environmental, and social aspects. Through the practice of energy conservation, people, organisations, and governments may attain many significant advantages that have a direct impact on tariff rates and total energy expenses.

- Energy conservation lowers the total need for electricity and other types of energy. The drop in demand might result in a more stable energy market, which may minimise the need for costly peak-load power plants that are only operational during times of high demand.
- Energy conservation is crucial in decreasing greenhouse gas emissions and addressing the effects of climate change. A growing number of nations are implementing laws and regulations with the goal of reducing carbon footprints and encouraging the use of sustainable energy practices.

4.11 Objectives of Tariff

- Recoup initial investment
- The expenses incurred for operation, supply, maintenance, and losses need to be recuperated.
- The cost recovered must be allocated among the customers.
- The expenses associated with metering, billing, collection, and other services need to be recuperated.
- There should be a mechanism for imposing penalties for a poor power factor.
- Achieve a favourable return on investment.
- Encourage users to adhere to their contractual load limits and discourage them from exceeding them.

4.12 Tariff and its Types

The following considerations should be taken while drafting a tariff:

- The customer's capacity for payment.
- Services provided, such as whether it's used for farming, agriculture, or lighting.
- The production's yearly cost, which includes operating, semi-fixed, and fixed expenses.
- The bill should be calculated using an easy approach.

i. LT (Low Tension) and HT (High Tension) Tariffs

- **LT Tariffs:** With a voltage demand of 440V or less. Example: residential and small commercial users.
- **HT Tariff:** For users that need voltages over 11kV. Large factories and industries are examples.

ii. Special Tariffs

- Introduced for certain consumer groups or durations.

iii. Time-of-Day Tariff

- Changes with time. Peak electricity prices may be greater than off-peak prices. This flattens the demand curve by encouraging consumers to operate off-peak.

iv. Peak-off-Peak Tariff

- Another Time-of-Day tariff that divides the day into peak and off-peak hours with varying charges.

v. Power Factor Tariff

- Promotes consumer power unification. A discount may be offered for power factor over a specific threshold and a penalty if below.

vi. Maximum Demand Tariff

- Based on consumer demand peak. A customer pays for his maximum demand (kW or kVA) and energy used. This encourages customers to reduce peak demand.

vii. Load Factor Tariff

- Tariffs based on consumer load factors, which are the average load to maximum demand over time. A greater load factor means a more consistent load.

viii. Availability-Based Tariff (ABT)

- Used by interstate bulk electricity buyers. A frequency-based tariff links grid frequency and electricity pricing. Frequency over a specific threshold indicates excess electricity, lowering rates. Periods of low frequency signify electricity shortages and higher rates.

***Example 4.3**: A consumer has a maximum demand of 200 kW at 40% load factor. If the tariff is Rs. 100 per kW of maximum demand plus 10 paise per kWh, find the overall cost per kWh.*

Solution: *Units consumed/year = Max. demand × L.F. × Hours in a year*

$$= (200) \times (0{\cdot}4) \times 8760 = 7{,}00{,}800 \text{ kWh}$$

Annual charges = Annual M.D. charges + Annual energy charges

$$= Rs\ (100 \times 200 + 0{\cdot}1 \times 7{,}00{,}800)$$

$$= Rs\ 90{,}080$$

$$\text{Overall cost/kWh} = Rs\ 90\ 080/7{,}00{,}800$$

$$= Re\ 0{\cdot}1285 = \mathbf{12{\cdot}85\ paise}$$

Example 4.4: *The following two tariffs are offered :*

(a) Rs 100 plus 15 paise per unit ;

(b) A flat rate of 30 paise per unit ;

At what consumption is first tariff economical ?

Solution: *Let x be the number of units at which charges due to both tariffs become equal.*

Then, $$100 + 0{\cdot}15x = 0{\cdot}3x$$

Or, $$0{\cdot}15x = 100$$

$$x = 100/0{\cdot}15 = 666{\cdot}67 \text{ units}$$

Therefore, tariff (a) is economical if consumption is more than 666·67 units.

4.13 Application of Tariff System to Reduce Energy Bill

a. Time of use Metering

- Time of use metering (TOU) is a system that divides the day, month, and year into different tariff slots.
- Electricity used during times of high demand is billed at elevated rates, while electricity consumed during periods of low demand is billed at reduced prices.
- Consumers may have an impact by reducing energy use during peak load periods and increasing it during off-peak loads, leading to automatic load management during peak load periods.
- By controlling the load demand, the supply agency may make approximate plans for their generating and transition infrastructure.

b. Domestic usage Meter

- Domestic users may utilise domestic variable rate metres that provide two rates, namely 'Peak' load and off-peak load.
- It will encourage household users to utilise electricity during periods of low demand and limit their consumption during periods of high demand to save energy and decrease the overall demand on the power grid.
- These installations use basic electromechanical switches that are employed with electrical storage heaters.

c. Getting Benefit by Improving Energy Efficiency

- Consumers have the option to install power factor correction equipment at their premises or installations to reap the advantages of a higher power factor, as specified by the tariff. Which will decrease the need for present load.
- H.T. customers are encouraged to use energy during periods of high load factors to optimise plant capacity utilisation and minimise the cost of energy production.

d. Energy Conservation by Improving Load Factor

- The load factor is the ratio of the actual amount of energy given to a system during a certain time to the maximum amount of energy that could be delivered by the system in that same time. Based on the duration, the load factor may be referred to as daily, monthly, annual, etc. This component always has a value that is lower than one.
- Improving the load factor, which implies bringing it closer to one, results in using more units for the same maximum demand or generating more units. This decreases the cost of generation per unit.
- If the generation plant operates its generating sets in a way that maintains a constant utilisation without any peaks or troughs in the load curve, it will attain a load factor of unity.
- Consumers should be provided with cheap prices for using energy during off-peak loads to enhance the load factor and decrease the cost of energy generation. The cost of labour per kilowatt-hour (kWh) of energy generation falls as the number of units created grows. This is because the manpower cost stays constant, regardless of the working load factor of the alternator at 25%, 50%, or 100%.
- Reducing the maximum demand on the plant may also enhance the load factor.
- Increasing production efficiency by minimising system losses may also enhance the load factor.
- Improving the load factor of the system may be achieved by encouraging users to adjust their peak demands to various hours throughout the day.
- Enhancements may be made by using energy management systems.
- Optimal energy utilisation may be achieved by reducing peak demands while maintaining a constant overall demand.

e. Advantages and Economy Achieved by Improvement of Power Factor.

Both the energy provider and consumer benefit from operating at a higher power factor due to the following reasons:

- The increase in provided load in kilowatts results in the more efficient utilisation of the prime movers' capacity and an increase in the kilowatt capacity of the generating plant.
- The power capacity of the transformers, as well as the transmission and distribution lines, is augmented.
- The efficiency of each plant is enhanced.

Example 4.5: *A Consumer has a maximum demand of 100 kW at 60% load factor. If the maximum demand tariff is ₹-150 per kW plus 20 paise per kW. Calculate the per unit cost & electrical energy for one year.*

Solution: $Unit\ Consumed\ per\ year = MD \times L.F \times hours\ in\ year$

$$Unit\ Consumed\ per\ year = 100 \times 0.6 \times 8760$$

$$= 525{,}600\ kW$$

$$Annual\ Charges = Annual\ MD\ Charges + Annual\ Energy\ Charges$$

$$I = Rs.(100 \times 150 + 0.2 \times 525600)$$

$$= 120{,}120$$

$$Overall\ cost\ per\ kWh = 120{,}120/525600$$

$$Overall\ cost\ per\ kWh = 22.85\ paise$$

***Example 4.6** the input power of three phase induction motor is measured as 10 kW. The value of voltage and current are 4.5 volt and 18 A respectively. Calculate the power factor.*

Solution: *Power P= 10 kW*

Line voltage V_L=4.5

Line Current = 18 A

$$Power, P = \sqrt{3}V_L\ I_L Cos\emptyset$$

$$Cos\emptyset = \frac{P}{\sqrt{3}V_L\ I_L}$$

$$= 10 \times 1000/\sqrt{3} \times 4.5 \times 18$$

$$= 0.77$$

SUMMARY

Co-generation is one of the methods of energy conservation. In many power generation and heating systems, waste of heat may be utilized for an efficient use of fuel. In this unit, concept, significance, advantages and disadvantages of co-generations are discussed in detail. Factors effecting co-generation and technologies used are also presented.

The rate at which electricity is supplied to the consumers is called tariff. In the present scenario, a substantial amount is paid by everyone towards tariff. Reducing electricity bills without compromising with the comfort, how tariff can be reduced through energy conservation is explained and discussed in this unit.

EXERCISE

Short Answer Type Questions

1. **Explain Co-generation and its significance.**
2. **Explain Topping cycle and Bottoming cycle.**
3. **State any two feature of topping cycle co-generation**
4. **What are the different types of co-generation?**
5. **Discuss different technologies used in co-generation.**
6. **How co-generation, reduces the tariff?**
7. **List co-generation systems based on sequence of energy used.**
8. **Discuss power factor tariff.**
9. **Define time off day tariff.**
10. **How maximum demand tariff is different from load factor tariff.?**
11. **Discuss factors governing the selection of co-generation system.**
12. **State the components of availability-based tariff.**
13. **Draw neat labelled sketch of gas turbine co-generation.**

Long Answer Type Questions

1. Discuss steam turbine co-generation, gas turbine co-generation and reciprocating engine co-generation.
2. Explain Topping cycle and Bottoming cycle.
3. What do you understand by tariff ? Discuss the objectives of tariff.
4. Why is tariff for power load less than the lighting load ?
5. What is the importance of power factor tariff ?
6. Illustrate the benefits of time off day and peak off day tariff relevant to energy cost along with its impact on energy bill.
7. Choose any four tariff schedule to reduce electricity bill of commercial consumer.
8. Make use of load factor and maximum demand tariff to minimize electrical consumption of electrical installation.
9. Summarize the factors considered while selecting the co-generation system.

MULTIPLE CHOICE QUESTIONS

1. What is co-generation?
   A. The use of a single energy source to produce both electricity and useful heat.
   B. Generating electricity using solar panels.
   C. A method of reducing electricity consumption.
   D. The process of generating power using wind energy.
2. Which of the following is a primary benefit of co-generation?
   A. Higher efficiency.
   B. Increased fuel consumption.
   C. Lower initial investment.
   D. Higher greenhouse gas emissions.
3. Co-generation systems are most used in which of the following industries?
   A. Textile.
   B. Steel.
   C. Food processing.
   D. All of the above.
4. What is the typical efficiency range of a co-generation system?
   A. 30-40%
   B. 50-60%
   C. 60-80%
   D. 80-90%
5. Which of the following fuels can be used in co-generation plants?
   A. Natural gas.
   B. Coal.
   C. Biomass.
   D. All of the above.

6. The by-product of co-generation often used for heating is known as:
   A. Cold air.
   B. Steam.
   C. Ash.
   D. Solar energy.
7. In which type of co-generation system is steam generated in a boiler and used to drive a steam turbine generator?
   A. Combined cycle.
   B. Topping cycle.
   C. Bottoming cycle.
   D. Brayton cycle.
8. What is a topping cycle co-generation system?
   A. Electricity is generated first, then the waste heat is used.
   B. Heat is produced first, then electricity is generated.
   C. Both electricity and heat are produced simultaneously.
   D. None of the above.
9. Which regulation typically governs co-generation in many countries?
   A. Environmental Protection Act.
   B. Energy Policy Act.
   C. Renewable Energy Directive.
   D. All of the above.
10. Which of the following is a significant barrier to the implementation of co-generation?
   A. High initial cost.
   B. Lack of fuel availability.
   C. Technical complexity.
   D. All of the above.

1A. What is a tariff in the context of energy consumption?
   A. A tax on energy use.
   B. A schedule of prices for electricity consumption.
   C. A rebate for using renewable energy.
   D. None of the above.

1B. Which tariff structure charges different rates for electricity use at different times of the day?
   A. Flat rate tariff.
   B. Time-of-use (TOU) tariff.
   C. Tiered tariff.
   D. Seasonal tariff.

1C. What is the purpose of time-of-use (TOU) tariffs?

A. To encourage energy consumption.

B. To promote energy conservation during peak hours.

C. To increase revenue for utility companies.

D. None of the above.

1D. Which type of tariff is designed to encourage off-peak electricity use?

A. Peak load tariff.

B. Off-peak tariff.

C. Seasonal tariff.

D. Flat rate tariff.

15. In a tiered tariff system, how are customers charged?

A. A flat rate regardless of usage.

B. Lower rates for higher usage.

C. Rates increase as consumption increases.

D. Different rates for residential and commercial users.

16. Which tariff system charges the same rate for electricity use regardless of the time of day or season?

A. TOU tariff.

B. Flat rate tariff.

C. Seasonal tariff.

D. Tiered tariff.

17. What is demand response in the context of electricity tariffs?

A. Immediate supply of electricity upon request.

B. Adjusting consumption patterns based on price signals.

C. Increasing demand during peak hours.

D. Reducing supply during off-peak hours.

18. Which entity typically sets electricity tariffs?

A. Utility companies.

B. Government regulatory bodies.

C. Consumers.

D. Manufacturers.

19. How do seasonal tariffs benefit electricity providers?

A. By maximizing revenue during low demand periods.

B. By balancing demand throughout the year.

C. By reducing operational costs.

D. None of the above.

20. Which tariff design is aimed at promoting renewable energy usage?
    A. Flat rate tariff.
    B. Tiered tariff.
    C. Feed-in tariff.
    D. Seasonal tariff.

Answer of Multiple Choice Questions

1	**A**	**2**	**A**	**3**	**D**	**4**	**C**	**5**	**D**
6	**B**	**7**	**B**	**8**	**A**	**9**	**B**	**10**	**D**
11	**B**	**12**	**B**	**13**	**B**	**14**	**B**	**15**	**B**
16	**B**	**17**	**B**	**18**	**B**	**19**	**B**	**20**	**C**

REFERENCES

1. BEE. "Energy Efficiency in Electrical Utilities" New Delhi, India: BEE; 2015.
2. BEE. "General Aspects of Energy Management and Energy Audit" New Delhi, India: BEE; 2015.
3. BEE. "Energy Efficiency in Thermal Utilities" New Delhi, India: BEE; 2015.
4. BEE. "Energy Performance Assessment For Equipment and Utility Systems" New Delhi, India: BEE; 2015.
5. R. K. Kakaras, A. Doukelis, and K. Giannakopoulos, "Industrial cogeneration: A selection procedure," *Energy*, vol. 28, no. 6, pp. 545-556, 2003.
6. S. Sanaye and T. K. Manesh, "Simulation and optimization of steam turbine cogeneration systems," *Appl. Therm. Eng.*, vol. 24, no. 17-18, pp. 2563-2572, 2004.
7. S. M. Guo, P. J. Mago, and L. M. Chamra, "Performance analysis of combined cooling, heating, and power systems using an absorption chiller and a gas turbine," *Appl. Therm. Eng.*, vol. 27, no. 15, pp. 2558-2565, 2007.
8. Y. M. El-Sayed and I. M. Tribus, "Thermoeconomic analysis and optimization of a cogeneration system," *Energy Convers. Manag.*, vol. 21, no. 1, pp. 85-98, 1981.
9. M. Lazaro, A. Dolado, D. Zalba, and J. M. Marin, "Reciprocating engines in distributed generation systems," *Energy Convers. Manag.*, vol. 51, no. 4, pp. 661-671, 2010.
10. A. Rentizelas, A. Tolis, and I. Tatsiopoulos, "Optimization of biofuel supply chains for the end use of heat and power co-generation," *Renew. Energy*, vol. 34, no. 3, pp. 873-881, 2009.
11. J. L. Silveira, M. J. Mendonça, and C. E. Tuna, "Thermoeconomic analysis method for optimization of combined heat and power systems. Part II," *Int. J. Therm. Sci.*, vol. 41, no. 2, pp. 209-214, 2002.
12. R. K. Ahmadi and H. D. Kamali, "Optimization of a hybrid CHP system based on exergy analysis and environmental impact," *Energy Convers. Manag.*, vol. 79, pp. 38-51, 2014.

13. F. A. Farret and M. G. Simoes, *Integration of Alternative Sources of Energy*, John Wiley & Sons, 2006.

14. D. Thollander, J. Palm, and P. Rohdin, "Improved energy efficiency in industrial energy systems," *Energy Policy*, vol. 38, no. 4, pp. 2098-2107, 2010.

15. M. J. B. Albadi and E. F. El-Saadany, "A summary of demand response in electricity markets," *Electr. Power Syst. Res.*, vol. 78, no. 11, pp. 1989-1996, 2008.

16. A. A. S. Galiana, K. C. Leong, and X. Y. Chen, "The regulatory and policy aspects of demand response and dynamic pricing," *IEEE Trans. Power Syst.*, vol. 29, no. 1, pp. 113-118, 2014.

17. P. Centolella, "The integration of price responsive demand into PJM wholesale power markets and system operations," *Energy J.*, vol. 30, no. 2, pp. 21-44, 2009.

18. J. Torriti, "Price-based demand side management: Assessing the impacts of time-of-use tariffs on residential electricity demand and peak shifting in Northern Italy," *Energy*, vol. 44, no. 1, pp. 576-583, 2012.

19. S. Borenstein, "The long-run efficiency of real-time electricity pricing," *Energy J.*, vol. 26, no. 3, pp. 93-116, 2005.

20. L. A. Greening, "Demand response resources: Who is responsible for implementation in a deregulated market?" *Energy*, vol. 33, no. 3, pp. 328-336, 2008.

5 Energy Audit of Electrical System

UNIT SPECIFICS

In this unit, the concept of energy audit and its implementation in electrical systems is discussed. The following aspects of energy auditing are presented here.

- Provision of regulations of energy audit in electrical systems described in energy conservation act.
- Procedural aspects of execution of energy audit and report writing.
- Instruments required to conduct the energy audit in electrical systems.

RATIONALE

Energy auditing of electrical systems and its implementation.

PRE-REQUISITES

Basic knowledge about electrical appliances and their energy consumption.

UNIT OUTCOMES

The outcomes of this unit are as follows

U5-O1: To understand the necessity of energy conservation and relative benefits in adoption of its practices described in energy conservation act.

U5-O2: To study the instruments required in the execution of energy auditing

U5-O3: To prepare the questionnaire for energy audit projects

U5-O4: To understand the methodology of energy audit.

U5-O5: To understand the procedure of writing energy audit report.

Unit outcomes	EXPECTED MAPPING WITH COURSE OUTCOMES (1- Weak Correlation; 2- Medium correlation; 3- Strong Correlation)				
	CO-1	CO-2	CO-3	CO-4	CO-5
U5-O1	3	2	3	-	3
U5-O2	-	2	2	-	3
U5-O3	1	2	1	1	3
U5-O4	1	2	1	1	3
U5-O5	-	-	-	-	3

5.1 Introduction

Energy saved is energy generated. According to the principle of energy conservation, energy is neither created nor destroyed, but it transforms from one form to another.

Energy is the driving force behind several aspects of our daily lives, including the operation of home appliances, automobiles etc. For example, lights, air conditioners, other equipments and appliances are powered by electrical energy.

The demand of energy is increasing day by day; therefore, it becomes necessary to conserve the energy. Energy conservation in simple terms means to avoid wastage of energy without sacrificing comforts and needs. Energy can be saved by the following simple methods

- Avoiding wastage of energy
- Improving efficiency of equipment
- Using alternate sources of energy

Energy auditing is an important aspect of energy conservation. Here in this unit, procedural aspects of energy auditing in an electrical system are described.

5.2 Energy Audit

The Energy Conservation Act, 2001 defines Energy Audit as "the verification, monitoring and analysis of use of energy including submission of technical report containing recommendations for improving energy efficiency with cost benefit analysis and an action plan to reduce energy consumption.

5.3 Significance of Energy Audit

- The main goal of an energy audit is to identify strategies for decreasing energy usage per unit of product production or reducing operational expenses.
- An energy audit establishes a reference point for effectively managing energy inside an organisation. It also serves as the foundation for developing a more efficient energy use strategy throughout the organisation.
- An energy audit provides a comprehensive analysis of energy and fuel used in any business, allowing for the identification of potential areas of waste and opportunities for improvement.
- The energy audit would provide a favourable direction for reducing energy costs, implementing preventive maintenance, and ensuring quality control in manufacturing and utility operations.
- An audit programme assists in monitoring and addressing fluctuations in energy prices, as well as ensuring the availability and dependability of energy supply.
- Energy auditing also aids in determining the most suitable energy mix, identifying energy saving technology, and implementing retrofitting measures for energy conservation equipment.
- The procedure of energy audit is described in Figure 5.1.

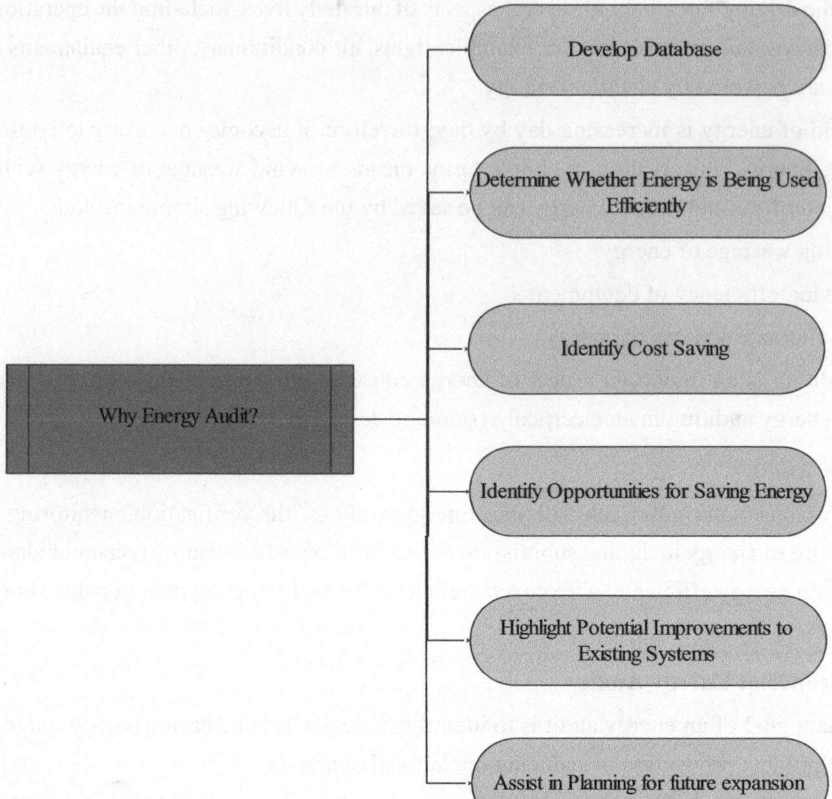

Figure 5.1 Methodology of Energy Audit

5.4 Energy Flow Diagram

Energy flow Diagrams are used to represent energy and its change graphically and statistically. This encompasses the basic energy sources used as raw fuels for input into a system, energy provision, conversion or alteration, energy losses, and energy consumption.

- An energy flow diagram, sometimes referred to as a Sankey diagram, is a specialized sort of flow diagram that represents the amount of energy by the width of its arrows. The length of the arrows is not correlated with the amount of energy.
- These diagrams illustrate the energy flow in a process and aid in determining the amount and quality of energy.
- Energy input originates from the left side of the figure. The graphic displays the output, usefulness, and energy leakages/losses.

The Figure 5.2 shows a Sankey graphical representation to illustrate the efficacy of an incandescent lamp. An incandescent lamp consists of a tungsten filament enclosed inside a glass bulb. The filament emits light when an electric current flows through it. Merely 10% of the energy generated manifests as light, while the remaining proportion is emitted as heat.

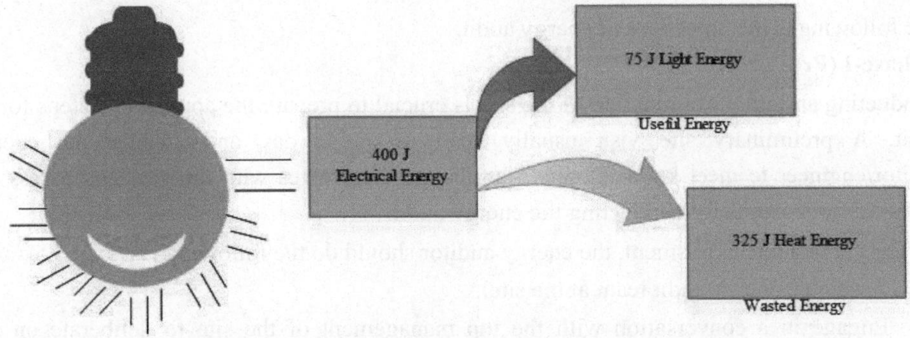

Figure 5.2 Sankey Diagram for Incandescent Lamp

The Figure 5.3 depicts a Sankey diagram that showcase the allocation of energy in a water pumping system. This system initially receives a full 100% of electrical input. The graphic representation provides a clear depiction of the efficiency and energy losses occurring at different phases. Approximately 45% of the energy is efficiently used to do work on the water. Nevertheless, there are several losses occurring inside the system. Pipe losses contribute to 12% of the energy, valve losses account for 8%, and pump losses make up 23%. In addition, coupling losses account for 2% of the total, while motor losses make for 10%. This visualisation emphasises the significance of the efficiency of each component in the overall functioning of the water pumping system. The width of the arrows represents the amount of energy flow and losses at each step.

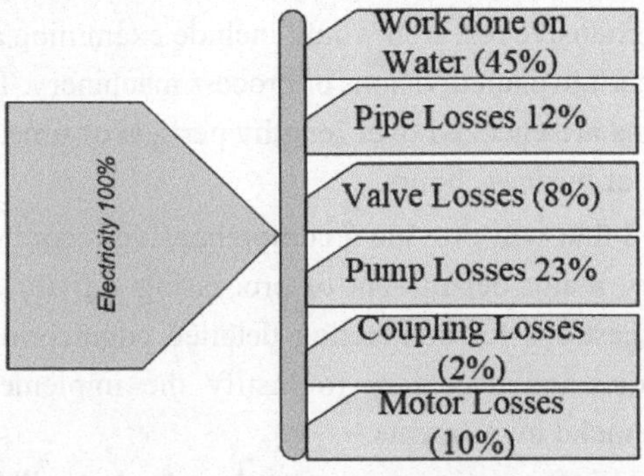

Figure 5.3 Sankey Diagram of Water Pumping System

5.5 Energy Audit Procedure

An energy audit is an essential resource for making informed decisions in the field of energy management. The purpose of this system is to achieve equilibrium between the total energy inputs and its utilisation, while also identifying all the energy flows inside a facility. It measures energy consumption based on its distinct operations. An Industrial Energy Audit is an essential component of a complete energy management system. It is described in the EC Act 2001 as: An "Energy Audit" refers to the process of verifying, monitoring, and analysing energy use. This includes providing a technical report that contains suggestions for enhancing energy efficiency, along with a cost benefit analysis and an action plan for reducing energy consumption.

The following is the procedure of energy audit.

i. Phase-I (Pre-Audit)

Conducting an initial examination of the site is crucial to prepare the appropriate steps for an audit. A preliminary site visit usually spans a single day and enables the energy auditor/engineer to meet key personnel, familiarise themselves with the site, and assess the necessary procedures for conducting the energy audit.

During the first site assessment, the energy auditor should do the following tasks:

- Assemble energy audit team at the site.
- Engage in a conversation with the top management of the site to deliberate on the objectives of the energy audit.
- Determine the primary areas inside the plant that uses the most energy, which will be inspected during the audit.
- Acquire site designs, if accessible, including building layout, steam distribution, compressed air distribution, power distribution, and other relevant information.
- Explore the site under the guidance of engineering/production personnel.
- Analyze the economic principles and policies linked to the suggestions of the audit.
- Proposing a schedule within a certain time window for complete energy audit.
- Raise awareness about energy audit via meetings and programmes.

ii. Phase II: Energy Audit Details

Completing a thorough audit might take several weeks to many months, depending on the site's complexity and nature. Extensive research would include examining and establishing material and energy balances for certain plant divisions or process machinery. To make sure that nothing is missed, plant operations are checked over lengthy periods of time, including on weekends, at night, and during regular business hours.

A report will be prepared that will provide a comprehensive record of the energy inputs and product outputs for every major department or processing activity. The audit report should conclude with clear suggestions for conducting detailed engineering studies and feasibility assessments. These studies are necessary to justify the implementation of conservation measures that require financial investments.

❖ **The following types of information are examples of what will be gathered during the comprehensive audit**

- Energy usage categorized by energy type, department, key process equipment, and end-use.
- Data on the balance of materials, including raw materials, intermediate products, finished products, and recycled materials. The audit team is required to gather the baseline data as presented in figure 5.4.
- Utilization of resources, incorporation of scrap or waste products, generation of by-products for subsequent use in other sectors, etc.
- Data on the cost of energy and tariffs
- Diagrams illustrating the movement of processes and materials.

- Production and dissemination of on-site utilities (e.g. compressed air, steam).
- Energy supply sources (e.g. grid power or self-generation)
- Possibility of substituting fuel, making process adjustments, and implementing cogeneration systems (combined heat and power production).
- Implementation of energy management protocols and training programmes to enhance energy awareness inside the organization.

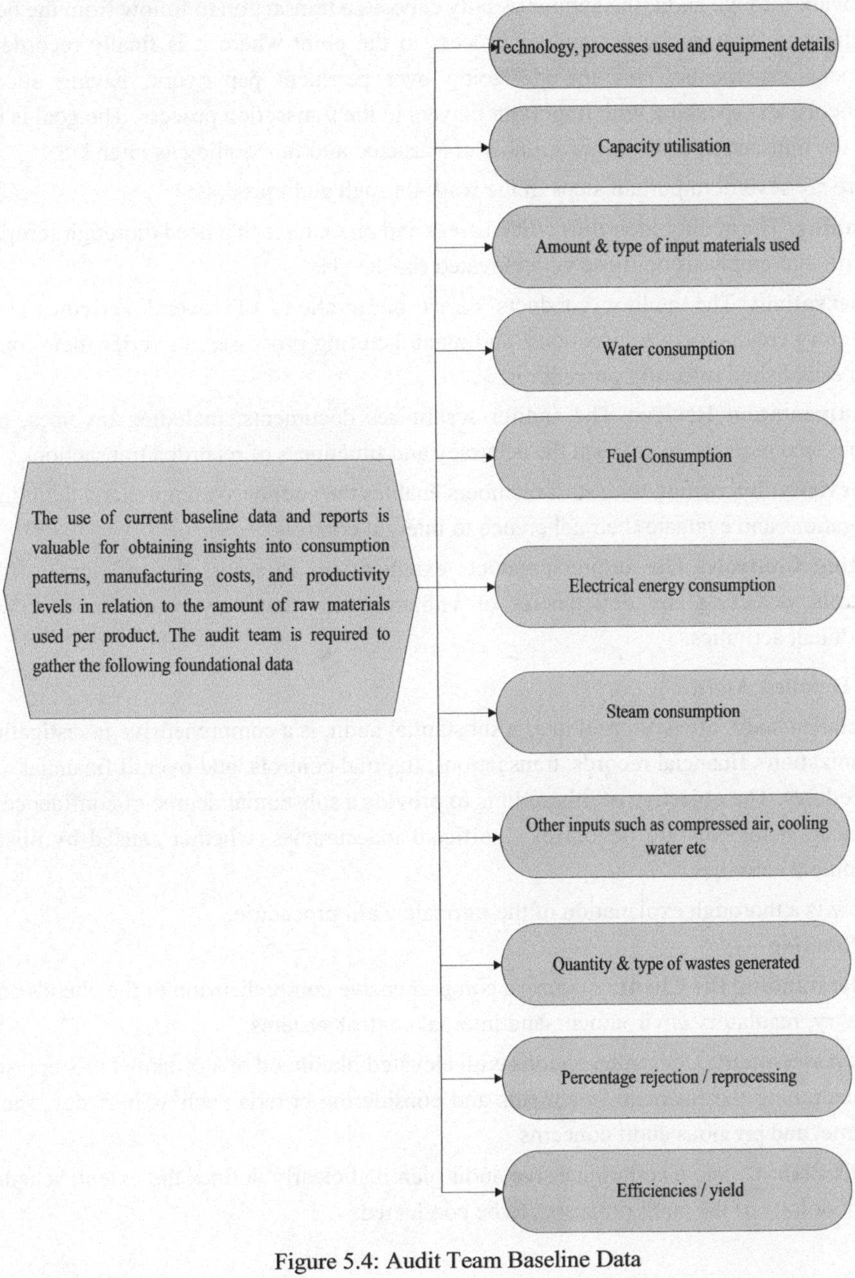

Figure 5.4: Audit Team Baseline Data

5.6 Walk-Through Audit

A crucial part of the auditing process is the walk-through audit, in which the auditor physically visits the client's location to examine and confirm the different systems, controls, and procedures in place. By using a hands-on approach, auditors may ensure the correctness and dependability of the financial statements by gaining a thorough knowledge of the organizations operational and control environment.

In a walk-through audit, the auditor usually chooses a transaction to follow from the beginning all the way through the accounting process to the point where it is finally recorded in the financial statements. This include going over pertinent paperwork, paying attention to protocols, and speaking with important players in the transaction process. The goal is to verify that the transaction controls are suitably constructed and functioning as intended.

There are several important steps in the walk-through audit process:

Planning: The auditor identifies crucial areas and procedures that need thorough scrutiny, with a particular emphasis on those with elevated risk levels.

Observation: The auditor conducts direct observations of several activities, including inventory counts, cash transactions, and manufacturing processes, to verify their compliance with established rules and procedures.

Documentation Review: The auditor scrutinises documents, including invoices, purchase orders, and receipts, to confirm the accuracy and timeliness of recorded transactions.

Interviews: Interacting with staff members enables the auditor to comprehend their duties and obligations and evaluate their adherence to internal controls.

Testing Controls: The auditor conducts examinations to assess the efficiency of internal controls, detecting any deficiencies or vulnerabilities that may result in inaccuracies or fraudulent activities.

5.7 Detailed Audit

A detailed audit, often referred to as a substantial audit, is a comprehensive investigation of an organization's financial records, transactions, internal controls, and overall financial reporting procedures. The objective of this audit is to provide a substantial degree of confidence that the financial statements are devoid of significant inaccuracies, whether caused by mistakes or fraudulent activities.

Below is a thorough explanation of the intricate audit procedure:

a. Planning

Understanding the Client: Acquire a comprehensive comprehension of the client's company, industry, regulatory environment, and internal control systems.

Risk Assessment: Determine regions with elevated likelihood of substantial misrepresentation by examining the financial statements and considering criteria such as intricacy, transaction volume, and previous audit concerns.

Audit Plan: Create a comprehensive audit plan that clearly defines the extent, schedule, and methodology of the audit processes to be conducted.

b. Fieldwork

Walk – Through Audit	Detailed Audit
Very simple, quick and less expensive.	It is expansion of simple audit, expensive, takes more time.
Only main issues are covered.	It focuses all the most suitable energy conservation measures for the system.
Basic information of energy system is collected in the premises.	The auditor collects utility bills of the year to find the suitable tariff structure, usage profiles etc.
Two resources: (i) Operation and maintenance staff collects data. (ii) Service utility provides this information.	As compared with walk in type, in this type, information is collected in more details.
It is also called as: (i) Preliminary audit. (ii) Screening audit. (iii) Simple audit.	It is also called as : (i) General audit. (ii) Site energy audit.

Internal Control Evaluation: Evaluate the structure and execution of internal controls. This include evaluating control methods, conducting staff interviews, and doing walk-throughs.

Substantive Testing: Conduct thorough examination of transactions and account balances to confirm their precision and completeness.

c. Verification Techniques

Inspection of Documents: Examine accompanying papers (such as invoices, contracts, and receipts) to verify the legitimacy of transactions and guarantee accurate recording.

Observation: Conduct visual inspections of tangible resources such as inventories and fixed assets to confirm their presence and assess their condition.

Inquiry: Perform interviews with management and staff to get explanations and insights about financial data and controls.

Recalculation: Conduct an independent verification of the mathematical correctness of financial data and calculations.

A Comparison between Walk – Through Audit and Detailed Audit

Example 5.1: *An electric heater of 230 V, 6kW, is used for water heating applications, calculate the electrical energy consumption per hours, if it is operated at 200 V. Assume that the power factor is 0.9.*

Solution: $P = VI \cos\phi$

$$=200 \times 24.15 \times 0.9$$

$$=4348\ W$$

$$Energy\ Consumption\ in\ one\ hours = \frac{4349 \times 1}{1000}$$

$$=\mathbf{4.35\ kWh}$$

5.8 Payback Period

Payback analysis is the most straightforward method for evaluating a proposal. The payback period refers to the duration, measured in years, needed to recoup the original investment (capital cost) by considering just the Annual Net Savings (Yearly benefits minus Yearly expenditures). After the payback time is finished, all the initial investment in the project will have been recouped, and any further cost reductions may be seen as pure 'profit'. A project gets more appealing as its payback time decreases. The duration of the maximum allowable repayment time is determined at the discretion of the firm.

The payback time may be determined by using the equation.

$$Sample\ Payback\ Period\ (Years) = \frac{Capital\ Cost\ of\ the\ Project\ (in\ Rupees)}{Net\ Annual\ Saving\ (In\ Rupees)} \quad ...5.1$$

Example 5.2: *A cogeneration system installation is expected to reduce a company's annual energy bill by Rs. 30 Lakhs. If the capital cost of the new cogeneration installation is Rs. 98 Lakhs, and the annual maintenance and operating costs are Rs. 15 Lakhs, what will be the expected payback period for the project?*

Solution: *Simple payback period*$= \frac{98}{30-15}$

$$= \frac{98}{15}$$

$$= 6.53 \text{ Years}$$

5.9 Energy Audit Instruments

To conduct an energy audit, a variety of equipment is necessary to measure all the essential parameters needed to achieve energy conservation. The energy audit equipment should be portable, user-friendly, and cost-effective.

The energy audit typically involves monitoring of following parameters:

- Voltage (V)
- Current (I)
- Power factor (PF)
- Active power (kW)
- Apparent power (demand) (kVA)
- Reactive power (kVAr)
- Energy consumption (kWh)
- Frequency (Hz)
- Harmonics, etc.

Other parameters of importance (other than electrical parameters) are:

- Temperature and heat flow

- Radiation
- Air and gas flow
- Liquid flow
- Air velocity
- Noise and vibration
- Dust concentration
- Total dissolved solids (TDS)
- pH value
- Moisture content
- Relative humidity
- Flue gas analysis – CO_2, O_2, CO, SOx, NOx
- Combustion efficiency, etc.

The energy audit equipment may be categories as:

1. Electrical instruments, used to measure various electrical properties, including current, voltage, power, power factor, and so on.
2. Mechanical instruments, used to measure mechanical quantities such as pressure, temperature, flow, and so on.

5.9.1 Electrical Measuring Instruments:

- Ammeters
- Voltmeters
- Power Factor Meters
- Digital Multimeter
- Frequency Meter

Other Importnat instruments used:

- **Clip on Digital PF Meter**, used to test power factor without causing any interruption to the connection.
- **Clamp on Ampere Meter**, used to measure current without disrupting the connections.
- **Harmonic Analyser**, used for the study of harmonics in a power system.
- **Clip on Digital Watt Meter**, used to measure power without the need to disconnect any connections. These instruments may be used online, for example, on motors without the need to stop the motor. Figure 5.5 displays a standard clip-on digital watt metre.

Figure 5.5: Clip on Digital Watt Meter

- **Lux Meters**

  The lux is a metric unit used to quantify the level of light, specifically luminance. A lux metre as shown in figure 5.6 is an instrument used to quantify luminance or the amount of light intensity. It precisely quantifies the level of brightness as seen by the human eye. A lux metre operates by using a photosensitive cell to detect and measure light intensity. Subsequently, the metre transforms this light into an electric current. The gadget can determine the lux value of the collected light by measuring this current.

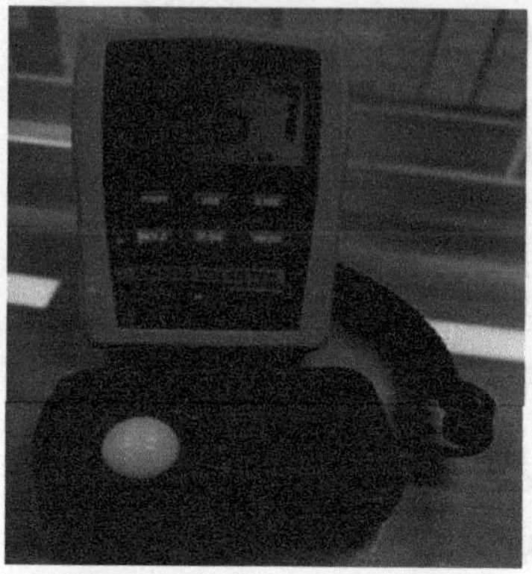

Figure 5.6: Lux Metre

5.9.2 Temperature Measuring Instruments

- Multiple temperature measuring devices are often required to monitor temperatures in offices and other locations where workers are present, as well as to measure the temperature of operational equipment.
- Affordable electronic thermometers with replaceable probes are now accessible for measuring temperatures at different locations in the system.
- Common kinds of temperature probes include immersion probes, surface temperature probes, and radiation protected probes used for monitoring genuine air temperature. Figure 5.7 is showing the temperature measuring instruments.

Figure5.7: Temperature Measuring Instruments

- **Contact Thermometer,** shown in figure 5.8 monitor temperatures of substances such as flue gas, hot air, and hot water by inserting a probe into the stream. A leaf type probe is used to measure surface temperature using the same equipment.

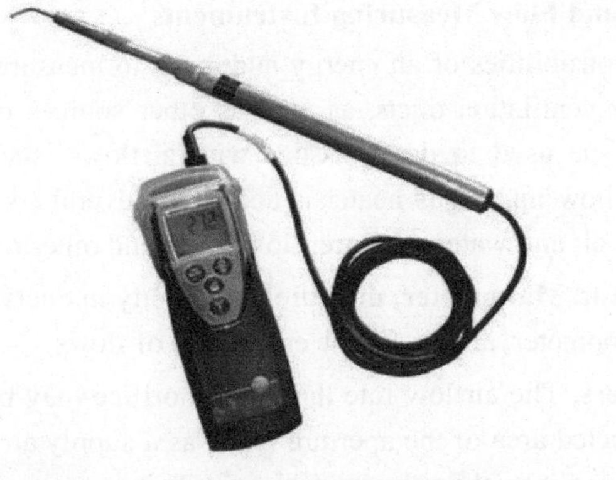

Figure 5.8: Contact Thermometer

Infrared Thermometer

An infrared thermometer as shown in figure 5.9 is a device that determines temperature by analyzing the thermal radiation, also known as blackbody radiation, released by the item being measured. Currently, there is a wide range of infrared temperature sensing devices accessible. These devices come in many forms, some of which are meant to be flexible and portable for handheld usage, while others are intended for permanent attachment to serve a specific function over extended periods of time. Infrared thermometers have a broad range of applications for measuring temperature like

- Identifying clouds to facilitate remote telescope operation.
- Inspecting mechanical equipment or electrical circuit breaker boxes or outlets for areas of excessive heat
- Verifying the accuracy and consistency of heater or oven temperature for calibration and control purposes.
- Identifying areas of high temperature or conducting diagnostic tests in the production of electrical circuit boards.
- Identifying areas of high temperature in firefighting scenarios.
- Monitoring the thermal behavior of materials throughout the heating and cooling process, to gather data for research and development purposes or to provide quality control in production.

Figure 5.9: Infrared Thermometer

5.9.3 Pressure and Flow Measuring Instruments

One of the responsibilities of an energy auditor is to measure the air flow from heating, air conditioning, or ventilation ducts, as well as other sources of air flow. Airflow measuring equipment may be used to detect issues with airflows, such as determining whether the combustion air flow into a gas heater is accurate. Several common examples of instruments used to measure air and water pressure, flow rates, and other related parameters include:

- **Pitot tube and Manometer,** measure air velocity in ducts by utilising a pitot tube and an inclined manometer, allows for the estimation of flows.
- **Anemometers,** The airflow rate through an orifice may be calculated by approximating the unobstructed area of the aperture (such as a supply air register or exhaust hood face) and multiplying it by the velocity of the air. This outcome is an approximation because of the challenges arise when trying to calculate the mean velocity of air and the unobstructed region for air flow. Regular calibrations are essential to ensure the precision of the equipment. The anemometer may also be used to optimize the face velocity of exhaust hoods by changing the door opening until the anemometer reveals the optimum airspeed. There are two kinds of anemometers that may be used to measure airflow:
- Vane anemometers and
- Hot-wire anemometers.

A digital anemometer is shown in figure 5.10.

Figure 5.10: Digital Anemometer

- **Water flow Meter**

  Flow meters are used in fluid systems, both for liquids and gases, to display the precise rate at which the fluid is flowing. If fitted with a flow control valve, they can regulate the rate of flow. Advance fluid flow meters utilizes the Doppler Effect and ultrasonic principles to measure flow without physical touch. There is a transmitter and receiver located on opposing ends of the pipe. The metre provides a direct measurement of the flow. This metre is capable of accurately measuring the flow of water and other fluids.

5.9.4 Miscellaneous Instruments

Combustion Analyzer

Combustion analyzer as shown in figure 5.11. is a portable instruments that can assess the combustion efficiency of furnaces, boilers, or other machinery that burn fossil fuels. There are two options to choose from: digital analysers and manual combustion analysis kits. Digital combustion analysis equipment conducts measurements and reads data. Combustion efficiency is expressed as a percentage. These instruments are intricately designed and come at a high cost. The manual combustion analysis kits often need many measurements, including exhaust stack temperature, oxygen concentration, and carbon dioxide content. Once these parameters are determined, the efficiency of the combustion process may be computed. The manual approach is time-consuming and prone to frequent human errors.

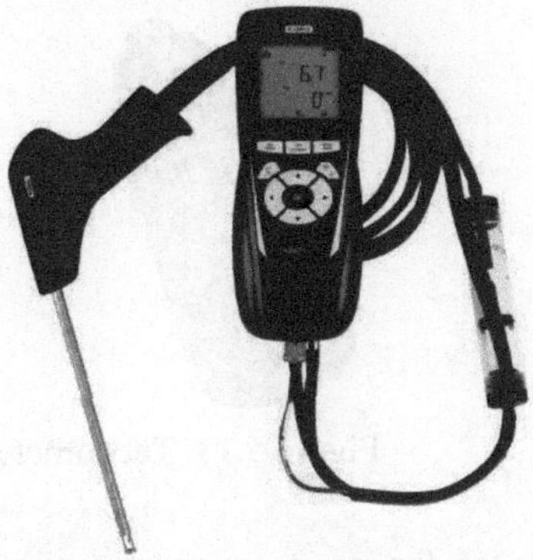

Figure 5.11: Combustion Analyzer

Fyrite Gas Analyzers

These devices are efficient, precise, and user-friendly tools for measuring and analysing carbon dioxide or oxygen. The Fyrite as shown in figure 5.12 absorbing fluid exhibits selectivity in chemically absorbing either carbon dioxide or oxygen. Thus, the Fyrite's precision falls well within the industrial and professional applications do not rely on complex sequential testing techniques. Furthermore, Fyrite values remain unaltered by the presence of most background gases in the sample.

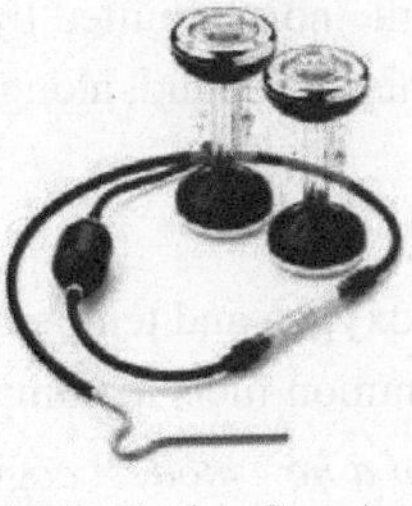

Figure 5.12: Fyrite Gas Analyzers

Tachometers

Speed measurements are crucial in any audit exercise since they may be affected by factors such as frequency, belt slip, and loading. A basic tachometer as shown in figure 5.13 is a device that makes physical touch and may be used in situations where direct access is feasible. Non-contact tools, such as stroboscopes, are more advanced and provide increased safety.

Mechanical stroboscopic instruments are devices equipped with mechanical shutters, known as choppers, which take the shape of either discs or hollow cylinders with slits. These apertures allow for the observation of the object. The frequency of the periodic motion of the item may be measured by measuring the speed of rotation of the disc at which the object observed through the shutter seems motionless. These devices are referred to as stroboscopic tachometers.

The primary benefit of the stroboscopic tachometer is that it allows for the measurement of angular rotation speeds of objects without requiring physical contact between the instrument and the object. As a result, it is possible to estimate the speeds of things that are observable but not readily reachable. This advantage also allows for the measurement of the velocities of low-power objects without the velocity being influenced by the usage of the instrument.

Figure 5.13: Tachometers

Leak Detectors

Compressed air is now one of the most expensive utilities in a plant. Implementing a straightforward leak detection and repair programme will significantly decrease unnecessary energy expenses. There are ultrasonic devices that may be used to identify leaks of compressed air and other gases. They are often imperceptible to human faculties.

The Ultrasonic Leak Detector is a portable and efficient device designed for detecting compressed air leaks. It is equipped with all the required characteristics for versatile usage in identifying and locating expensive air leaks. The Ultrasonic Leak Detector is a comprehensive package that includes a top-notch flexible sensor. This sensor is affixed to the tip of a flexible steel pipe, allowing it to effectively detect ultrasonic sounds in difficult-to-reach locations.

The device translates the ultrasonic noise emitted by a leak into an audible sound that can be perceived by humans, such as a hissing sound, along with other indications such as beeping or an LED display.

Fuel Efficiency Monitor

This device detects the levels of oxygen and temperature in the flue gas. The microprocessor utilises the calorific values of common fuels to compute the combustion efficiency.

Example 5.3: *The construction of a new modest cogeneration plant is anticipated to decrease the company's yearly energy expenses by Rs.5,66,000. The payback time for the project may be calculated by considering the capital cost of the new boiler installation, which is Rs. 32,10,000, and the yearly maintenance and operating expenditures, which amount to Rs. 52,000.*

Solution: *Capital cost of Project: . 32,10,000*

Net Annual Saving: Yearly Expenses-Yearly Maintenance

: 5,66,000-52,000= 5,14,000

$$Sample\ Payback\ Period\ (Years) = \frac{Capital\ Cost\ of\ the\ Project\ (in\ Rupees)}{Net\ Annual\ Saving\ (In\ Rupees)}$$

$$= \frac{3210000}{510000}$$

$$= 6.25\ Years$$

5.10 Energy Audit Report Format

After conducting a thorough energy audit, the energy manager or auditor should provide a report to the top management to promote effective communication and efficient implementation. The following text presents the components and organisation of a standard energy audit report. The following structure is typically applicable to most circumstances. The industries or fields. However, the structure may be suitably modified to fit the specific needs of a particular organisation.

Report on

DETAILED ENERGY AUDIT

Table of Contents

4.1 Flow chart showing flow rate, temperature, pressures of all input - output streams
4.2 Water balance for entire industry
5.0 Energy Efficiency in Utility and Process Systems
5.1 Specific energy consumption
5.2 Boiler efficiency assessment
5.3 Thermic fluid heater performance assessments
5.4 Furnace efficiency analysis
5.5 Cooling water system performance assessment
5.6 DG set performance assessment
5.7 Refrigeration system performance
5.8 Compressed air system performance
5.9 Electric motor load analysis
5.10 Lighting system
6.0 Energy Conservation Options and Recommendations
6.1 List of options in terms of no cost, low cost, medium cost and high cost, annual energy savings and payback
6.2 Implementation plan for energy saving measures/Projects

ANNEXURE

A1. List of instruments

A2. List of Vendors and Other Technical details

The following worksheets (refer Table 5.1 & Table 5.2) can be used as guidance for energy audit assessment and reporting in Executive Summary.

Table 5.1 Summary Of Energy Saving Recommendations

S.No.	Energy Saving Recommendations	Annual Energy (Fuel & Electricity) Savings (kWh/MT or kL/MT)	Annual Cost Savings (Rs. Lakhs)	Capital Investment (Rs. Lakhs)	Simple Payback Period
1					
2					
3					
4					
Total					

Table 5.2 Types and Priority of Energy Saving Measures

	Type of Energy Saving Options	Annual Electricity / Fuel Savings	Annual Savings	Priority
		kWh/MT or kJ/MT	(Rs. Lakhs)	

A	No Investment (Immediate) • Operational improvement • Housekeeping			
B	Low Investment (Short to Medium Term) • Controls • Equipment modification • Process change			
C	High Investment (Long Term) • Energy efficient devices • Product modification • Technology change			

SUMMARY

Since the demand of electricity is increasing every day, therefore the consumer's electricity bill is also increasing. By adopting and practicing energy conversations methods, a substantial consumption of electricity and its bill can be reduced without compromising with the quality of life and comfort. Energy Audit is the process of transforming conservation concepts into tangible outcomes by providing technically viable solutions that consider economic and organizational factors, all within a defined time frame. Here in this unit different aspects of energy audit, its benefits, instruments used to perform energy audit and economical analysis with payback period are discussed. Report writing is an import aspect of any study. Energy audit report format with questionnaire for energy projects are also presented in the end of the unit.

EXERCISE

Short Answer Type Question

1. What do you mean by energy audit?
2. What is the significance of an energy policy?
3. Define 'energy management'.
4. What is the objective of energy management?
5. Give a typical energy audit reporting format.
6. List steps involved in 'detailed energy audit'.
7. List any four instruments used in energy audit with their application.
8. List four relevant instruments to carry out energy audit in electrical laboratory.
9. Distinguish between Energy conservation and Energy audit based on activities.
10. What is the difference between a walk-through audit and a detailed audit in the energy audit procedure?

Long Answer Type Question

1. Explain various forms of energy and Law of conservation of energy.

2. Explain the various principle of Energy Management.
3. Give the Energy Conservation Act's definition of an energy audit and discuss its significance for industry.
4. Describe the purpose of a Sankey diagram and how it is used to visualise energy losses and flows.
5. Write down at least three common tools used in energy tests and explain what they are used for.
6. Conduct the energy audit of your home by using utility bill and appliances used in the home. Identify the area of energy conservation and suggest the scope of energy audit. Based on the study, prepare a questionnaire and present an economic analysis of energy audit, the expenditure incurred in carrying out energy audit and justify it with payback period.
7. State the definition of energy audit as per energy conservation act.
8. Outline questionnaires to carry out energy audit of electrical workshop.
9. Describe with flow chart, the detailed energy audit procedure.
10. Outline the steps involved in conducting an energy audit, including the procedures for walk-through and detailed audits, and discuss the format of an energy audit report.

Multiple Choice Questions

1. What is an energy audit as per the Energy Conservation Act?
   A. A financial audit of energy expenses
   B. An analysis of energy flows to improve efficiency
   C. A review of energy policies
   D. A survey of renewable energy sources
2. Which instrument is used to measure electrical energy consumption?
   A. Thermometer
   B. Anemometer
   C. Wattmeter
   D. Barometer
3. What is the primary purpose of an energy audit?
   A. To increase energy consumption
   B. To reduce energy efficiency
   C. To identify energy-saving opportunities
   D. To install renewable energy systems
4. Which of the following is a key instrument in a detailed energy audit?
   A. Hygrometer
   B. Power analyzer
   C. Altimeter
   D. Chronometer
5. What does a Sankey diagram represent?
   A. Financial flow

B. Information flow

C. Material flow

D. Energy flow

6. Which of the following is NOT typically included in an energy audit questionnaire?

A. Types of lighting systems

B. HVAC usage

C. Employee salaries

D. Operating hours of equipment

7. What is the first step in the energy audit procedure?

A. Data collection

B. Detailed audit

C. Implementation of measures

D. Walk-through audit

8. What does the Simple Payback Period (SPP) measure?

A. The time taken to repay the initial investment from energy savings

B. The time taken to achieve maximum efficiency

C. The duration of an energy audit

D. The period over which energy consumption is measured

9. Which tool is used to measure the power factor in an electrical system?

A. Oscilloscope

B. Power factor meter

C. Lux meter

D. Sound level meter

10. What kind of audit provides a quick snapshot of energy-saving opportunities?

A. Walk-through audit

B. Detailed audit

C. Financial audit

D. Environmental audit

11. What is a key component of the final energy audit report?

A. List of all employees

B. Company's financial statement

C. Organizational chart

D. Detailed recommendations for energy-saving measures

12. Which of the following instruments is used to measure light levels?

A. Thermocouple

B. Lux meter

C. Ammeter

D. Manometer

13. What does a detailed energy audit include that a walk-through audit does not?
    A. Visual inspection
    B. Energy bill analysis
    C. Instrument measurements
    D. Employee interviews
14. Which device is used to record energy consumption over time?
    A. Digital multimeter
    B. Energy logger
    C. Thermometer
    D. Hygrometer
15. What aspect of an electrical system is often a focus during an energy audit?
    A. Power factor
    B. Voltage levels
    C. Current flow
    D. Frequency stability
16. In the context of energy audits, what does HVAC stand for?
    A. High Voltage Alternating Current
    B. Heating, Ventilation, and Air Conditioning
    C. High Value Asset Control
    D. Hybrid Vehicle Accumulator
17. Which of the following is an energy conservation measure?
    A. Installing high-efficiency lighting
    B. Increasing the thermostat setting
    C. Extending operating hours of equipment
    D. Reducing insulation in buildings
18. What does a power analyzer measure?
    A. Electrical power quality
    B. Sound levels
    C. Temperature variations
    D. Air pressure
19. In an energy audit, what is the purpose of using a data logger?
    A. To measure instantaneous power consumption
    B. To track energy usage patterns over time
    C. To calibrate other instruments
    D. To record ambient temperature
20. Which phase of an energy audit involves the implementation of identified measures?
    A. Preliminary audit
    B. Detailed audit
    C. Post-audit
    D. Follow-up audit

21. Which of the following comes under mandatory labeling programme
    A. diesel Generators
    B. induction motors
    C. tubular Fluorescent Lamps
    D. LED lamps
22. An energy audit as defined in the Energy Conservation Act 2001 does not include
    A. action plan to reduce energy consumption
    B. verification, monitoring and analysis of use of energy
    C. submission of technical report with recommendations
    D. implementation of all the recommendations of energy audit
23. Which of the following instrument is used for assessing combustion efficiency ?
    A. lux Meter
    B. pitot tube & manometer
    C. ultrasonic flow meter
    D. fyrite
24. Which of these is non-price method of energy conservation?
    A. Direct quantity rationing
    B. VAT
    C. Fuel taxes
    D. Energy audit
25. Which of the following lamp would have the highest electrical energy cost for 50000 hours
    A. LED
    B. Incandescent
    C. CFL
    D. It dose not depend on the type of the lamp
26. Which of the following lamp is most economical over 20 years period
    A. LED
    B. Incandescent
    C. CFL
    D. It dose not depend on the type of the lamp

Answer of Multiple Choice Questions

1	B	2	C	3	C	4	B	5	D
6	C	7	D	8	A	9	B	10	A
11	D	12	B	13	C	14	B	15	A
16	B	17	A	18	A	19	B	20	D
21	C	22	D	23	D	24	D	25	B
26	A								

REFERENCES AND SUGGESTED READINGS

1. BEE. "Energy Efficiency in Electrical Utilities" New Delhi, India: BEE; 2015.
2. BEE. "General Aspects of Energy Management and Energy Audit" New Delhi, India: BEE; 2015.
3. BEE. "Energy Efficiency in Thermal Utilities" New Delhi, India: BEE; 2015.
4. BEE. "Energy Performance Assessment For Equipment and Utility Systems" New Delhi, India: BEE; 2015.
5. B. L. Capehart, W. C. Turner, and W. J. Kennedy, *Guide to Energy Management*, 8th ed. Boca Raton, FL: CRC Press, 2020.
6. A. Thumann and T. Niehus, *Handbook of Energy Audits*, 9th ed. Lilburn, GA: Fairmont Press, 2012.
7. P. Ian Shapiro, Energy audits, ASHRAE J. 15 (2009) 18–27.
8. D. R. Wulfinghoff, *Energy Efficiency Manual*. Energy Institute Press, 1999.
9. A. Thumann, W.J. Younger, Handbook of Energy Audits, The Fairmont Press, Inc., 2008.
10. Krarti M. Energy audit of building systems: an engineering approach. third ed. Boca Raton, FL: CRC Press, Taylor and Francis Group; 2020.
11. T. Al-Shemmeri, *Energy Audits: A Workbook for Energy Management in Buildings*. Chichester, UK: Wiley, 2011.
12. M. Krarti, *Energy-Efficient Electrical Systems for Buildings*. Boca Raton, FL: CRC Press, 2017.
13. L. C. Witte, P. S. Schmidt, and D. R. Brown, *Industrial Energy Management and Utilization*. New York, NY: Hemisphere Publishing Corporation, 1988.
14. G. Mazur, *Electrical Systems for Facilities Maintenance Personnel*. Tinley Park, IL: American Technical Publishers, 2010.
15. R. E. Brown, *Electric Power Distribution Reliability*. Boca Raton, FL: CRC Press, 2009.
16. S. Doty and W. C. Turner, *Energy Management Handbook*, 9th ed. Lilburn, GA: Fairmont Press, 2015.

Appendices

Table 1-A Physical quantities and their Units

Physical quantities	Name of Unit	Symbol of Unit
Acceleration	Meter per second squared	m/s^2
Amount of substance	Mole	mol
Area	Square meter	m^2
Capacitance	Farad	F
Concentration	Molar	M
Density	Kilogram per cubic meter	kg/m^3
Distance	Meter	*m*
Electric current	Ampere	A
Electric charge*	Coulomb	C
Electric field intensity	Newton per coulomb	N/C
Electric resistance	Ohm	Ω
Emf	Volt	V
Energy	Joule	J
Force	Newton	N
Frequency	Hertz	Hz
Heat	Joule	J
Illumination	Lux (lumen per square meter)	lx
Inductance	Henry	H
Luminous intensity	Candela	cd
Magnetic flux	Weber	Wb
Mass	Kilogram	kg
Pressure	Pascal (newton per square meter)	Pa
Power	Watt	W
Potential difference	Volt	V
Temperature	Kelvin	K
Time	Second	s
Velocity	Meter per second	m/s
Volume	Cubic meter	m^3
Work	Joule	J

Table 1-B SI Units

Physical quantities	Name of Unit	Symbol of Unit
Activity	Curie	C_i
Electric charge	Coulomb	C=A.s
Electric potential	Volt	V=W/A
Electric capacitance	Farad	F=A.s/V
Electric resistance	Ohm	Ω=V/A
Exposure	Rongtan	R
Force	Newton	N= $Kg.m/s^2$
Illumination	Lux	*Ix= Im/m^2
Inductance	Henry	H=V.s/A
Luminous flux	Lumen	Im=cd.sr
Magnetic flux	Weber	Wb=V.s
Power	Watt	W= J/s=N.m/s
Radiation: dose	Rad	Rad
Work, energy, quantity of heat	Joule	J= N.m

Table 1-C Physical quantities with Unit symbol

Physical quantities	SI Unit	Symbol of Unit
Acceleration	Metre per second square	m/s^2
Angular velocity	Radian per second	rad/s
Angular acceleration	Radian per second square	rad/s^2
Area	Square unit	m^2
Density	Kilogram per cubic metre	kg/m^3
Dynamic viscosity	Newton second per metre square	$N \cdot s/m^2$
Electric field strength	Volt per metre	V/m
Frequency	Cycle per second	s^{-1}
Kinetic viscosity (diffusion coefficient)	Metre square per second	m^2/s
Luminance	Candela per square	cd/m^2
Magnetic field strength	Weber per square metre	Wb/m^2
Magnetic field strength	Ampere per metre	*A/m*
Surface tension	Newton per metre	N/m

Physical quantities	SI Unit	Symbol of Unit
Pressure	Newton per square metre bar	N/m^2 10^5 N/m^2
Thermal conductivity	Watt per metre kelvin	W/mK
Velocity	Metre per second	*m/s*
Volume	Cubic metre	m^3

Table 1-D General conversions

Multiply by	To Obtain	From	Multiply by
	To Convert	To	
2.54	Inches	Centimetres	.3937
30.48	Feet	Metres	.0328
.914	Yard	Metres	1.094
1,609.3	Miles	Metres	.000621
1,853.27	Nautical miles	Metres	.000539
6.45	Square inches	Sq	.155
0.093	Square feet	Centimetre sq	10.764
.836	Square yard	Metres	1.196
16.39	Cubic inches	Sq metres	.061
28.3	Cubic feet	Cubic centimetre	.0353
6.24	Cubic feet	Litre	.1602
.765	Cubic yard	Gallons	1.308
.3732	Pound (troy)	Cubic metre kilogramme	2.68
31.10	Ounces (troy)	Grammes	03216
.4536	Pound (avoir)	Kilogrammes	2.2045
7,000	Pound s (avoir)	Grains (troy)	.000143
28.35	Ounces (avoir)	Grammes	.0352
.065	Gram	Grammes	.1538
50.8	Cwt.	Kilogrammes	.01968
1,01 6.0	Tons	Kilogrammes	.000984
4.546	Gallons	Litres	.22
10	Gallons of water	Pounds	. 1
.454	Pound of water	Litres	2.202
70.3	Lb per sq m	Gm/sq cm	.0142
2.3	Lb per sq in	Head of water (ft)	.434

Multiply by	To Obtain	From	Multiply by
	To Convert	To	
.7	Lb per sq in	Head of water (m)	1.4285
.068	Lb per sq in	Atmospheres	14.7
1.575	Tons per sq in	Kgm/sq mm	.635
4.883	Lb per sq ft	Kgm/sq metre	.205
.593	Lb per cub yd	Kgm/cub metre	1.686
16.02	Lb .per cub ft	Kgm /cub metre	.0624
.0998	Lb. per gallon	Kgm/li tre	10.02
.138	Foot lb	Kgm·m	7.23
.33	Foot tons	Tonne metres	3
1.014	Horse power	Force de cheval	.9861
746	Horse power (british)	Watts	.00134
33,000	Horse power	Ft· lb/min	1/33000
76	Horse power	Kg ·m/sec	.01316
44	Watts	Ft· lb /min	.0227
0.1	Watts	Kg· m/sec	IO
0.252	B·th·u	Kg calories	3.97
14.7	Atmospheres	Lb/sq inch	.068
0.90	German candles	Eng li s h cand le s	1.1111
9.55	Carcels	Candle	0.1047
.737	Jo u le s	T1· lb	l. 357
88	Mile/hour	Ft/min	.01136
197	Rnetre/sec	Ft/ mi n	.00508
1.8	C·h·u	B·th·u	.5555
.0000208	Centipoise	Lb force sec sq ft	48000

Table 1-E General conversions

To Obtain	From	Multiply by
Angstrom	M	10^{-10}
Atmospheres	kg/m^2	10332
Bars	kg/m^2	1.02×10^4
BTU	joule	1054.8
BTU	kwh	2.928×10^{-4}
Circular miles	m^2	5.067×10^{-10}

To Obtain	From	Multiply by
Cubic feet	m^3	0.02831
Dyne	newton	10^{-5}
Erg	joule	10^{-7}
Erg	kwh	0.2778×10^{-13}
Gauss	tesla	10^{-4}
Grams (force)	newton	9.807×10^{-3}
Horsepower (metric)	watts	735.5
Lines /sq. inch	tesla	1.55×10^{-5}
Maxwell	weber	10^{-8}
Mho	siemens	1
Micron	meter	10^{-6}
Miles	km	1.609
Miles	cm	2.54×10^{-3}
Poundals	newton	0.1383
Pounds	kilogram	0.454
Pounds (Force)	newton	4.448

CO and PO Attainment Table

Course outcomes (COs) for this course can be mapped with the programme outcomes (POs) after the completion of the course and a correlation can be made for the attainment of POs to analyze the gap. After proper analysis of the gap in the attainment of POs necessary measures can be taken to overcome the gaps.

Table for CO and PO attainment

Course Outcomes	Attainment of Programme Outcomes (1- Weak Correlation; 2- Medium correlation; 3- Strong Correlation)						
	PO-1	PO-2	PO-3	PO-4	PO-5	PO-6	PO-7
CO-1							
CO-2							
CO-3							
CO-4							
CO-5							

Index